THE MILLENNIAL KINGDOM
(THE FIRST RESURRECTION)

THE TIME OF CHRIST ON EARTH:
The Visible Kingdom of the Church

SATAN'S LAST STAND

The Final Sentencing

THE SECOND DEATH

THE NEW
CREATION

THE NEW
JERUSALEM

THE NEW WORLD

THE SECOND
RESURRECTION

1000 years

THE CONSUMMATION OF HISTORY

THE MOST REVEALING BOOK OF THE BIBLE: MAKING SENSE OUT OF REVELATION

by

VERNARD ELLER

WILLIAM B. EERDMANS PUBLISHING COMPANY

Grand Rapids   Michigan

Reprinted, August 1982

Library of Congress Cataloging in Publication Data

Eller, Vernard.
  The most revealing book of the Bible: making sense
out of Revelation.

  1. Bible. N. T. Revelation—Commentaries.
I. Title.
BS2825.3.E57   228'.07'7   74-2495
ISBN 0-8028-1572-3

CONTENTS

THE MOST
REVEALING
BOOK OF
THE BIBLE

CHAPTER ONE

Revealing What?

A technical and authoritative exegesis of the book of Revelation this is not. Our purpose is more to amble through it as a book to be read and enjoyed rather than treating it as a corpse to be dissected or a cipher to be broken.

Revelation is here called "revealing" not because it displays attractive figures for calculating the time of the end, but because it highlights some of the most engaging contours of the gospel.

And right at this point lies the nub of our entire book. What the book of Revelation is intended to reveal, we will contend, is *the gospel*, the good news of who Jesus Christ is and what he accomplishes—this rather than secret information regarding the when and how of events from the hidden future.

The first consideration impelling us this way is the title of the book itself. You will not learn what that title is, however, by looking in your Bible at the table of contents, a title page, the heading of the book, or whatever—whether you find it reading THE REVELATION OF ST. JOHN THE DIVINE or any variation thereof. It is clear that John himself would not have approved such a title: the person it names is not the one he has any interest in drawing attention to.

I can testify from firsthand experience that publishers like to change a book title from the way the author had it; it gives them a sense of power. But John was clever enough to beat this game by incorporating his title into the text itself. The title of Revelation is its opening phrase: "APOCALYPSIS JESU CHRISTUS—which God gives to him." John does not get around to naming himself until somewhere on down the line—and then only as the last in a series of transmitters of the revelation, certainly not as its author, instigator, or possessor. *Apocalypsis* is the Greek word translated "the revelation," denoting an unveiling, a disclosure, a making known; and the book is presented as an *apocalypsis* of Jesus Christ. The phrase apparently is meant to carry two senses. The phrase "which God gives to him" makes it plain that Jesus is to be understood as the Revealer, the prime possessor and bearer of the revelation. But the likelihood is that John also wants to designate him as the *content* of the revelation. Jesus Christ is both the Revealer and that which is being revealed. The remainder of John's book would support this interpretation; he understands that he has been given a message from the Lord Jesus, which message, in turn, tells us who this Lord Jesus is, what he represents in the totality of his being and work, his history past, present, and future.

This being so, in his title John also has given us the primary principle for interpreting his book. Even though he works at it from a perspective somewhat different from that of the rest of the New Testament, John is essentially at one with those other authors, namely in his desire to proclaim and expound the person of Jesus Christ, the same Jesus to whom they witness in their ways. It follows, then, in our effort to understand John, the first question always to ask is "What is he trying to tell us about Jesus?" Consequently, we should test our interpretation by attempting to correlate it with what we otherwise know of Jesus. We shall insist, then, that at every point the attempt be made to read John as giving us a revelation *of Jesus Christ* which is to be harmonized with the larger revelation of Christ which is the New Testament itself—this, rather than as a revelation of future history to be correlated, now, with "signs," i.e., whatever can be observed in today's world and in the political events of the twentieth century.

Although it will take the remainder of our book to find out how successful this principle of interpretation can be, it is obvious here at the outset that it will point us to something quite different from the currently popular mode of reading Revelation. That mode we shall call "calendarizing," an effort to fit the events of John's visions into the world-historical calendar of the recent and coming events that constitute our own socio-political experience.

It is most apparent, of course, that an interpreter is calendariz-

ing when he makes an outright prediction of a date for the return
of Christ, the end of the world, or whatever; but it still would
come under our definition of calendarizing if he chose not to cut
it that fine but made his prediction only for an approximate
period. Indeed, it is quite possible to calendarize without mentioning time at all. For instance, if one were to identify, say, the
Antichrist as a particular historical person, or the kings mentioned
by John as representing modern nations, this still would have the
effect of locating his visions on our time-scale and on the calendar
of our history. We do not mean to deny that John's events could
or will happen in our history; we do mean to deny that either
John or God has any intention of enabling *us* to locate them in or
detail them as a part of our historical future.

To this point we have averred only that, in his title, John has
pointed us in a direction other than calendarizing and that we
intend to follow that lead. Of course, we have yet to *demonstrate*
that the book itself tends more this way than to calendarizing. But
before we proceed to that, it will be appropriate to show that the
New Testament as a whole very much discourages calendarizing
and that, in fact, calendarizing has the effect of undermining the
very eschatological stance (attitude toward last things) which the
New Testament is intent to teach.

There is one very obvious but often ignored fact out of church
history which should drive us back to the New Testament to check
out this matter of calendarizing. That is, the contemporary scholars who now are so sure they have the Revelator's picture nailed
down to an historical when, where, and how—these are by no
means the first calendarizers to have made such a claim. We
currently are riding a surge, but this same sort of interest has
waxed and waned over the long centuries. And every single calendarizer up to this generation has been proved wrong—dead wrong.
The cumulative batting average for no one knows how many
thousand self-proclaimed pros is .000. Of course, those presently
at the plate say, "But now the evidence is so much clearer; now
the signs are unmistakable; this time we've got it, I guarantee
you." Yes, but know for a fact that all of the former calendarizers
were just as certain, said the very same thing in their own day.
They were reading the same book of Revelation, were just as
capable observers of history, were just as open to the Holy Spirit,
had just as convincing arguments.

There is, of course, the fact that some Bible prophecies *have been* fulfilled. We do not propose to go into the matter here except to observe that the nature of those prophecies was such that, *when the event itself took place,* they could be cited as confirmation that it *had been prophesied* ahead of time. However, there is no evidence of what would be a quite different phenomenon, namely that the prophecies ever made it possible for anyone to make an accurate *prediction* as to just when, where, and how the event would occur. The accomplished fulfillment of some Bible prophecies provides no excuse or justification for contemporary calendarizing.

If all those previous attempts to make Revelation produce an accurate calendarized reading unanimously have come to naught, perhaps the question should occur as to whether calendarizing is the means by which God intends us to read that book. At least, white rats try some other way of getting through a maze after they have gone down the same blind alley so many times. In any case, it won't hurt to go back to the New Testament manual to see whether calendarizing actually was what the instructions called for.

As we turn to the New Testament, we will look first at those sayings attributed to Jesus in which he specifically counsels against trying to get at the secrets of God by doping out "signs"—which is precisely what calendarizing does. We don't propose to do anything like detailed analysis at this point, debating whether it can be proven that Jesus actually did make each of these statements, whether one or another of them might not be interpreted so as to be irrelevant to our issue, etc. We are going to cite quite a number of scriptures but have no desire to hang a great deal of weight on any one of them. We will go through them rapidly and then talk about their *cumulative* thrust; and even this will constitute only a rather minor step in our overall argument. So please save your rebuttals until we have had time to draw the full picture. We will treat the texts in their New Testament sequence, even while recognizing that many are simply parallel reports of the same saying.

In Matthew 12:36ff., Jesus is talking about the coming day of judgment, and some doctors of the law and Pharisees ask him for a sign. Jesus responds, "It is a wicked, godless generation that asks for a sign; and the only sign that will be given it is the sign of the prophet Jonah." Matthew 16:1-4 reports a very similar incident in almost the same words, adding only, "So [Jesus] went off and left them."

Mark 8:11-13 gives us the same kind of situation with only a slightly different response: "Why does this generation ask for a sign? I tell you this: no sign shall be given to this generation." Mark 13:5-6 reads, "Jesus began: 'Take care that no one misleads you. Many will come claiming my name, and saying, "I am he"; and many will be misled by them.' " And then, in verses 21-23:

> Then, if anyone says to you, "Look, here is the Messiah," or, "Look, there he is," do not believe it. Imposters will come claiming to be messiahs or prophets, and they will produce signs and wonders to mislead God's chosen, if such a thing were possible. But you be on your guard; I have forewarned you of it all.

(What we have quoted here from Mark 13 is paralleled almost word for word in Matthew 24:4-5.)

Luke 11:29ff. is almost an exact restatement of the first incident we reported from Matthew. Luke 17:20-24, then, reads:

> The Pharisees asked him, "When will the kingdom of God come?" He said, "You cannot tell by observation when the kingdom of God comes. There will be no saying, 'Look, here it is!' or 'there it is!'; for in fact the kingdom of God is among you." He said to the disciples, "The time will come when you will long to see one of the days of the Son of Man, but you will not see it. They will say to you, 'Look! There!' and 'Look! Here!' Do not go running off in pursuit. For like the lightning-flash that lights up the earth from end to end, will the Son of Man be when his day comes."

Again, in Luke 21:7-8:

> "Master," they asked, "when will it all come about? What will be the sign when it is due to happen?" He said, "Take care that you are not misled. For many will come claiming my name and saying, 'I am he,' and, 'The Day is upon us.' Do not follow them."

John 21:20-23 is an example of a somewhat different type but of similar effect. The conversation is dealing with matters of eschatological destiny, and Peter asks Jesus about what is to happen to one of the other disciples. Jesus answers, "If it should be my will that he wait until I come, what is it to you? Follow me." At that point the Gospel writer breaks in to tell us that some of the early Christians understood this to mean that the disciple would not die. He then comments, "But in fact Jesus did not say that he would not die; he only said, 'If it should be my will that he wait until I come, what is it to you?' "—a rather clear instance of Jesus squelching curiosity about details of the end.

Finally, in Acts 1:6-8, following the resurrection, in Jesus' last conversation with his disciples, they put to him the question, "Lord, is this the time when you are to establish once again the sovereignty of Israel?" Jesus answers, "It is not for you to know about dates or times, which the Father has set within his own control."

Putting them all together, they spell something less than enthusiastic support from Jesus or the church that produced the Gospels for any effort at getting one up on things and trying to write history before it happens. Would our present-day calendarizers claim that they are free to ignore this counsel? Would they claim that the author of Revelation, under God's leading, ignored it?

Granted, at other points in the Gospels (and sometimes right alongside our passages) Jesus does talk about and even identify some signs of the end. How are we to reconcile the presence of these two types of text?

Some scholars would do it at a stroke by denying that Jesus ever spoke of signs and by attributing all such references to later interpolators. That solution strikes me as being too neat and easy, and unjustified. My best help, then, is to suggest that most if not all of the signs Jesus acknowledges are of a sort different from those that could be used as a basis for calendarizing the future. Rather, they are of the sort involved when we say, for example, "The demonstrations taking place on campus are a *sign* of student unrest." In such case the "sign" is simply the outward, visible side of an event which also includes deeper, less visible, but more significant aspects.

The "sign" is an indicator that enables us to understand the full implications of what *is happening*—but certainly not a means of calculating what is *yet to happen*. And if such is the case here, then Jesus' acknowledgement of *these* signs in no way contradicts his warning regarding *those*.

But there is another way of coming at the whole matter; we need not draw our final conclusion at this point. We can ask the question: does the New Testament suggest any reason *why* Jesus should be opposed to calendarizing? We shall see that the answer comes back: yes, to calendarize is to undercut the very eschatological stance Jesus was intent to teach.

This new consideration turns our discussion in the way it ought to go—away from the merely negative of what Jesus opposed and toward the positive of what he encouraged. These positive teachings, again, we find scattered throughout the Gospels; but we do not propose to ferret out them all. Matthew includes pretty much everything in this regard that the other Gospels do; and his work has the advantage of drawing Jesus' eschatological teachings together into one passage rather than leaving them scattered. Matthew 24–25 will tell us what we want to know.

The key presupposition (supported both by texts we have examined and by those we are yet to examine) is given its definitive statement in 24:36, "But about that day and hour no one knows, not even the angels in heaven, *not even the Son;* only the Father" (italics mine). Calendarizers argue that Jesus is saying, in effect, "Go ahead with your predictions, but don't try to cut it as fine as the day or the hour!" But particularly when we see the total context of Jesus' thought, such an interpretation is shown to be sheer sophistry.

Because no one (not even Jesus himself) knows "when," the consequence for the Christian believer follows as stated in verses 42-44 (as crucial a text as any used in this book):

> Keep awake, then; for you do not know on what day your Lord is to come. Remember, if the householder had known at what time of night the burglar was coming, he would have kept awake and not have let his house be broken into. Hold yourself ready, therefore, because the Son of Man will come at the time you least expect him.

Rather plainly, the reason Jesus is opposed to calendarizing is that it leads people into thinking they know something they have no chance of knowing. The reason they have no chance of knowing it is that God never intended they should. And the reason he does not want them to know is that, if they did, there no longer would be any cause for them to be *constantly* awake and *perpetually* ready. If I "know" when the end is to happen, then, of course, until the time actually comes, there is not the slightest reason to "hold myself ready." And to plead, "But I don't know the exact day and hour," doesn't affect the situation in the slightest. No, calendarizing comes through as an attempt to pull an end run on God and find out what he expressly indicated is not to be found out.

The matter does not hang exclusively on the passage quoted; it is followed by a collection of three parables, each bearing directly upon the point. The first, in 24:45-51, is the story of a servant whom his master left in charge of the household staff. He (on the basis of his calendarizing calculations) "knew" that the master would be *a long time* coming and so used the interim to really live it up and misuse his fellow servants. But the master came back *early*, and the servant was caught in sad shape.

Conversely, the second parable, found in 25:1-13, is the familiar story of the wise and foolish maidens. The wise maidens equipped themselves for perpetual readiness; but the foolish maidens (on the basis of their calculations) "knew" that the bridegroom would come *soon* and so neglected to carry any reserves of oil. It turned out, however, that the bridegroom returned *late*, and the maidens were unprepared.

That these adjacent parables should be the precise converse of each other is significant; it forces one to the conclusion that the only possible stance is that of perpetual (both early *and* late) readiness.

The third parable, 25:14-30, is that of the talents. The useless servant was so sure (on the basis of his calculations) that the master would come right back that he felt it sufficient simply to protect the coin that had been entrusted to his care. But as you might guess, he was caught just the way every calendarizer has been; the master's delay made it clear that he should have invested (made use of) the money.

This teaching of a perpetual readiness based precisely upon the fact that we have absolutely no information about the "when" of the end does not come through as the stance only of Jesus; we find the same thought reiterated consistently throughout the New Testament. It shows up typically as a two-part affirmation. The first thought is that "the time is short"; the second that the time of the end will be a surprise, with Jesus coming as a thief in the night.

Both affirmations, of course, are prominent in the Gospels. But then, in Paul, strong assertions about the shortness of the time are found in Romans 13:11-13 and 1 Corinthians 7:29-31—these coupled, in turn, with 1 Thessalonians 5:1-2, "About dates and times, my friends, we need not write you, for you know perfectly well that the Day of the Lord comes like a thief in the night." Later writers also emphasize the shortness of time in Hebrews 10:25, 36-37 and James 5:8. The First Epistle of Peter comes through very strong on the shortness of the time, "The end of all things is upon us" (4:7 and 17), and perhaps implies the surprise aspect, "Awake! be on the alert!" (5:8-11). Second Peter reverses the emphasis, being very strong on surprise: "The Day of the Lord will come; it will come, unexpected as a thief" (3:8-10), but only implying the shortness of the time: "Look eagerly for the coming of the Day of God and work to hasten it on" (3:11-13).

Finally, the book of our particular interest, Revelation, says in its very first verse that these things "must shortly happen" and, in its next-to-last verse, "I am coming soon"; and it repeats the thought any number of times between those two statements. But also, regarding the surprise aspect, 16:15 (a crucially placed statement) reads: "That is the day when I come like a thief! Happy the man who stays awake and keeps on his clothes, so that he will not have to go naked and ashamed for all to see!" and 3:3b says much the same thing. (By the way, is it plausible that an author who includes such a statement at two points in his book could be writing the very same book for the purpose of telling us *when* the day was to come: "Jesus *wants* to come like a thief, but here are the data you need to calculate the time of his coming"?)

Here, then, is a double theme, rooted in the teaching of Jesus but permeating the New Testament as a whole. The "surprise" element, of course, accords very well with the basic counsel of perpetual readiness. However, the "time is short" element is another matter. It *could* be interpreted—and perhaps on first reading normally would be interpreted—as a calendar claim: "I *know*, have specific information as to when the end is coming; and it is right away now." If that is what these statements intend, we have problems.

In the first place, the "time is short" element then stands in direct conflict with its counterpart "surprise" element. How are we to handle that? In the second place, if these truly are calendar claims, then they are all *false* claims and all these writers were just plain wrong; they said something was going to happen "very soon," and it still hasn't happened almost two thousand years later. That being so, it would seem risky business for modern calendarizers to base *their* calculations upon the very works of *those* calendarizers who have been so thoroughly discredited by history. Or do our modern calendarizers claim the competency to use the evidences of Jesus, Paul, and the other apostles and writers but succeed where they failed?

Obviously, the preferable alternative is to see whether it is not possible to understand this "time is short" element as something other than a calendar claim. There is one good line of evidence indicating that it never was meant as calendarizing. If we peg the idea as originating in the teaching of Jesus and then trace it through Paul, the writing of the Gospels themselves, and on down into the later epistles and writings, then we have documentary evidence that the expectation was current in the church during almost every decade from A.D. 30 on to the end of the century. Yet, through this period, writers could continue to state the expectation (and readers continue to accept it) without apparent difficulty over the fact that their predecessors had been stating the same expectation for some time—a time that was stretching out to something like seventy years. Clearly, the statement about the shortness of the time was not being understood as a calendarizing claim—that would have forced the unavoidable conclusion that too many leaders had been too wrong too often.

But if they are not calendar claims, what do these statements intend? Let me suggest some possibilities. It may be that these different writers were meaning to say, "*For all we know*, the time is short," or "Although we have absolutely no 'knowledge,' we ought always *to assume* that the time is short (and be ready to go on assuming that as long as necessary)." This would be a proper way of describing and fostering perpetual readiness: "Precisely because I don't know, I had better operate under the continual assumption that the time is short."

Similarly, some events are such that in their very nature they display the character of "soonness," no matter when they may be scheduled to occur; they are so big that their own moment cannot contain them; they bulge over even into the present. A little child could lead us into understanding how "Grandma is coming" is a "soon" event whatever the calendar indication might be.

The suggestions above would indicate that the "time is short" expectation is to be understood as a *subjective description* rather than an *objective claim;* the statement refers to the stance of the subject (the believer) rather than to the factuality of the object (the historical time-scale). But at the same time I am firmly convinced that, in the minds of the early Christians, this idea of "soonness" also carried another significance that involves much more of objectivity.

It is not the case that the writer is looking *ahead,* peering into the dim future and seeing the end making its approach, thus to proclaim, "The time is short; the end is at hand." Rather, he is looking *back,* there to see all that God *already has done* in the way of bringing his promise to fulfillment; he sees the arrival and work of God's Messiah, his atoning death and victorious resurrection, he sees the coming of the Holy Spirit, the creation of the new faith community and its missionary outreach, and he says, "The day is far gone, and the time is short. No matter what the dates or times which the Father has set within his own control, it is evident that the 'distance' (i.e., what needs yet to take place) between what God has done and what yet must happen is short; the end could come at any time; the time indeed is short."

And note well, this is a statement Jesus could make in his day and it be entirely true and proper. Paul can make the same statement some years later; it is still just as true and proper. Seventy years after Jesus it can be made again—still true and proper. We can make it today, as the centuries stretch into millennia—still just as true and proper as it was in the mouth of Jesus. Indeed, the obligation of the church is to keep on making that statement until the end itself closes off the words. It is when the church fails to announce that the time is short that she has fallen away from the truth of the matter.

And this brings us to the point of the entire argument. Our study has demonstrated that a sense of eschatological expectancy permeated the entire New Testament church and its literature. Further, although we have not done so, it would be easy to show that every aspect of that church's life and thought was driven by the motor of such expectancy. This eschatological expectancy was both the motivation and the content of Jesus' preaching, service ministry, and atoning work. It is the basis of New Testament ethical teaching. It was the source of the early church's life and the explanation of her distinctive character. It was the dynamic and definition of her mission in the world. The New Testament itself is both the fallout from and the exploration of the implications of this early Christian eschatological expectancy. And one of the central values of our study of Revelation should be an increased understanding of what these assertions mean and how true they are.

A critical consideration follows; contemporary Christianity is truly Christian only insofar as it shares this eschatological expectancy; outside of it there hardly are grounds for claiming the name "Christian"—any more than a candy that does not taste of lemon can claim to be "lemon-flavored." Christianity is "Christness"; and the essence of the New Testament understanding of Jesus Christ lies in his being as eschatological promisor, agent, firstfruit, and guarantee of the oncoming kingdom of God.

To restore to the church, then, a vital sense of this expectancy is all-important. Insofar as the calendarizers are concerned to do this, they deserve approbation and support—if only they were willing to give some attention to the ethical, political, theological, and ecclesiological implications of the same. But because they have chosen an unbiblical, unchristian means of establishing that expectancy, they have skewed their whole effort.

Consider that an expectancy based upon a calendarizing claim is completely vulnerable to disappointment, disillusionment, and despair—as assuredly it has happened to every calendarizer up to the present time. "I was *sure* I knew when the end would be. I became highly expectant about that coming. But now, that date has come and gone; my information was false and my expectancy a delusion. Wrong—all wrong! I have no basis left for faith or expectancy." Disappointed expectations can have no effect other than to blight and kill the Christian life.

Then consider, on the other hand, that the biblical expectancy of perpetual readiness is entirely immune to such disappointment. "Yes, I expect the Lord soon. I know he is coming, but he never even intimated that I should know when. So if he comes today, great!—that's what I'm expecting. If he doesn't come today—I'll expect him tomorrow. He can't break an appointment with me, because he never made one. The day God chooses will be 'soon' (and soon enough for me) as long as it is *Jesus* who comes."

Both the calendarizers and those who are perpetually expectant want to say, "Jesus comes—yes, he comes *soon!*" But there is all the difference in the world between saying it because one thinks he has broken a code and extracted inside information on the matter and saying it because he doesn't know and so, on faith, assumes always that the next moment might be it. And it seems clear which is the stance the Bible itself affects and recommends.

There is, also, another respect in which calendarizing tends to skew things. The interest of most calendarizers seems to begin and end in speculation about what is *going to happen then.* Biblical eschatology puts more of its emphasis upon what the expectancy of those future events has to say about *the quality of my life and action now:* What should I do to be ready? We will find the book of Revelation coming through very strong in this respect.

We need, finally, to give consideration to what the calendarizing approach implies about the nature of the Bible. The calendarizer must assume that the book of Revelation, for example, is written in code: the biblical author uses esoteric, symbolic language, but he actually is talking about present-day entities, alignments, and events. There are here references to the present situation in the Mideast—Jews, Arabs, Russia, China, the European Common Market, et alia.

If this is so, it follows that no one had any chance of truly understanding Revelation prior to the present day when the actual referents came into existence. Only *we* have had any chance of understanding Revelation, so, obviously, God must have intended the message of the book only for us—to tell us that the end will happen in our day. Yet certainly, if God intended the message for our ears alone, he could have found a way of delivering it directly to us. But that he chose to put it into circulation almost two thousand years before there was the remotest chance of anyone's understanding it implies some very wicked things about God.

We know beyond question to whom the Revelator's writings originally were addressed and delivered. Revelation 1:4 reads: "John to the seven churches in the province of Asia." Elsewhere the seven churches are named, and there is nothing mystic or ethereal about them. They were actual, concrete, everyday little congregations in first-century Asia Minor; the cities (or ruins of the cities) in which they existed can still be located today. However, it is not true that the book was John's word *to them* if they had no way of knowing what he was talking about. If the suggestion is that John *thought* he was writing to the seven churches and only God knew that the message actually was reserved for late twentieth-century Christians, then God was playing with both John and the churches. If the suggestion is, rather, that John *knew* he was writing only for the twentieth century, then he was not being truthful when he said that he was writing "to the seven churches in the province of Asia." What kind of God is it who would lead generations upon generations of Christians to read a book, believing that they had the word of God and were being addressed by it, while, the whole time, God knew that it was a locked secret which they didn't even have the wherewithal to understand? If calendarizing is the method by which Revelation is meant to be read, then God and no one else is responsible for the crushed expectations of all past calendarizers; he gave them a puzzle for which there was no way they could get anything but a false solution.

Flatly rejecting all such implications, we propose another basic principle for our study of Revelation. We take with all seriousness John's assertion that he is writing *to the seven churches in the province of Asia.* Therefore, any interpretation of his words that patently would not have been a possibility for the original readers cannot be accurate. Or, to put it the other way around, we can accept as accurate an interpretation of John's words only if his original readers could have understood it so, too. Indeed, if anyone is eavesdropping or looking over anyone else's shoulder in this matter, it is us moderns and not our first-century brethren. Revelation is not, in the first place, God's word *to us*—with them used merely as a vehicle for getting it to us. In the first place, it was God's word *to them;* and they, knowing John personally and being part of his historical and cultural milieu, had a better chance of understanding the book than we do. It is God's word *to us* by indirection (although not, by that token, any less the word of God) as we find ourselves able to identify with those Christians and discover that what was written for their benefit can be of great benefit to us, too.

CHAPTER TWO

The Gospel According to
John the Revelator

We still are in process of setting up guidelines and clearing the ground preparatory to plowing through Revelation. But now we turn a corner of sorts. We have been working at the somewhat *negative* matter of explaining why we will *not* take the popular approach to the book—although, at the same time, we were developing the *positive* orientation for the sort of perpetual expectancy that is basic to our study. Now, however, we will become entirely positive in looking directly to Revelation itself.

It may be helpful to be told what we are going to find in Revelation even before we look. So here follows a list of what I consider the most basic insights the book has to offer. None of these is different from what is to be found elsewhere in the New Testament; but the nature of Revelation gives it an advantage, perhaps, in pointing up and emphasizing them.

(1) Revelation helps get the Christian gospel into its proper context. We discover that the good news does not center upon—and is not limited to—discrete, scattered, isolated transactions between God and various individuals. "Salvation" includes much more than just getting myself taken care of; the Christian interest involves much more than enjoying merely "what Jesus has done *for me.*" No, God's action must be seen in a much broader, all-inclusive frame of reference.

(2) Because of God's role within it and his authority over it, the entire sweep of human life and history must be viewed as a meaningful sequence. The riddle of human existence never will be broken—simply *cannot* be broken—as long as one's sense of history amounts to "the history of *me*" and his sense of time to an

awareness of "now." And the attempt to identify "now" as "the end" does not change the situation. Indeed, the current Jesus Movement penchant for calendarizing is probably just one more manifestation of our societal philosophy that there is no real meaning or significance outside of "the now generation." Only the now is real; so, unless the end is now, it isn't real and relevant; ours *must* be the last days.

But no, Christianity—and particularly the book of Revelation— avers that "the real" is a totality encompassing human existence from Creation to New Creation and that the meaning of any particular "now" is to be found not in itself, but in its relationship to the totality. Thus, because it is part of the one historical process that is reality, "the end" can be of great significance for "now" without its actually having to occur now. The reality to which Revelation points is the reality of the historical *whole*, not simply of a particular historical *moment* within (or beyond) it.

(3) Yet the calendarizers are correct in stressing that "the end" is of primary importance. However, that importance is not to be found simply in the moment of the end itself but in the fact that its presence gives an "end-state orientation" to the sequence as a whole. The meaning of history lies essentially in that it is a process pointed toward a goal; and that goal determines the meaning of history's first moment (the creation) and its present moment (the "now") just as much as it does its last moment (the end itself). The Bible—as a whole, as well as in its various parts—is very much an end-state oriented book. And the great contribution of Revelation is in helping us read it that way. Jesus, by centering his entire message and ministry upon the coming of the kingdom of God, pointed us in this direction. Revelation, by picturing history *from* its end, simply drives the lesson home.

The key is in learning to think *eschatologically*—and this calls for a word of explanation. *Eschaton* is the everyday New Testament Greek word which means simply "the end." However, in biblical parlance the term is used in a more technical sense as a reference to the consummation and end of history itself. *Eschatology*, then, is thought and doctrine concerning the end, last things. Customarily "eschatology" has shown up as a final chapter of books on systematic theology and as the final lecture in seminary courses in the same. The content of such eschatology usually amounts to speculation concerning the end-time events.

But this understanding marks a distortion of biblical eschatology. Far from being a minor chapter within Christian theology, eschatology there is the basic stance that governs the theology as a whole. It deals not simply with the events of the end-time but is much more concerned with how the presence of *that* end affects the very constitution of the gospel and every aspect of Christian thought. And it is right here, in stressing eschatology as a total end-state orientation, that Revelation can be most contributive. The book obviously is "eschatological"; yet, if a person can get out of the calendarizing blinders and look at it with open eyes, he will discover that it consists of very much more than just speculation regarding last things. It is a revelation of Jesus Christ—the totality of Jesus Christ in the totality of his mission and ministry, his death and resurrection, his living lordship, and his coming again—all *from an eschatological perspective*. It is an explication and proclamation of the gospel—*from an eschatological perspective*. It is instruction in Christian discipleship—*from an eschatological perspective*. It is a portrayal of the church—*from an eschatological perspective*. Revelation is written within the same eschatological perspective, the same end-state orientation, as the rest of the New Testament; but it is done in such a way as to make that orientation much more clear, explicit, and self-conscious than is the case elsewhere.

A NOTE FOR THE ESCHATOLOGICALLY RESISTANT

The demand that one look at life and history (and even oneself) from an end-state orientation may strike you as esoteric and unnatural. But consider that you are quite willing to think in these terms in other connections. Any "game"—a chess game, for example—is very much an end-state oriented operation. The rules of play in chess decree that the sole goal of the procedure is to bring the opponent's king into checkmate. Only moves that contribute to that end are "good" moves; and they are "good" only to the degree they do so contribute. How many other men I capture, how many of my own men I manage to protect, how soon I get one of my men into his king row, how quickly or slowly I make my moves, how many different pieces I use, how much my play impresses the spectators—these and all other factors have significance only insofar as they contribute to my checkmating his king. That end is the measure for everything that happens within the game itself, from first move to last.

And just so, John affirms that the one end that gives significance to human history, and the one norm by which can be measured the extent to which any event within it is "good," is the coming of the kingdom of God. With the Revelator's help, we still will need to say a great deal about what that kingdom is and how it comes; so wait until you see how Revelation handles an end-state oriented presentation of world history before you decide whether or not you "like" eschatology.

(4) When the Revelator affirms that history is end-state oriented, for him this is identical with the affirmation that God is Lord. The particular end-state for which he sees history destined is "the kingdom of God," i.e., the situation of God's ruling as king, the time when all things are ordered according to his desire and plan, when his will is done on earth as it is in heaven. And it is because the wherewithal for that rule already is present *in God* and, through his mighty acts, already is making itself felt in the world, that it confidently can be proclaimed as the end-state that *will be*. It is because God always has been Lord and even now is Lord that the end of history can with certainty be described as his lordship consummated.

Yes, the Revelator does also affirm that *man*, created in the image of God, likewise has a freedom, ability, and power to make his mark in history. We will see how significantly he recognizes and honors this fact. Nevertheless, John must say that, in the final analysis, the outcome of history is determined by the will of the Lord God rather than the activity of men.

(5) Because the Lord of history is this God, and because its end-state is the accomplishment of *his* will, it follows that the action of the drama is *universal* in its scope. A major motif of the Revelator's account is its "universalism." Do not, at this point, go reading a lot of implications into the term. It is by a very careful exegesis of many texts from throughout the book that we will let John himself draw the implications. At present, by the term "universalism" we mean to affirm only the very fundamental concept that the Revelator intends his as being the *one* story of history, the *one* end-state that is to encompass all things. His is not presented as the story of just one particular people, one faith, one

race, one planet (?). He does not leave room for alternative universes to have other stories going other ways to other ends. Because the Lord of history is one, history itself is one, and John's is the one story of mankind.

Of course, any person is free either to accept or reject the truth of the story presented in Revelation. But the thing he cannot do is accept it as one among a number of the true understandings to which men have come regarding history. Essential to Christian eschatology, with its affirmation of God's lordship, is a claim of universality; so it must be *either* the New Testament view of history (represented, in our case, by Revelation) *or* a view derived from secular historiography *or* a view from one of the mystical, non-eschatological religions *or* something else. The universality of the Revelator's claim prohibits mixture.

(6) If God is the Lord of history and the one whose kingdom constitutes its end, it follows that man, on his own, has not the ghost of a chance of discovering history's purpose or of bringing it to pass. His call, rather, is to come to God, learn of him, be directed by him, and become molded and enabled through him—this rather than striking out on his own, no matter how nobly inspired and well intentioned the effort. Thus John's book is presented as being a *revelation* from God rather than merely creative insights of the author himself. And if the book's witness is to be authentic, the reader must accept it on the same terms. This is not to deny that there may be present earthbound, human, Johannine elements as the book stands in its written form. But unless God was involved in *revealing* the truth of its overall message, the book is without authority, for its subject matter clearly lies beyond human competency.

(7) Absolutely basic to John's understanding is the conviction that the Lord God has willed JESUS CHRIST to be the one through whom history's end-state be revealed—and not only revealed but also put in motion—and not only put in motion but also brought to consummation. The story of history is to be the story of Jesus Christ; God's lordship is to be *his* lordship. This relationship is portrayed most explicitly, of course, in that the achievement of history's end-state is signalized as *the return of Christ.* However, it is very important to realize that this yet-to-come Jesus Christ is not some sort of mythic construction put forward as a representation of a golden-age ideal. He is identified

as the entirely concrete, down-to-earth personage who became flesh among us, whom we have heard, felt, seen, and known in all his historical actuality. Likewise, because of his resurrection from the dead, the Jesus Christ known to contemporary Christians here and now as a vital presence of action and power also is to be identified as this same person.

That Christian eschatology is the story of this Jesus Christ gives it an utterly unique character. Jesus Christ—the entire New Testament knows—is preeminently an eschatological figure. But it is not that he suddenly *becomes* eschatological with his appearance at the end of the age. No, his every appearance and his continual presence always have been and ever will be eschatological—oriented toward and significant in relation to the end-state of all things.

Because Jesus Christ has been, is, and will be present in these ways, history suddenly has been given a unity and continuity. The future (that end) is not something detached and different from the present (this "now"). The end does not have to come in this generation for the book of Revelation to have meaning for us. The presence of the already-come, always-come, yet-to-come (in every tense "coming") Jesus Christ ties us into that future—whenever God decides it should happen.

Jesus Christ—and not any human efforts eventuating in the perfection of man—spells the continuity of history. Jesus, in his career within history, was the proclaimer and teacher of the coming kingdom of God; this was the core of his message. More, his works were those of the kingdom—wiping tears, putting an end to death, to mourning and crying and pain. More still, if the kingdom is the situation of God's will being perfectly done, then where Jesus was, the kingdom was: "It is meat and drink for me to do the will of him who sent me until I have finished his work" (John 4:34). Also, in his resurrected presence as the Lord who even now is with us, Jesus still signifies the kingdom of God. "When anyone is united to Christ, there is a new world; the old order has gone, and a new order has already begun" (2 Corinthians 5:17).

It is the presence of this one who is our Eschaton that makes our own moment of history eschatological, no matter where it happens to fall upon the calendar of God. For John, eschatology is precisely and nothing other than the *apocalypsis* (revelation) of

Jesus Christ—this much more essentially than any prediction of socio-political events, whether of this-worldly or other-worldly origin.

(8) That it is the return of Jesus Christ that marks the eschaton says something very important about the *character* of the end-state. Who Jesus Christ *is* determines what that situation *shall be;* what we already have come to know as his character and style will be the character and style of the end-events. How he acted in first-century Palestine will be how he acts in last-century Every-where.

This point is particularly crucial for our reading of Revelation. Some aspects of the Revelator's description of the Christ of the Return sound, upon first reading, like a radically different Jesus from that of the Gospels. But Jesus Christ is a constant in John's calculus—is *the* constant in John's calculus. And for him, the character of the historical man Jesus defines the content of the theological entity "Christ." So it is inconceivable that this author could understand Jesus Christ as changing character with the change of the times. If, then, it is possible to find an exegesis that maintains this constancy, it always is to be preferred over any other. Yes, there is room in Jesus of Nazareth for judgment and redemptive sorts of punishment; and there is room for them in Revelation. What there is not room for in either is cruelty, vindictiveness, gloating, or vengeful punishment.

(9) When the Lord God and his will are made as all-in-all as the Revelator chooses to make them, there is sometimes the temptation to play down the reality and power of that which is the opposite of God and resistant to him. We think to glorify God by giving the impression that everything is going his way. How beautiful is the world on its road to the kingdom; how beautiful, mankind attaining the likeness of its Master!

The Revelator doesn't fall for this one (nor do the other New Testament writers). He is acutely aware of the presence (and *threat*) of sin and evil and treats them with appropriate seriousness. The fullness of God's salvation is not, for him, explained in terms of a lack of opposition; quite the contrary. God's glory is *enhanced* by its having been polished in hard-fought encounter with very powerful and entrenched enemies.

Revelation is the more helpful to us for taking such a view. Not only is it more biblical, it also is more in accord with our own experience in the world. The book is for real, talking about the world we know and with which we must contend.

(10) Yes, the coming of the kingdom must entail an all-out struggle against the opponents of God. Nevertheless, John displays total confidence that the victory will be God's. However, that claim does not represent mere optimistic projection on John's part. Not at all; God's final victory is *guaranteed,* because the completely decisive battle *already has been fought and won.* Jesus did the fighting on Good Friday; God confirmed the victory on Easter. There lies the turning point of world history; all that went before was prologue, all that follows (including the coming of the end itself) is epilogue. Jesus' death-and-resurrection was "it"; thereafter, God's war for the world can go to its appointed end. Thus it is in reference to this event (and none other) that John reports a voice from heaven: "Now is the hour of victory for our God, the hour of his kingdom coming in power, when his Christ comes to his rightful rule!" (Revelation 12:10).

A very important implication follows. The Revelator cannot portray any new and subsequent face-off between God and Evil and still be true to his revelation—not even a final showdown at the end. Any such would detract from what Jesus did at Calvary, would imply that that victory had been something less than sufficient. Contrary to the way Revelation usually is read, we will find John being entirely consistent in this regard; it is a point we will want to watch.

(11) Finally, because the important victory already has been won and because the Victor is himself present and active, it follows that the end-state right now is proceeding out of the Christ-event, the kingdom at this moment is in process of becoming actual. This is not to discount the importance of or expectancy for "that day," the time when the heretofore "coming" kingdom shall in all truth "be" as it is in heaven. However, it is to affirm—as Revelation most certainly does—that eschatological reality is to be *tasted* as well as waited for. And this, in the final analysis, is why the Christian can afford to be *perpetually* expectant, can be happy in his eschatology whether God has named this as the last generation or not. Right now we are in the Eschaton which he *is,* no matter when the eschaton of "that great gettin'-up morning" arrives. Even so, come, Lord Jesus!

The eleven points above are so completely assumed and so pervasively implied in Revelation that they are too big to fit into a commentary regarding a particular verse; so we have presented them here. Now you can (and ought to) read them out of the book as a whole.

I am convinced that most of our popular calendarizers would themselves accept most of the points presented here. They probably would admit that they are true to the book of Revelation and might even agree that they are more fundamental than matters of date and detail. Yet I maintain that calendarizing curiosity carries the focus of interest away from these essentials and over to controversial side-issues. Calendarizing commentaries tend to distract from the most basic ideas of Revelation; the hope is that this one can come down on them with both feet.

We now are ready to read our way through Revelation—except that we ought to make a few observations regarding the book's overall structure and method.

Two charts to which we will make repeated reference are included in this book. They have been printed just inside the covers so that they can be located easily without having to keep a finger in the place. The Time-Line of the Revelator's Construct of History is in the front. An Outline of the Book of Revelation is in the back. There is no need to study the charts now; we will use them as we go along.

We are going to make one important assumption regarding the formal structure of Revelation. It is a matter that cannot be conclusively proven either way; but our alternative seems to make better sense of things. We assume that not all the events John describes are meant to constitute a single, straight-line sequence, each scene following directly upon the heels of the one before. Rather, at points, John takes the liberty of doubling back, going another time through a period already covered, giving us a new angle on it, using a somewhat different imagery. His might be called a "spiral approach," circling back (as a good teacher does) to fill in and fill out a concept by coming at it in different ways. The chart inside the back cover makes evident where the doubling back occurs.

This observation leads to one of a more general sort. Throughout his book our author displays a certain freedom, flexibility, and imagination. After all, his material is presented as "visions"—and visions are the stuff from which poetry (and not a travel guide) is made. The book is a masterpiece in its use of imagery and word pictures. And we ought to have the courtesy to read the book after the manner in which the author presents it. Yet most exegesis forces him to plod precisely when he is trying to soar. It is the old problem of not being able to see the forest for the trees. We tend to read scripture with a close, analytic mind-set that focuses not just on *trees*, even, but on the makeup of the bark and leaves. No wonder we fail to appreciate the vista of the forest and the joy of a walk through it!

The need to read and think in terms of "scenic views" rather than "factual analysis" is particularly crucial regarding a "vision book" like Revelation. We should be ready to turn our imaginations and spirits loose to run with the author rather than continually forcing him to halt with: "What does that mean?" "How is that phrase to be interpreted?" "Why did you color that horse red?" "Is that a reference to the ten nations of the European Common Market?" Revelation calls for readers who are dreamers, not nit-pickers. So let John draw his pictures, and then you scale your meditation to their large lineaments. Indeed, the form customary to commentaries may not be the best for handling Revelation—so we will try to keep ours from becoming a customary commentary.

In this regard, neither I nor any other commentator should claim to be able to explain every verse of the book and satisfy every problem concerning it. I, for one, am more than willing to say, "I don't know," to any number of questions that may be asked. Even so, our understanding of the book as a whole certainly should be controlled by the big ideas that are clear, emphatic, and repeated rather than by the obscure allusions that give us trouble. So again, let us not force John to plod by demanding an explanation of every jot and tittle before we are willing to enjoy his big scene.

A great deal of the Revelator's imagery and even phraseology comes from the Old Testament; evidently he knew that volume virtually by memory. But the *manner* in which he uses these references is more noteworthy than simply the fact *that* he uses them. Although filled with such borrowings, his book is by no means a mere pastiche or patchwork. He has digested the material and made it his own; when he uses it, he uses it in his own way, for his own purposes, enhancing the uniqueness of his own vision. In some cases we can be helped to understand the Revelator by examining the Old Testament source of the reference; and we shall do this where it seems helpful. But more frequently it is the case that his creativity is such that one can learn much more by studying the context within which he *places* the reference than the one from which he *took* it.

There is, however, another consideration that sometimes makes the identification of Old Testament allusions important. When the Revelator uses a quotation, he, of course, is not himself responsible for the exact wording involved. Assuredly, he selected the quote because he wanted its main idea; but the wording may carry some implications he would have avoided had the phrasing been strictly his own. The reader should be willing to grant John a little more latitude when he is working with the earlier tradition than when he is speaking entirely for himself.

One basic aspect of John's "poetic," imaginative approach is found time and again throughout his book. It is the "symmetrical" relationship he develops between the kingdom of Good and the kingdom of Evil. On point after point after point, even down to rather small details, a feature regarding the Good will have its counterpart regarding Evil. The main structure of this symmetry we will outline now; details we will note as we come to them.

THE GOOD	over against	THE EVIL
(1) God the Father		(1) Satan, the dragon
(2) Jesus Christ, the Lamb		(2) Antichrist, the beast
(3) The Holy Spirit		(3) The False Prophet, the second beast
(4) The Woman Clothed with the Sun		(4) The Great Whore
(5) Jerusalem (Old and New)		(5) Babylon

The symmetrical approach seems, indeed, to be a very effective and accurate way to portray Evil. Evil comes through as a perverted, mirror image of the Good. And this is the explanation of its power and attractiveness. Evil is not sheer ugliness but rather counterfeit beauty; that is why it is so dangerous. And John's symmetry is designed to emphasize the *counter*feit aspect. Evil is the negative of the positive print which is the Good, the dark image of that which is light, the demonic inversion which spells perversion.

This basic principle within Revelation could be called "dualism," except that that term usually implies some sort of equality between the powers involved. John's symmetry won't allow such. Counter to the organization, advancement, and edification of the Good stands the chaos, regression, and deterioration of Evil. In Jesus Christ, the Good appears as power hidden in apparent weakness; the *counter*feit is Evil's apparent power that hides its true weakness. Besides, John wants to tell us that the Evil we encounter already has been defeated in Jesus' death and resurrection. Revelation doesn't come anywhere close to portraying a dualistic, fifty-fifty chance between Good and Evil. For John, the only power left to Evil is that of *seduction*—that and nothing more. Seduction is a power to contend with, of course— particularly for us who are so vulnerable to it—but it isn't something that puts the outcome of history into doubt.

There is one other feature of the Revelator's work which is just as significant as his symmetry. It is his symbolic use of *numbers*. In this instance, too, his Old Testament constitutes a rich tradition behind him; but, again, he uses it with particular power and effect. His primary number is SEVEN. Tracing clear back to the seven-day creation account of Genesis 1, it represents wholeness, unity, harmony, order and is thus the number of Good and of God. Over and beyond the sheer number of times "seven" appears in John's text, a glance at the outline inside the back cover will reveal to what extent Revelation itself is *structured* over the number seven. It could well be called *The Book of Sevens*. John has done this deliberately; it is a potent way of proclaiming: "History is built on *sevens* and is going to come up *sevens*. God is Lord, and the world is his!"

Much less prominently, THREE also occurs as a good, God

number. There is some evidence that John, this early, is beginning to read trinitarian implications into it.

But John thinks symmetrically; so, if Good has its number, Evil must have its, too. The number is THREE-AND-A-HALF. It may be that the Revelator derived this from Daniel's "a time and times and half a time" (Daniel 7:25 and elsewhere). But it may also be that both authors understood it the same way: 3 1/2 is a "broken" 7. The pattern is right; Evil appears in a perverted image of the Good, and its number is the broken version of the Good number; it is *counter* in every respect.

There is one other prominent number in the Revelation glossary. TWELVE is the number of the church, Zion, the people of God. John explicitly derives it from the twelve tribes of the old Israel *and* the twelve apostles of the new Israel, which is the Christian community. That the number twelve has this double referent is John's way of making a most important theological affirmation. Although, at the time he was writing, Jews and Christians were very much at each other's throats, John insisted that this situation did not mark God's ultimate will and plan. Through Jesus Christ, he intends to bring them together into the one people of God; and the one number, twelve, with its bilateral reference, is the sign of the essential unity.

A further general observation about the structure of Revelation should be made. The time-line chart inside the front cover suggests that John's account covers two basic periods. (1) The Énd-Time, leading up to the end itself, begins with the close of Jesus' earthly ministry and continues until his return (the point of demarcation). (2) The End Itself includes the events consequent upon his return. Now according to both John's chronological indicators and the number of key events involved, the second period is longer and carries more weight than the first. Yet, in terms of the ˙writing space he devotes to each, the first period gets eighteen chapters to three for the second—or approximately fifteen pages to less than three for the second.

The rationale for this apparent disproportion seems clear. Both John's original readers and we ourselves are living in this first, end-time period which lies between Jesus' historical incarnation and his eschatological coming again. This is the period that concerns us specifically; in a very real sense, the rest is out of our hands. And John's primary purpose in writing is to give practical instruction for the situation in which his readers actually find themselves. Thus the very proportioning of his book is evidence that John did not share with contemporary calendarizers their primary concern of doping out events that are of no real relevance to present obligations and opportunities.

Not only in specific preparation for writing this book, but as part of my ongoing education, I have read a good many books about Revelation. Many were worthless; but from many others I undoubtedly have derived insights that have become so assimilated as my own that their point of origin no longer can be identified. I am not volunteering now to undertake the research that would be necessary simply to give credit to whom credit is due. Anyone who recognizes something he thinks belongs to him can consider himself thanked.

However, the one book I found most helpful and upon which I am most dependent is that by the Swiss-American scholar, Mathias Rissi, *Time and History* (John Knox Press, 1966). Even so, the form and style of his book was such as to make it hard to use and of virtually no help to lay readers. Besides, it is now out of print and generally unavailable. My presentation is enough different in kind that it is as much as impossible for me to spot and credit each specific dependency; but I do want to acknowledge the debt and tender my gratitude.

THE REVELATION
OF
JESUS CHRIST

— Made Known to John

In the translation of
THE NEW ENGLISH BIBLE

1:1-20

The Introduction
to the Book

THE COMMISSION

1   This is the revelation given by God to Jesus Christ. It was given to him   (1:1-3)
so that he might show his servants what must shortly happen. He made
2   it known by sending his angel to his servant John, who, in telling all
that he saw, has borne witness to the word of God and to the testimony
of Jesus Christ.
3   Happy is the man who reads, and happy those who listen to the
words of this prophecy and heed what is written in it. For the hour of
fulfilment is near.

John begins by establishing the authority of his book. As we
already have noted, he does so by invoking (contrary to the
translation printed here) "*apocalypsis Jesu Christus*—which God
gave to him." We noted, too, that this phrase probably is meant to
carry a double meaning: Jesus Christ is both the revealer of the
revelation and the one revealed in it.

The ultimate recipients, the ones for whose benefit the revelation is intended, are Jesus' "servants." Here is our first reference
to Christians, or the church; such references constitute a very rich
and important train of thought for John (and for us); we will want
to give them particular notice. The Greek word could as accurately
be translated "slaves"—that's what "servants" were in those days.
In John's vocabulary a Christian is above all "a slave of Christ."
Certainly, the term is not meant to carry any implications of
"involuntary servitude"; but it does suggest the quality of dedication, loyalty, and obedience that his followers owe to the Master.
They have been bought at a price.

The content of the revelation is to be "what must *shortly*
happen." As we observed earlier, if this was meant as a calendar

claim, it was a false one; those words were written in the first century to Christians of that day. However, as a basis for an eschatological stance, the words are always true and always urgent. When will the end come? John didn't know; and Jesus, the Revealer, had said *he* didn't know. But in your perpetual expectancy, you *act* as though it is soon; from a Christian perspective, these are things that "must shortly happen."

The revelation comes to John by means of an "angel." The word "angel" means "messenger," and we ought to keep our sights on this modest definition. The imagery of wings, halos, background music, and unearthly beauty is a tradition that has developed since John's day; and indeed, we will discover in Revelation several passages expressly designed to keep angels down to the "messenger" or "servant" level. Angels do appear in the book with great frequency; but we dare not grant them any importance in and of themselves. As message bearers, their presence always should direct our attention to the message rather than to the bearer.

In receiving this revelation-message, John calls himself "Jesus' servant John." There is not the slightest doubt but that the author of the book was a man named John; there is nothing but doubt when it comes to identifying John Who? Most commentaries would spend a great deal of time in the introduction arguing about John Who? We choose to do it briefly here—largely because we don't know and care only little.

The traditional understanding has been that this is the Apostle John, disciple of Jesus, son of Zebedee, brother of James. That poses some difficulties, however. Our John does not name himself as the apostle—and here would have been a most logical place for him to do so. He clearly is interested in establishing the authority of his book; and to have reminded the readers of his apostolicity would have contributed to that interest. Further, our author treats Jesus, the kingdom, the nature of history, etc., out of an entirely different frame of reference than does the author of the Gospel of John; and the experts tell us that the two even write quite different styles of Greek.

But these observations are presented not so much to eliminate John the Apostle as simply to keep the question open. The important thing is that this book is presented as a revelation of Jesus Christ and has been accepted by the church as such. The claim can be tested only by asking whether what Revelation tells us about Christ jibes with what we know of him otherwise. Having the identity of the human author would be of no help on that score; the book does not consist of historical report, so there is no relevance to the question of his being an historical eyewitness. Either Revelation carries its own authority (with the author named simply "John") or else it carries no authority at all; the identity of the author wouldn't change anything. In many cases we want to know the identity of the author for the light it would throw on the circumstances of the book's being written; but in this case we already are much more certain regarding those circumstances than we have any hope of becoming in regard to the identity of the author. He is John; that's as much as we need to know.

John says that he has "borne witness to the word of God and to the testimony of Jesus Christ." Both "bear witness" and "testimony" reflect the same Greek root *martyr*. John uses it here in reference to himself and to Jesus; a bit later he will use it in reference to Christians generally. It is one of his key concepts—and one, along with "slaves," to go into our collection headed "What does it mean to be a Christian?"

The word will be recognized as the source of our English word "martyr"; yet the translators are correct, the Greek word means "witness" or "testimony." But the English word means "one who is *killed* because of his faith"; how did we get from the one meaning to the other? The answer seems plain: time was that, when a Christian made his good witness for Jesus Christ, he was very likely to get himself killed in consequence. As a result, the meaning of the word gradually slipped off from the person's witness and onto the fact of his getting killed.

For the Greek of Revelation, the translators are correct in going for "witness"; but we need only to note with what consistency John mentions death in close proximity to his word *martyr*, and it is evident that the slippage already has started and the word must be allowed to point both ways at once. For John, then, *martyr* denotes a quality of "witness" that is so deep and dedicated that the testifier is willing to face death for the sake of it. John is clear that a primary call of the Christian is to be a "martyr"—not necessarily *to be* killed but to make the witness that risks it. We will see, too, that John's use of the term suggests that this witness goes beyond simply talking to others *about* Jesus to include living the sort of life that *demonstrates* that one is his slave.

John here uses the phrase "the testimony of Jesus (*martyria Jesu*)"; it becomes a specialized term to which he returns time and again. It seems to carry a double meaning: It can refer to the testimony Christians make *to* Jesus, the testimony that he is Lord, Savior, etc. However, it can also refer to a testimony he himself made (or makes). Jesus, too, is a *witness*—and what he witnesses to is the coming of the kingdom of God. These two interpretations of *martyria Jesu* are different but they are not in conflict; when we witness to Jesus as the Eschatological One, we also are witnessing to the kingdom to which he witnessed; one way we witness *to* him is by joining him in *his* witness. John will use the phrase to carry all these meanings—and likely does so here.

"Happy is the man who reads . . . " is a beatitude couched in the same terminology as Jesus' beatitudes of the Sermon on the Mount. Seven of them appear scattered throughout Revelation. This "seven" may be accidental—but then again, it may not be. (By the way, if the message of this book is that the world will end in the last quarter of the twentieth century, what does John have in mind in calling first-century Christians to "heed" or "keep" it?)

And again, "the hour of fulfillment is *near*."

THE GREETING

(1:4-8) John to the seven churches in the province of Asia.   4

Grace be to you and peace, from him who is and who was and who is to come, from the seven spirits before his throne, and from Jesus   5
Christ, the faithful witness, the first-born from the dead and ruler of the kings of the earth.

To him who loves us and freed us from our sins with his life's blood, who made of us a royal house, to serve as the priests of his God and   6
Father—to him be glory and dominion for ever and ever! Amen.

Behold, he is coming with the clouds! Every eye shall see him, and   7
among them those who pierced him; and all the peoples of the world shall lament in remorse. So it shall be. Amen.

'I am the Alpha and the Omega', says the Lord God, who is and who   8
was and who is to come, the sovereign Lord of all.

John is entirely specific as to whom his writing is directed, the Christians of seven little congregations near the Aegean Coast of

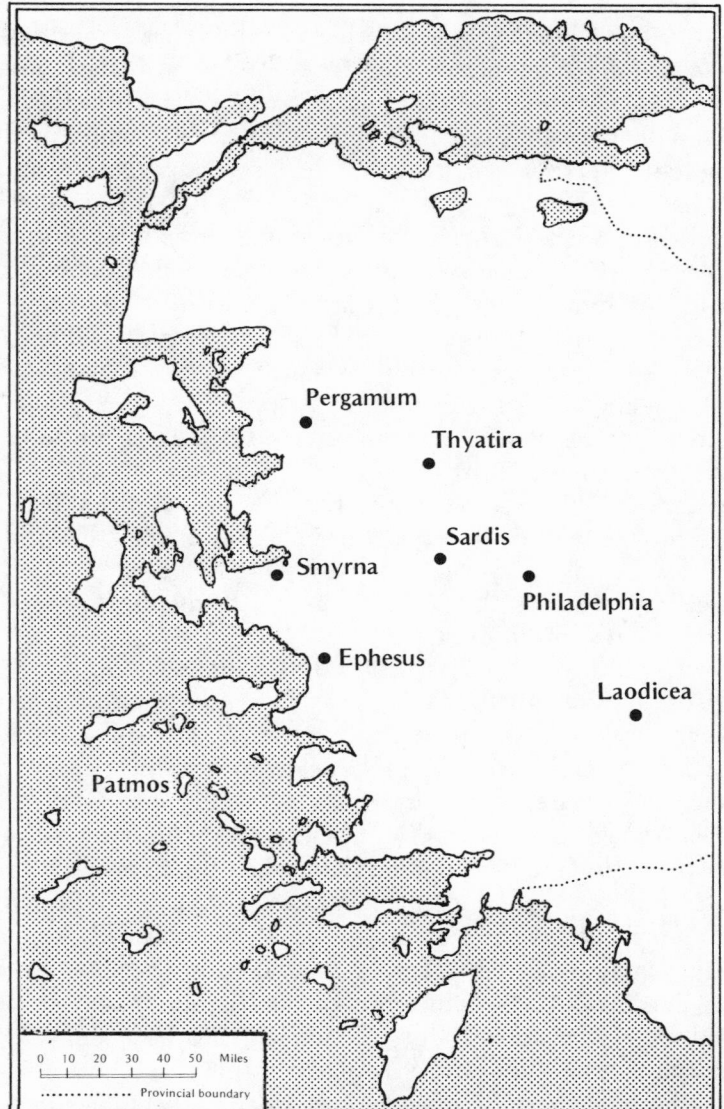

THE PROVINCE OF ASIA (Western Part)

Asia Minor (see the map). There is not the slightest doubt that these were actual, down-to-earth Christian gatherings that John knew well and with whose people he was entirely familiar. John is writing *to them*, and there is nothing to indicate that he ever had any other readers in mind.

Before long, John's book will become quite esoteric—peopled with angels and demons, moving from heaven to hell, describing strange and incredible events—but it opens in the midst of ordinary, mundane reality: a leader of the first-century church writing to the congregations he probably had helped organize and of which he was in charge. This link with actuality, this anchor into normal history, is a vital orientation for understanding the book as a whole. There is no evidence at all to indicate that John intends these as anything except the actual congregations he names—not periods of world history or anything of the sort. When John speaks plainly, read him plainly; we will have problems enough when the going *does* get rough.

John greets his churches in the name of God. In so doing, he recognizes the basic "threeness" of God—although we should be aware that he was writing before the church had developed anything like the formal theological definition we call "the trinity." The titles he gives to the "persons" of God are of particular significance; consider that John is here *introducing* some of the major characters of his drama.

God the Father he calls (in a wording that gets closer to the symmetry of the original Greek than does the translation above) "him who was and who is and who comes." Primarily, of course, this is an affirmation of God's lordship over all of history, past, present, and future (which is John's particular interest). Also, it emphasizes the "comingness" of God, the fact that always there is *more* to be expected from him than what we have experienced thus far (another of John's particular interests). But still another meaning may be involved as well. The God of the Old Testament bore the name "Yahweh." It was derived from the root "to be," and in Exodus 3:13-14 is interpreted as meaning "I am," or "I am who I am." Now John adopts the ancient "to be" name of God but suggests that, under the revelation that has come in Jesus Christ, the name of God must be expanded to become *three*-fold (a good, God number, recall) and incorporate the past and the future of "was" and "comes" as well as the present of "I am." John's is a bold and thought-provoking stroke.

God the Holy Spirit John apparently refers to as "the seven spirits before his throne." This, also, may be a brand-new usage (John is nothing if not original); at least we are not at all accustomed to hearing the Holy Spirit referred to in the plural. And yet the way John uses the concept here and elsewhere strongly indicates that it is the Holy Spirit he has in mind. He seems able to treat the Spirit as either singular or plural—or both. And he may be onto a very important insight.

When referred to in the singular, it is, of course, the unity, the oneness, of the Spirit that is affirmed; there is but *one* Spirit of God. However, when referred to in the plural, an equally important truth about the Spirit is affirmed: he is not confined to one place at one time and one mode of operation. His oneness is not a limitation as ours is or even as the oneness of the historical Jesus was. The Spirit is more than and can be other than just speaking in tongues, or physical healing, or strange miracles. He is present and active not just among certain groups within the church or only within the church itself. He *is* singular, but he *acts* plural. And if plural, the only option is that he be a "seven." The Holy Spirit is completeness, harmony, order, and integrity; he *is* God.

(In this whole matter, John may be thinking the thoughts of his progenitors after them. Throughout the Old Testament, the Hebrew word for "God" actually is a plural form.)

Jesus Christ comes last because John wants to give him particular emphasis; and the titles are of particular significance. They form a *three*-fold sequence (Jesus also rates a God number) of which the *sequence* is as important as the titles themselves.

Jesus is, first, "the faithful witness (*martyr*)." This, I believe, is the only place in Scripture that such a title is ascribed to him; but it is as significant as any other. Jesus did maintain his faithful witness to the coming kingdom of God even unto death—death on a cross. He was an authentic martyr; and this title describes his career during his public ministry, up to and including the crucifixion.

But because Jesus was faithful in his martyr-witness, God crowned it with a resurrection; so Jesus is also, John tells us, "the first-born from the dead." That term "first-born" clearly implies that others are to follow in consequence of Jesus' being born from the dead; Jesus' experience is not to be understood as his alone but as involving his followers as well. Although this relationship is specified only in this second title, other references make it plain that John understands it so regarding all three. Jesus was *the*

faithful witness, but his followers are called to be faithful witnesses with him. If he is the first-born from the dead, they are to
be the latter-born.

In consequence of his resurrection, John says in the third place,
Jesus is "ruler of the kings of the earth." Jesus is *Lord.* Note the
linkage between the three titles: each is dependent upon those
that preceded it; each points to the one that follows it. Notice,
also, that John says Jesus *is* ruler of the kings of the earth, not
that he some day will *become* such. Yet when we get into John's
account, the evidence would all seem to point the other way. "The
kings of the earth"—who, we will see, represent earthly power and
authority, militarism, exploitation, and repression—form a clique
which plays a very major role in John's story; we will want to keep
an eye out for them. After all, they did manage to execute Jesus;
and John portrays them as playing hob with humanity and the
church—even challenging God himself. How can John say that
Jesus *is* their ruler?

We are here at the heart of John's message, particularly as he
intended it for the seven churches. It is: things aren't what they
seem! From everything the seven churches could see (and most of
us can see) it appears clear that "the kings of the earth" are where
the action is; theirs is the clout that makes things happen; theirs
are the actions determining the course of history. That we buy this
view of things is confirmed by the assumption of contemporary
Christian activism that, if things are going to be changed at all,
they will have to be changed *there.* All our efforts are directed at
influencing "the kings of the earth"—with very little to show in
the way of accomplishment. (With all his talk about the kings of
the earth, John gives not the slightest hint of any Christian call to
be out trying to influence them—either to change or to subvert
them. John, rather, little more than stands around and watches
them fall to pieces from their own internal weakness.)

No, things are not what they seem! Contrary to their own
inflated opinion, that crew does not hold the reins of history.
John's very first notice of the kings of the earth is to proclaim that
they have a *ruler*, they are being ruled. That ruler—because he is
also the martyr-witness who has been born from the dead—already
has won the decisive victory and established his control. Recall the
pattern we described earlier: God's is real power clothed in apparent powerlessness; Evil's is apparent power which is really power-

lessness. Things are not what they seem! Jesus *is* Lord—and that
not only of us slaves who accept his lordship but of everyone else,
up to and including the kings of the earth.

Although it is not said here, the pattern still holds: the things
these titles say of Jesus are, each in its own way, reiterated in the
experience of the Christian. Because he is ruler, we, in some sense,
are too. We no longer have to be ruled by the kings of the earth
and can't be forced to accept their premise that what they control
constitutes the power of history.

"Jesus Christ, the faithful witness, the first-born from the dead,
and ruler of the kings of the earth": who ever has spoken more of
the truth about him in fewer words?

John proceeds to dedicate his book to this Jesus Christ, ascribing praise to him particularly for what he has done in behalf of
John and his readers. It was in giving himself on the cross that he
demonstrated his love and won for them their freedom. He has
made (not *will someday make* but already, in his death and
resurrection, *has made*) of them a royal house of priests—and it is
here, rather than with "the kings of the earth," that true *royalty*
resides. The reference is to Exodus 19:6, where the promise is in
the *future* tense and addressed to those who made the covenant at
Sinai. John, no doubt, means to suggest that, through Jesus Christ,
God's *promises* to Old Testament Israel are being fulfilled in the
new Israel of the Christian church. Elsewhere, also, John calls the
Christians "priests." Fundamentally, a priest is one who has been
set aside for the service of God. This likely is all that John intends;
he never gives any indication that he values cultic, liturgical, or
sacramental modes of thought; and indeed, he specifically cuts the
temple out of his New Jerusalem.

We need to make some explanation of the phrase "for ever and
ever" so that we can use it later. The translation—demanding, as it
does, the sense of *endlessness*—is not wholly accurate; the literal
reading is "aeons of the aeons." Now in most cases—as here—the
implication of endlessness undoubtedly is appropriate. But we will
find some instances in which the more literal understanding,
namely that of a very long yet limited period of time, is called for.
We need to keep the language free to express what the Greek
actually says.

Verses 7-8, returning to John's prime theme, proclaim Christ in
his "soon-coming." Although his "comingness" is a constant qual-

ity in Christ, here the reference more specifically is to his *parousia*, the very event of his eschatological arrival. This event, announced here for the first time, will be continually pointed to by John; and the description of it will mark the turning point of his book.

Parousia is the ordinary Greek term for a "coming," or "advent"—but it comes to be applied to the eschatological arrival of Christ which we commonly call "the *second* coming." But not just any coming in anywhere qualifies as a *parousia;* the Greek word carries specific connotations that can be helpful to us. A *parousia* is an entrance that immediately changes the situation into which the entrance is made. While the teacher is out of the room, a great, wild eraser fight gets going. When she steps back in, that's a *parousia!* Have you ever seen an eraser stop in mid-air? (Note that, although the word *eschaton* [the end] has not at all the same meaning as the word *parousia* [a coming], in Christian eschatology the one event is understood as the sign of the other. The two terms get used on an exchange basis, if not synonymously.)

The dominant theme of this present treatment of the parousia is its *universality.* Christ's appearance shall be of decisive effect for *everyone*—not just those who await and desire it, John specifies, but even those who are so opposed to the presence of Christ that they took him out of the picture in the first place.

We already have said something about "universalism" (see page 28 above) and now need to say more. We are going to take special note of each of John's universalistic statements as we come to them; but we are not going to comment upon the overall character of his "universalism" until we have all the evidence in hand and can address the matter as a whole. However, we need to keep open minds and be aware that calling a text "universalistic" can suggest any one of a number of things. It could denote any of the following:

(1) that the gospel of Christ is intended for *all* men, depending only upon whether they choose to accept it;

(2) that God's action through Jesus Christ will be of decisive effect for *all* men—not necessarily implying that it will be of the same effect for all;

(3) that God will save *all* men, whether they make any acknowledgment of Jesus Christ or not;

(4) that, there being no ill effect in failing to acknowledge

Christ, at the end it will become apparent that, in their own ways, *all* actually have acknowledged him and been saved;

(5) that, even after death, in spite of and even through God's just punishments, the way still is open for men to repent, acknowledge Christ, and be saved—and thus there remains the *possibility* that *all* will choose to be saved.

It quickly will become apparent that John has no use for the universalism of Nos. 3 and 4. We will now begin sorting out his texts regarding the other three possibilities. The present passage affirms at least No. 2. Whether it intends to suggest anything more depends upon one's reading of the phrase "all . . . shall lament in remorse." That *could* mean that some people will be lamenting the crucifixion out of their love for Jesus, and others, unrepentant, simply because they will be punished for having killed him. However, it could as well mean that *all* had come to heartfelt repentance over Jesus' death and out of a love toward him. The phrase itself comes from Zechariah 12:9-10; there it explicitly is not applied to *all* peoples—but it does just as clearly denote true repentance and love.

It would be unwise to try to draw a firm conclusion on the basis of this one verse; so leave the matter open and hold this passage to go along with many others to come.

In verse 8, God enters the scene to affirm what has just been said about the coming of Jesus. He takes as title the first and last letters of the Greek alphabet, a way of saying, "I am the Lord of all and cover the whole." It should be noted that elsewhere John ascribes this same title to Jesus; he never allows any distinction of status or honor between God the Father and God the Son. Also, there appears again the threefold title of the God who was, who is, and who comes. The placement of this allusion to the coming of God likely can be taken as an indication of John's understanding that the parousia of Christ *is* the coming of God; when Christ comes, he is Immanuel ("God *with* us").

JOHN AND THE REVEALER

(1:9-20) I, John, your brother, who share with you in the suffering and the 9
sovereignty and the endurance which is ours in Jesus—I was on the
island called Patmos because I had preached God's word and borne my
testimony to Jesus. It was on the Lord's day, and I was caught up by 10
the Spirit; and behind me I heard a loud voice, like the sound of a
trumpet, which said to me, 'Write down what you see on a scroll and 11
send it to the seven churches: to Ephesus, Smyrna, Pergamum, Thyatira, Sardis, Philadelphia, and Laodicea.' I turned to see whose voice it 12
was that spoke to me; and when I turned I saw seven standing lamps of
gold, and among the lamps one like a son of man, robed down to his 13
feet, with a golden girdle round his breast. The hair of his head was 14
white as snow-white wool, and his eyes flamed like fire; his feet 15
gleamed like burnished brass refined in a furnace, and his voice was like
the sound of rushing waters. In his right hand he held seven stars, and 16
out of his mouth came a sharp two-edged sword; and his face shone like
the sun in full strength.

When I saw him, I fell at his feet as though dead. But he laid his right 17
hand upon me and said, 'Do not be afraid. I am the first and the last,
and I am the living one; for I was dead and now I am alive for evermore, 18
and I hold the keys of Death and Death's domain. Write down therefore 19
what you have seen, what is now, and what will be hereafter.

'Here is the secret meaning of the seven stars which you saw in my 20
right hand, and of the seven lamps of gold: the seven stars are the angels
of the seven churches, and the seven lamps are the seven churches.

Everything thus far has been prelude—although not by that token
waste motion. John has been about the crucial work of defining
his key concepts, setting his major themes, getting us oriented for
the book proper. It is most appropriate, then, that that book
proper open with a scene in which the revealing Christ comes to
John with his revelation.

"I, John, your brother": he still wants to be known as a
brother, one with his hearers, rather than an apostle. The next
phrase, a particularly significant one, could more closely be translated: "joint participant with you in the suffering and the sovereignty and the endurance (steadfastness) of Jesus." John is writing
to Christians of the end-time (which is our situation, also) and is
characterizing what is to be his and their experience during this
period. He wants to say not merely that he and they are "joint
participants" in these things but that together they participate in
these things *with Christ*. The Christian experience is an extension

of Jesus' own experience; and it is only because they are "with him" that they have any chance of coming through.

The three experiences named here have some correlation with the three titles earlier ascribed to Christ. His "suffering" was, of course, the other side of his martyr-witness. His "sovereignty" is the lordship of the risen Christ, his being ruler of the kings of the earth. The Christian is to share in both. The middle term of being "born from the dead" is not mentioned here; but it is the only way of getting from suffering to sovereignty, and John knows that Christians participate with Christ in this one, too.

The suffering and the sovereignty—we end-time Christians are caught between these two, we live out of a strange mixture of the two (as Jesus himself did). We usually think of the two as contradictory and incompatible—and yet we do experience both, and both together. Yes, in Christ we do know at least moments of sovereignty, times when we are on top of things. Yet there is always the suffering—so inextricably mixed in that there is no way to get the one without taking the other. And when, in our "celebrations," we try to pretend that things are otherwise, to act as though life is endless joy and gaiety, we know we are faking it. Yes, there is the suffering. Nevertheless, we know that, in Christ, suffering is never just suffering; there are elements of sovereignty, of victory over it even while hurting under it.

Always, in every experience, the suffering *and* the sovereignty. In some ways, life would be more manageable, easier to cope with, if it were one or the other—or at least if they were separated so that we could know which we were supposed to be doing at any given moment, suffering or reigning. But no, they come in, under, and through each other. And the only thing that can hold them together—rather, the only thing that can hold *us* together under the tension is John's third factor, the patient endurance, the steadfastness, of Jesus. Time and again, we will discover, it is this to which John calls his readers; it becomes one of his most consistent themes. From Jesus they must learn and by Jesus they must be enabled to hang in, hold on, and bear up. It is perhaps the Christian's greatest need—the patient endurance of Jesus.

And this emphasis, in itself, leads one to suspect that the reiterated proclamation, "He is coming *soon*," was never meant as a guarantee that it will all be over tomorrow. The two ideas belong together—just as we read both from the same chapter of Revelation. With his help we can *endure*—but, even so, come, Lord Jesus!

The one John meets in this scene is hard to pin down; he defies description, is too big for words. But where the meeting takes place is easy; it can be located on any map (see page 45 above). Hear what John is saying as he works to anchor his celestial visions into this-worldly, first-century Asia Minor; it is important to his purpose.

He was on Patmos, he tells us, because he had preached God's word and—as every Christian is called to do—had borne his *martyria Jesu*, the martyr-witness that both testifies to Jesus and joins him in *his* witness. The assumption usually is made that John had been indicted by the state and was under detention in a penal colony on Patmos, doing forced labor in the mines. That conjecture may be correct; but note well, there is *nothing* of this in the text. We are in trouble when we start taking our conjectures as facts and then make of them a principle of interpretation.

In this case, the line of error goes so: John was arrested and imprisoned *by the Roman state* (the text does not say this). John's readers of the seven churches were under pressure *from the Roman state* to participate in Caesar worship (there is no text indicating this). The beast-riding whore of Revelation 17 is *the Roman state* (this will take more discussion but probably is not the case). The book of Revelation is basically a treatise on Christ and the state, with particular reference to *the Roman state* (it isn't so!). Yes, the state does figure in Revelation, in such symbols as "the kings of the earth," but always in general rather than specifically Roman terms and never as a major focus. So don't let John be captured by the current tendency to see the state as the focus of all evil.

"It was on the Lord's day": this is the one and only reference in Scripture to the fact that Christians had made Sunday their day of worship—not that it hadn't happened earlier but that there just hadn't been occasion for saying so. John was "caught up by the Spirit" (in the singular). That the voice is "like a trumpet" may indicate that it signals the beginning of the end; in John (and the Bible generally) trumpet calls are used to announce decisive moments. The seven churches to which the revelation is addressed are named specifically. A look at the map (page 45) will indicate that the order marks the loop John normally would take in visiting his churches or a messenger take in circulating the scroll. That John is to write on "*a scroll*" suggests that the letters were circulated not separately to the individual churches, but all together, as they presently are in the book.

Among "seven standing lamps" the Revealer takes his place; and these, we are told, represent the seven churches. Lamps, of course, are meant to give light; and the reference, most likely, is to the church's role as martyr-witness. The lamp thus constitutes a very good symbol for the church, and John will use it that way again elsewhere.

That Christ the Revealer is described as "one like a son of man" is important. The phrase comes from Daniel 7:13, where it identifies an eschatological figure who comes "with the clouds of heaven." That John here specifically applies the term to Jesus makes it as much as certain that, when he uses the phrase again at a later point, he still has Jesus in mind. The subsequent description is constituted from Old Testament allusions; and no matter how the imagery affects our modern sensibilities, it is intended to communicate great beauty and glory. Try reading it through the eyes of biblical man rather than your own.

In his right (his dominant) hand, he held "seven stars," which, we are told, are the "angels" of the churches, their heavenly messenger-representatives. John has his point covered two ways. When Christ is thought of as a presence on earth, his place is among the lampstands of the churches. When he is thought of as a being in heaven, he has the churches' angel-telephone right in his hand. Either way, Jesus is *with* his church and never away from it. This is a precious thing for end-time, suffering-sovereignty Christians to know—ourselves as much as those of the Asia Minor congregations.

"Out of his mouth came a sharp two-edged sword." That is one it would be good for us to know, whether we think it precious or not. It symbolizes the power of *judgment*—and it belongs. The historical Jesus demonstrated it. Used as he used it, it is entirely consistent with his love, grace, goodness, and mercy—is in fact a necessary concomitant of these. Discipline, chastisement, and judgment are very much a part of John's picture of Jesus; if they won't fit into yours, it's because yours isn't a picture of the real Jesus. Consider, too, that that "sword-tongue" goes back to Isaiah

49:2, where it belongs to the suffering servant of Yahweh. It can represent the stroke of sharp discrimination between truth and falsehood rather than simply slaughter and punishment.

As a fringe benefit, we have here a caution against simple-minded literalism. In verse 16, Jesus has a sharp two-edged sword for a tongue; in verse 17, he speaks—a neat trick indeed. Then "he laid his right hand upon me"—the same hand that already had seven stars in it. Obviously, John does not intend that his images be interpreted simple-mindedly.

As Jesus comes to the Revelator, the very first words he speaks are, "Do not be afraid!" That's just like Jesus—just what he did speak in Palestine, just what he speaks to us, just what end-time Christians need to hear.

"I am the *living* one; for I was dead and now I am alive for evermore, and I hold the keys of death and Hades." The Revealer's introductory words are crucial ones. They present the theme of "life and death," an important aspect of John's symmetrical method and a most pervasive theme of Revelation as a whole.

Jesus is "the living one," and it is his *resurrection* that qualifies him as such. To call him "the living one" says much more than that he simply is one who is alive—a number of us might qualify on that count. No, John is thinking in terms of the *quality* of life; we can outline the structure of his thought, which is merely touched upon here but developed further as the book proceeds.

"First-order life" is that quality of natural life that we all enjoy as a matter of course. It probably should be listed on the side of the Good, but it has no moral significance in itself. That a person is alive is no indication that he is good or approved of God; good people and bad people, believers and unbelievers, share this quality of life without distinction. Just so, "first-order death," although it is a *counter*part to be listed under the Bad, is equally devoid of moral significance. Biological death comes to good and bad alike and apparently at random; bad people often live long, and good people often die young. Normally, the simple fact that a person has died says nothing one way or the other about the state of his faith and morals. Because they are of this neutral, chance character, John does not attach any great significance or give particular attention to life and death on this level. For example, he does not—as many thinkers do—see the moment of first-order death as marking either the ultimate consummation of the Christian's beatitude or the ultimate loss and prohibition of the same for the nonbeliever. For him, physical death is a comparatively minor transition.

What truly interests John is "second-order LIFE" and "second-order DEATH"—matters of totally *moral* significance. Here is a quality of LIFE that has nothing of death or "dyingness" about it. Such is not the case with first-order life; there, the moment of birth also marks the onset of deterioration, gradual death. And not only from a biological standpoint—our experience of life inevitably includes as well the deterioration and death of family relationships, other social relationships, the relationships of society itself; we often witness and sometimes experience a dying of morals and spirit. As the suffering and sovereignty are completely intermixed, so are life and death; for us, life is three parts death.

But John knows a quality of LIFE that has nothing of death about it—marked, therefore, he tells us later, by the total absence of tears and death and mourning and crying and pain. It is life, life, life—all life—nothing but LIFE! And once one enters this LIFE, he is totally and forever immune to the further threat of any sort of death. For John, the way to this LIFE—the only way to it—is *resurrection.* When, in his first appearance and speech in Revelation, Jesus says, "I am the living one," he actually is proclaiming: "I am the source of LIFE; it is in me—and only in me—that true, second-order LIFE is to be found; I am the LIVING one!" And it is because he was dead and now is alive for evermore that he qualifies as the living one; it was his death-and-resurrection that did it.

Consequently, it follows in John's thought, for us to be resurrected in Christ and with Christ is the one way for us to enter LIFE. I am sure John would not deny that, through Christ, one can *begin* to taste and experience second-order LIFE even in the midst of first-order life-and-death. Nevertheless, his main thrust is toward the total experience of LIFE that comes only upon a resurrection from the dead—and this, in turn, comes only through him who is "first-born from the dead" and into him who is "the LIVING one." For John, LIFE does not come as an *evasion* of death but as a going through it and coming out victorious on the other side. In this regard, it will be important to keep an eye on John's use of the concept "resurrection." Consistently, for him, it denotes this graduation into LIFE; he would never speak of a "resurrection to judgment," "the resurrection of the unjust," or anything of the sort.

It is not mentioned here, but later John will complete his symmetry by speaking of second-order DEATH. It is *death* that carries total moral significance. The *counter*part of LIFE, it is an experience constituted of nothing but deterioration, damnation, tears, mourning, crying, and pain; it is death with nothing of life about it.

Because Jesus is "the LIVING one" who was dead but now is alive for evermore, he also can say, "I hold the keys of death and Hades." "Hades," here, is not to be equated with what we normally call "hell." "Hades" is a Greek concept denoting merely "the realm of the dead." In this reference, then, death represents not so much an individual experience as an active power. "Death and Hades" signifies, therefore, "death and all that goes with it"—all the deterioration, brokenness, pain, and tears to which we already referred. John regularly presents "Death and Hades" as a pair—one of man's most fearful enemies.

But Jesus holds their keys. The intended picture is probably that of a jail cell. Through his resurrection, Jesus got the power over them, and they came under his charge. What freedom they still enjoy is at his sufferance; and when the right time comes (which isn't quite yet), he has everything necessary to lock them up and throw those keys far, far away. The important thing to note is that these words portray a victory *won in the past* but finally to be worked out at some point *in the future*. Yet certainly nothing like a *new* victory is called for. This is John's picture throughout. Death and Hades are still around (as we can well attest); but Jesus, even now, is Lord; he holds the keys. Things aren't what they seem!

2:1–3:22

The Revealer's Letters to Seven Actual Churches of the End-Time

Christ the Revealer dictates to John a letter for each of the churches. They are filled with specific details with which the original readers would have been completely familiar and with which we are almost completely unfamiliar. The frame of reference obviously is first-century Asia Minor and not a twentieth-century end of history.

A couple of general observations should be made before we look at the letters individually. First, it becomes plain that at least some of the congregations had been, were being, and would be persecuted. It is, of course, quite possible that the state was one of the agents of such persecution. However, the text nowhere specifies that; and it nowhere hints that a problem was constituted by the state's demand that Caesar be recognized as divine. This may be because Revelation is an earlier book than usually assumed and mandatory Caesar-worship had not yet become the policy of the Empire. In any case, church-state relations are not the primary concern.

Second, to get at what *is* the primary concern: it clearly regards the internal life of the congregations, namely their tendency to tolerate and follow false teachers, lose their sense of expectancy, drift into complacency, and generally allow their love of Jesus to cool. Then—as now—it seems to have been the case that the coming of persecution from the outside was as likely to steel Christians in their faith as lead them to renege; the greater threat was that the faith would become eroded through carelessness and

59

lack of upkeep. And so, then—as now—the Revealer's prime concern is with *apostasy*, the losing of one's relationship to him.

Yes, persecution must be met and handled. Yes, sins of various sorts must be avoided. But above all, watch your fidelity to Jesus, maintain your relationship to him. For it is only in him you will find the wherewithal for meeting presecution and avoiding sins, only in him you have the means of forgiveness and a way out. So take care to stay close to him.

Now "apostasy" is not a word widely used in the church today—and that is just as well if it is a case of our sitting in self-righteous judgment as to which of our brethren are loyal to Jesus or not. But even so, apostasy is *the* threat to us as it was to the seven congregations addressed by the Revealer. Both individuals and congregations do drift away from their strict loyalty to Jesus, even now are drifting away. And whether we call it by name or not, whether we show any concern over it or not, *apostasy* is what it is, the most serious situation Jesus Christ would warn about. Yes, most of the details of the seven letters are lost to us; we simply do not know enough about the historical situation. But the primary counsel of those letters is as much to the point as if Jesus were addressing them to the congregations where we live and in which we would be the hearers.

Each of the seven letters is constructed over a set pattern, the constituent elements of which are these:

(a) there is a phrase identifying the speaker as the Revealer, taken in each case from the vision by which he was just introduced;

(b) he says, "I know (your situation)," and proceeds to make an evaluation of the congregation;

(c) on the basis of that analysis, words of commendation or chastisement are given;

(d) there comes the formula: "Hear, you have ears to hear, what the Spirit says to the churches";

(e) there is a promise for the victors, i.e., those who remain faithful and do not apostatize.

From the fourth letter on, the order of the last two elements is reversed. If there is any significance to the switch, it escapes us.

1. TO EPHESUS

1 'To the angel of the church at Ephesus write:

(2:1-7)

' "These are the words of the One who holds the seven stars in his
2 right hand and walks among the seven lamps of gold: I know all your
ways, your toil and your fortitude. I know you cannot endure evil men;
you have put to the proof those who claim to be apostles but are not,
3 and have found them false. Fortitude you have; you have borne up in
4 my cause and never flagged. But I have this against you: you have lost
5 your early love. Think from what a height you have fallen; repent, and
do as you once did. Otherwise, if you do not repent, I shall come to
6 you and remove your lamp from its place. Yet you have this in your
7 favour: you hate the practices of the Nicolaitans, as I do. Hear, you
who have ears to hear, what the Spirit says to the churches! To him
who is victorious I will give the right to eat from the tree of life that
stands in the Garden of God."

It is most unlikely that "those who claim to be apostles" were
claiming to be among the number of Jesus' original twelve. Rather,
they would claim to be "those who were sent (of God)," which is
what the word "apostle" means. They may be the same people as
the "Nicolaitans" mentioned in verse 6; but that doesn't tell us
much, because we have no knowledge of the Nicolaitans outside of
these letters in Revelation.

Logically, a "Nicolaitan" would be a follower of "Nicolas"—
whoever he might be. But the name "Nicolas" is itself built upon
the Greek root found in the very next verse, *nikontes*, "him who is
victorious," or "the *victor*." And this concept of "victor" is one
that is central not only to these letters but to Revelation as a
whole. So whoever the Nicolaitans may have been, and whatever
the line they were peddling, the Revealer classifies them with the
thousands upon thousands of deceivers who, throughout the history of the church, have claimed to possess the key to personal
success and victory. Nicolaitans (victory-promisers) are still very
active among us; you can give specific name to those who would
tempt you.

But Jesus says that to go with the Nicolaitans is apostasy and
that true victory is found only in fidelity to him. There is but one
Victor—the faithful witness, first-born from the dead, and ruler of
the kings of the earth—and the victory-claiming Nicolaitans are not
of him. And so the word to the church at Ephesus (and to us) is
"Repent!" This word, particularly prominent in this letter, also is

prominent in the book as a whole. "Repent" means to "turn around," or "come back"; and it is the one solution for apostasy. To go after any victory-promiser but Jesus is apostasy; to repent is to turn back to him. And to the one who, through repentance, finds his victory in Jesus, the promise is LIFE—in this case, the right to eat from the tree of life that stands in the garden of God. In Adam, mankind lost access to this tree and the second-order LIFE it represents. Here it is promised to those who become victorious by remaining steadfast to Christ. At the very end of his book, John will refer to this tree of life once more.

2. TO SMYRNA

(2:8-11)   'To the angel of the church at Smyrna write: 8
            ' "These are the words of the First and the Last, who was dead and
            came to life again: I know how hard pressed you are, and poor—and yet   9
            you are rich; I know how you are slandered by those who claim to be
            Jews but are not—they are Satan's synagogue. Do not be afraid of the   10
            suffering to come. The Devil will throw some of you into prison, to put
            you to the test; and for ten days you will suffer cruelly. Only be
            faithful till death, and I will give you the crown of life. Hear, you who   11
            have ears to hear, what the Spirit says to the churches! He who is
            victorious cannot be harmed by the second death."

The Revealer nowhere shows any desire to evaluate a congregation according to the organizational criteria we would be inclined to use. And so, although admittedly hard pressed and poor, the church at Smyrna is judged to be rich. How so? Plainly, rich in her faithfulness to Jesus.

John, we now should note, was writing in a day different from ours: the Jews were slandering the Christians rather than vice versa. (Not long after the time of John, Christians proceeded to do a notable job of slandering and persecuting in their turn. Jewish-Christian relations might go better today if *both* groups would confess that they have been guilty as opportunity presented itself.)

But the book of Revelation stands above and points beyond this bilateral slandering. For John, "Jew" is a very highly respected and valued term. Indeed, he sees the Christian church as a continuation of Judaism and the end-state of history as involving reunification of the two into the one people of God. Nevertheless, given his faith as to who Jesus is, John can draw no other conclusion but that the Jew who refuses to accept the fact that God has designated Jesus as the awaited Messiah is not being true to his own Judaism, is not (in this action) a *true* Jew, no matter what he may claim on other grounds. The Christians who accept this fulfillment of the Old Testament promises are thus more faithful to the Jewish tradition than are the Jews who refuse and oppose it. And to the extent that these Jews slander and persecute the church, to that extent they have apostatized from their own God-given faith and become "Satan's synagogue."

This is John's theological analysis, but he nowhere draws the conclusion that the Christians are free to retaliate (or even defend themselves) against these Jews. Don't let them shake your faith in Jesus; but for the rest, God can take care of them. And what God has in mind to do, we will discover later, is to bring them to the truth, help them become *true* Jews once more, and through Jesus Christ, restore them to the one people of God.

John's interpretation undeniably is a *Christian* one; as such it cannot be acceptable to believing Jews. But neither can John be accused of anything like anti-Semitism, the encouragement of scorn and hatred toward a person because of his racial background. Either Jesus is the one who Revelation claims him to be or he is not; thus he should receive either the ultimate loyalty of all men or of none. There is no way men even can *be* Christians and Jews without the necessary inference that the other group is way off the track in its assessment of Jesus. But this difference (which if, from the one side, is to be called "anti-Semitism," from the other must just as truly be called "anti-Christianity") is not where the human-relations problem lies. "Anti-Semitism" must refer, not to the basic theological distinction, but to the attitudes and actions one takes toward Jews as persons. The Christians in Smyrna were under attack by some of the Jews, but there is no evidence that John taught or approved the hatred of anyone.

Smyrnean Christians, we are told, will be thrown into prison and put to the test. Jesus' promise of victory is never that of exemption *from* suffering but always of the strength and help that will see one *through* suffering. The "ten days" probably is the customary reference for "a short time" rather than a calendar prediction. But the upshot is that faithfulness *unto death* (not simply "as long as you happen to live" but "even to the extent of accepting death as a consequence of faithfulness") is the way to LIFE. Here is stated the paradox that is basic to the Revelator's concept of second-order LIFE—a restatement, perhaps, of Jesus' "He who loses his life for my sake will find it."

"The second death" refers to what we earlier called "second-order DEATH." John will enlarge upon the idea later; but part of the promise to the victor is immunity from the second death.

3. TO PERGAMUM

(2:12-17)   'To the angel of the church at Pergamum write: 12
           ' "These are the words of the One who has the sharp two-edged
           sword: I know where you live; it is the place where Satan has his   13
           throne. And yet you are holding fast to my cause. You did not deny
           your faith in me even at the time when Antipas, my faithful witness,
           was killed in your city, the home of Satan. But I have a few matters to   14
           bring against you: you have in Pergamum some that hold to the
           teaching of Balaam, who taught Balak to put temptation in the way of
           the Israelites. He encouraged them to eat food sacrificed to idols and to
           commit fornication, and in the same way you also have some who hold   15
           the doctrine of the Nicolaitans. So repent! If you do not, I shall come   16
           to you soon and make war upon them with the sword that comes out
           of my mouth. Hear, you who have ears to hear, what the Spirit says to   17
           the churches! To him who is victorious I will give some of the hidden
           manna; I will give him also a white stone, and on the stone will be
           written a new name, known to none but him that receives it."

The Revealer here identifies himself as the one with the two-edged sword; and the particular theme of the letter is *judgment* against apostasy. Pergamum is "the place where Satan has his throne," for this city was a center for a number of pagan religions. The temptation for the church members here was syncretism, the watering down of their Christianity by importing into it ideas taken from other faiths and philosophies; the concrete examples of Balaam and the Nicolaitans are cited. Syncretism—involving for us, perhaps, more of borrowings from political, psychological, and social philosophies than from religious ones—is no less a danger now than then. It is apostasy and incurs judgment.

We do not know the story of the martyr-witness Antipas, who here, in Christ, merits the same title that earlier was given to Christ himself; we wish we did.

Balaam, obviously, is a derogatory name used to identify some false teacher with the Old Testament apostatizer Balaam. Whether the Balaamites and the Nicolaitans are the same group, related groups, or two different groups, we cannot tell. In any case, their impulse was to lead people away from true loyalty to Jesus. The reference to "fornication" could be to literal sexual promiscuity; however, it could with more likelihood be, as John elsewhere uses it, a picking up of the Old Testament custom of using "fornication" to speak of a promiscuous chasing of other gods.

The concluding promise to the victor seems to be constructed, in this instance, from allusions to the Old Testament period of Israel's wandering in the wilderness (which also, by the way, is where the story of Balaam is to be found). The "manna," the bread from heaven, is sustenance from God. The white stone may refer to the lot-sign that designated God's positive, "yea" decision through the Urim and Thummim (Exodus 28:30). An old Jewish tradition says that the name of God was inscribed on the Urim and Thummim. Later references to Christ's "own new name" (3:12) and "a name known to none but himself" (19:12) make this reference particularly meaningful. The emphasis is upon the "comingness" of Christ; and the promise is that the victor will come to know more of Christ, know him more intimately and completely, than presently is possible. He is the Christ of "more to come."

4. TO THYATIRA

18   'To the angel of the church at Thyatira write: (2:18-29)

' "These are the words of the Son of God, whose eyes flame like fire
19   and whose feet gleam like burnished brass: I know all your ways, your love and faithfulness, your good service and your fortitude; and of late
20   you have done even better than at first. Yet I have this against you: you tolerate that Jezebel, the woman who claims to be a prophetess, who by her teaching lures my servants into fornication and into eating food
21   sacrificed to idols. I have given her time to repent, but she refuses to
22   repent of her fornication. So I will throw her on to a bed of pain, and plunge her lovers into terrible suffering, unless they forswear what she
23   is doing; and her children I will strike dead. This will teach all the churches that I am the searcher of men's hearts and thoughts, and that I
24   will reward each one of you according to his deeds. And now I speak to you others in Thyatira, who do not accept this teaching and have had no experience of what they like to call the deep secrets of Satan; on

you I will impose no further burden. Only hold fast to what you have, 25
until I come. To him who is victorious, to him who perseveres in doing 26
my will to the end, I will give authority over the nations—that same
authority which I received from my Father—and he shall rule them with 27
an iron rod, smashing them to bits like earthenware; and I will give him 28
also the star of dawn. Hear, you who have ears to hear, what the Spirit 29
says to the churches!''

As with Balaam, "Jezebel" is a code name identifying some person
with the Old Testament queen who was particularly noted for her
effort in leading Israel away from the faith and into idolatry. The
references to her fornication, her lovers, and her children are
probably not literal but, rather, suggestive of the Old Testament
model for describing those who teach false religion and lead others
into apostasy. What might have been the relationship between this
Jezebel, the Balaam at Pergamum, and the Nicolaitans, we simply
are unable to say.

The Christian victory, it is made more explicit in this case,
comes through participation in "the endurance of Jesus," involves
holding fast until he comes; and the promise is that the victor will
also participate in "the sovereignty of Jesus." The reference to
ruling the nations with an iron rod (which John uses a number of
times) is from Psalm 2:9. In this instance particularly, it sounds
very cruel and bloodthirsty. Nevertheless, if such is the interpretation, it stands quite out of harmony with the overall picture of
Jesus that John presents. We must assume, then, that at this point
he would not want to be taken with complete literalness. The
Christian sovereignty over the nations is in outlasting them, watching them deteriorate and go to smash through their own corruption; this—rather than our setting out to do the smashing with iron
rods, bombs, or anything of the sort—is John's picture. But, yes,
the promise *is* that the victor will see the nations go under, to be
replaced by the rule of Jesus Christ.

In 22:16, Jesus calls himself "the morning star"; that the
morning star here is given to the victor, then, may intend Christ's
gift of himself. The morning star is also the herald of the dawn and
thus a symbol of hope.

5. TO SARDIS

(3:1-6)

1 'To the angel of the church at Sardis write:
' "These are the words of the One who holds the seven spirits of God, the seven stars: I know all your ways; that though you have a
2 name for being alive, you are dead. Wake up, and put some strength into what is left, which must otherwise die! For I have not found any
3 work of yours completed in the eyes of my God. So remember the teaching you received; observe it, and repent. If you do not wake up, I shall come upon you like a thief, and you will not know the moment of
4 my coming. Yet you have a few persons in Sardis who have not polluted their clothing. They shall walk with me in white; for so they
5 deserve. He who is victorious shall thus be robed all in white; his name I will never strike off the roll of the living, for in the presence of my
6 Father and his angels I will acknowledge him as mine. Hear, you who have ears to hear, what the Spirit says to the churches!"

More than the church at Smyrna, the one at Sardis may be like what *we* know. There, "though hard pressed and poor—yet you are rich!" Here, "though you have a name for being alive, you are dead!" Any church you ever have seen? The Revealer does not judge by outward organizational standards but only by the measure of fidelity.

Revelation belongs to the New Testament tradition of perpetual readiness and not to the calendarizers. As in the Gospel teachings, Jesus still warns that his coming will catch apostate sleepers unawares—in soiled robes.

Better they should be clothed in white robes, which are, throughout Revelation, the symbol of purity and victory. The promise to the victor, in this instance, is not only the white robe but an interesting play on the concept "name." There are two (just two) alternatives: either, in the presence of the Father and his angels, Christ will acknowledge your name, or else your name will be struck off the roll of the living, i.e., of those destined for second-order LIFE. An important implication follows, one the remainder of the book will bear out: the roll of the living is kept on an up-to-date basis, names can be added and (as here) names can be deleted—it all depends upon the person's fidelity. Hear, you who have ears to hear!

6. TO PHILADELPHIA

(3:7-13)   'To the angel of the church at Philadelphia write: 7
           ' "These are the words of the holy one, the true one, who holds the
key of David; when he opens none may shut, when he shuts none may
open: I know all your ways; and look, I have set before you an open   8
door, which no one can shut. Your strength, I know, is small, yet you
have observed my commands and have not disowned my name. So this   9
is what I will do: I will make those of Satan's synagogue, who claim to
be Jews but are lying frauds, come and fall down at your feet; and they
shall know that you are my beloved people. Because you have kept my   10
command and stood fast, I will also keep you from the ordeal that is to
fall upon the whole world and test its inhabitants. I am coming soon;   11
hold fast what you have, and let no one rob you of your crown. He   12
who is victorious—I will make him a pillar in the temple of my God; he
shall never leave it. And I will write the name of my God upon him, and
the name of the city of my God, that new Jerusalem which is coming
down out of heaven from my God, and my own new name. Hear, you   13
who have ears to hear, what the Spirit says to the churches!"

The Revealer now identifies himself as the one "who holds the key
of David," the converse, perhaps, of the earlier "keys of death and
Hades." The reference is to Isaiah 22:22, which also speaks of
opening in a way that none shall shut. The allusion is used here to
suggest that Christ opens or shuts the entrance to eschatological
promise. And the small, weak church at Philadelphia has before it
a sort of eschatological opportunity that no persecution or seduction can close off.

John refers to the church's Jewish opponents as before. That
they will fall down at the church's feet is not the threat of
conquest and enslavement but the promise that they will come to
recognize the truth of that for which the church stands.

And "because you keep the word of my endurance, I will also
keep you." The message is plain: we do not (*can* not) endure out
of the strength of our own endurance; we keep close within *his*
endurance and so are kept *by him*. What we are to be kept *through*
are the end-time trials which John will describe shortly.

The promise to the victor, in this instance, is built around the
imagery of the temple. He shall stand as a very element of the
house of God. The name of God will be written upon him as the
high priest wore on his forehead a golden plate inscribed "Holy to
the Lord." He will be addressed for delivery to the new Jerusalem

(the description of which climaxes the book). And he will bear the new, "more to come" name of Christ. (Later scenes will refer to the Christians' being sealed with these names; John is tying these letters into the rest of his book.)

7. TO LAODICEA

(3:14-22)

14 'To the angel of the church at Laodicea write:
' "These are the words of the Amen, the faithful and true witness,
15 the prime source of all God's creation: I know all your ways; you are
16 neither hot nor cold. How I wish you were either hot or cold! But because you are lukewarm, neither hot nor cold, I will spit you out of
17 my mouth. You say, 'How rich I am! And how well I have done! I have everything I want.' In fact, though you do not know it, you are the
18 most pitiful wretch, poor, blind, and naked. So I advise you to buy from me gold refined in the fire, to make you truly rich, and white clothes to put on to hide the shame of your nakedness, and ointment
19 for your eyes so that you may see. All whom I love I reprove and
20 discipline. Be on your mettle therefore and repent. Here I stand knocking at the door; if anyone hears my voice and opens the door, I
21 will come in and sit down to supper with him and he with me. To him who is victorious I will grant a place on my throne, as I myself was
22 victorious and sat down with my Father on his throne. Hear, you who have ears to hear, what the Spirit says to the churches!" '

Perhaps deliberately, the Laodicean letter is something of a summary, hitting with somewhat more power than the others. The church as a whole (now as then), what does it add up to? Not outright, bold apostasy; it hasn't enough guts for that. But neither can it be called faithful and true—as the Amen himself is called in the verse preceding. No, more like weak tea that is too flavorless to drink as tea, yet strong enough to be ruined as water—not hot enough to invigorate, nor cold enough to refresh.

Verses 17-18 invite an interpretation that may be too neat to be true, but we'll share it anyhow. The ancient city of Laodicea was noted for three things: (1) its wealth—it was a banking center; (2) its wool—sheep galore; and (3) its medicine—site of a medical school. Likewise, the Laodicean church considered itself: (1) rich, (2) well attired, and (3) healthy; whereas the Revealer knew it was (1) poor, (2) naked, and (3) blind. What the Laodiceans need is: (1) gold, not of the sort in their banks but that which goes through the fire of suffering with Jesus; (2) white robes woven of Christian fidelity rather than Laodicean wool; and (3) eye ointment to heal the sort of blindness the pagan medical school encouraged rather than cured.

Verse 19, then, is crucial: Christ's reproof and discipline are a mark, a necessary aspect, of his *love*. Both the church and the world need to be punished—as much as cry out for punishment. Unpunished, they no doubt will simply continue their drift toward destruction. With reproof and discipline, they might just answer the challenge to be on their mettle and repent. In the pages to follow, John will portray a great deal of trauma and suffering. In the effort to understand and justify it, we need continually to remember what is said here: "All whom I love I reprove and discipline. Be on your mettle therefore and repent."

Verse 20 is probably the favorite and most-used verse in the book; but also, it probably intends much more than we customarily see in it. The verb tenses are important. Jesus stands knocking *now* (present tense). If he who has ears to hear also has enough get up and go to answer that knock, Jesus *will* (future tense) come to supper with him. The reference could be to the Lord's Supper; it could be to the great wedding supper of the Lamb (the eschatological banquet mentioned by John and known throughout the Bible); it could be both, there being evidence that they were thought of together and seen as related. But the implication is clear that how you jump to the door at Jesus' present knocking determines whose your table will be when suppertime comes—and this was the very word the lazy Laodiceans needed to hear (and lazy churches today as well).

The promise to the victor is also more powerful in this instance—and with emphasis, again, upon the verb tenses. "You *will be* victorious and have a place on my throne . . . as (and because) I *already was* victorious and sat down with my Father on his throne." His victory—in the cross and resurrection—is the power and accomplishment of ours. And in that victory he sat down with the Father *on his throne*—can it be sheer coincidence that the next chapter opens with a vision of the throne of God? John builds beautifully; and his transitions are neat indeed.

THE GREAT DISJUNCTURE THAT ISN'T

Truth to tell, John is better at writing transitions than I am at reading them. To this point, Revelation has been firmly anchored to John on Patmos and the seven congregations of first-century Asia Minor; after this point, we hear of them no more. Now, as it were, we leap off into space and things go unreal; there is little or nothing we can latch on to as linkage with our own experience or history.

For a long time I felt the discontinuity of this break (with a decided preference for the first part of the book) and felt it as a decided flaw in the work. What possible transition is there between the one part and the other? John has given us two different books rather than one.

But finally I got ointment for my blind eyes, and now I see (or think I do). John has been focusing on seven lowly little churches in a minor part of the world at a less than epochal time in history. That focus has been fine enough even to give us allusions to some of the grubby individuals involved—Balaam, Jezebel, and the Nicolaitans—those along with not so grubby John and Antipas. In Chapter 4, then, the picture suddenly cuts away from all this to heaven and the throne of God.

However, what John intends, I now am convinced, is nothing other than to tell his churches: "Look, my friends, whether you recognize it or not, your history is part of the great and universal mission being directed from God's throne. What you do and what happens to you is an integral and meaningful part of the wonderful thing God is doing with the cosmos, through Christ, to Evil, for mankind. My story starts with you and ends with all things being made new—but it is *one* story! Until you can understand what it is you're part of, you're bound to see yourself and your efforts as lowly; you're defeated before you even get into the game. But look at it once with me from the true perspective of God's throne, and you'll see that because of Jesus there's no way we can lose—*no* way!"

What better transition could one ask for?

4:1–5:14

The Control
of History
in the End-Time

As we move into this scene in the throne room of God, be very aware that John's motive in writing and ours in reading is not simply the satisfaction of curiosity as to what a certain spot in heaven may or may not look like. No, John still is making an affirmation regarding the nature and meaning of history, ours as well as his own. And the essential fact about this history is that it is controlled *from here*. Its center is to be found here rather than in itself; it displays more of the character of a railway car that must be hitched to its engine than an automobile that is self-contained. God is Lord, and history is subject to him. Surely his lordship is powerful and glorious; but John's picture also affirms that it is wise, benevolent, and beautiful—worthy of boundless praise and adoration. Always read John as relevant; this part of the book was addressed to the seven churches just as much as the earlier part was.

THE THRONE OF GOD

1   After this I looked, and there before my eyes was a door opened in   **(4:1-11)**
heaven; and the voice that I had first heard speaking to me like a
trumpet said, 'Come up here, and I will show you what must happen
2   hereafter.' At once I was caught up by the Spirit. There in heaven stood
3   a throne, and on the throne sat one whose appearance was like the
gleam of jasper and cornelian; and round the throne was a rainbow,
4   bright as an emerald. In a circle about this throne were twenty-four

73

other thrones, and on them sat twenty-four elders, robed in white and
wearing crowns of gold. From the throne went out flashes of lightning   5
and peals of thunder. Burning before the throne were seven flaming
torches, the seven spirits of God, and in front of it stretched what   6
seemed a sea of glass, like a sheet of ice.

In the centre, round the throne itself, were four living creatures,
covered with eyes, in front and behind. The first creature was like a   7
lion, the second like an ox, the third had a human face, the fourth was
like an eagle in flight. The four living creatures, each of them with six   8
wings, had eyes all over, inside and out; and by day and by night
without a pause they sang:

'Holy, holy, holy is God the sovereign Lord of all, who was, and is,
and is to come!'

As often as the living creatures give glory and honour and thanks to   9
the One who sits on the throne, who lives for ever and ever, the   10
twenty-four elders fall down before the One who sits on the throne and
worship him who lives for ever and ever; and as they lay their crowns
before the throne they cry:

'Thou art worthy, O Lord our God, to receive glory and honour and   11
power, because thou didst create all things; by thy will they were
created, and have their being!'

"After this," verse 1 opens; John customarily uses the phrase to
mark a break in the action and introduce a new scene. The
Revealer appears again, with details very reminiscent of his first
appearance. There he came to John on Patmos; here John goes to
him in heaven; the same Jesus Christ, he is the continuity between
earth and heaven, the continuity of John's entire story.

"In heaven stood a throne." Thrones are very big in Revelation,
getting mentioned in chapter after chapter. They represent, of
course, sovereignty and lordship. And it is significant that John is
much more interested in the fact of the throne than he is in telling
us what God looks like; a little imagery of glory is all he gives;
John has no room for idle curiosity about things that don't
concern us. Further, it is the case that every personage and group
appearing in Revelation is represented in symbolic form, is given
its own particular symbol—*except God*. John knows that there is
no symbol great enough to express what "God" means. To call
him anything other than "God" would be to falsify.

Through the scene as a whole, imagery recalling the Old Testament temple is combined with that which suggests the throne

room of a royal palace. There is no conflict in this, because the
heart of the temple was the Holy of Holies, in which sat the
ancient Ark of the Covenant, which itself was understood to be an
image of the throne of God. John consistently treats the temple as
the royal "house of God" rather than as a cult center involving
animal sacrifice, the activity of holy priests, and all such.

Close about God's throne are twenty-four elders on *thrones*,
wearing *white robes* and *golden crowns*—all symbols of victory and
sovereignty. Twenty-four, note well, is a *twelve* number which, we
will see, inevitably denotes the church. In this case, it is a *double*
twelve—most likely John's way of affirming that the true church
consists of both the twelve tribes of the Old Testament people of
God and the twelve apostles of the New Testament church (in
21:12-14, John specifies the unity of these two groups).

We are told, then, that in the reality heaven represents (the
reality which, at present, is "coming to be" on earth as it "already
is" in heaven), the church has the sovereignty, and its place is in
the front rank around the very throne of God—good things for the
little congregations of Asia Minor (and us) to know. Also, we
discover, the primary function of the double-twelve church is to
magnify and honor the God who makes her what she is—so get
with it on earth as it is in heaven!

That flashes of lightning and peals of thunder proceed from
God's throne may be meant to recall his appearance on Sinai and
the pillar of cloud and fire that led Israel through the wilderness.
The Holy Spirit, placed in closest conjunction with the throne of
God, goes plural again; the description as "seven flaming torches"
may even intend Pentecost's "tongues like flames of fire." The
"sea of glass" may come from the sea of the Old Testament
temple even though it is described in quite different terms.

The four living creatures come through as the strangest part of
the picture; but they need not; there is nothing mysterious about
them. They date back to the first chapter of Ezekiel, where each
has four wings rather than six and has all four faces rather than
each having a different one of the four. From there, they go back
to Isaiah 6 and his great vision of God in the temple, where an
undesignated number of seraphim (undoubtedly pictured much
more like John's and Ezekiel's living creatures than the way we
draw seraphs) had six wings each and cried, "Holy, holy, holy!"
From there they go back to the old Ark of the Covenant (Exodus

25:18-20; 37:7-9; Psalm 80:1) where two cherubim (again, more like living creatures than what we call cherubs), presumably with two wings each, were made of beaten gold as decoration upon that symbolic throne of God. John's four living creatures are a composite of these. Christian tradition comes to make each of the faces representative of one of the four Gospels; but it undoubtedly was long after John's day this happened.

The wealth and depth of the tradition John draws upon here indicates that his is not simply a first-century Christian God; the God he would portray is the same one the ancient Hebrews knew when they set the golden cherubim to watch his throne. The living creatures form the foremost honor guard of God, indicative of his majesty and glory and also showing that he is Lord of the supernatural world as well as the natural. That they are "covered with eyes" we might choose to express by saying that God has satellites outfitted with TV sensors to keep him in touch with what is happening all over the world. The song they sing combines the thrice holy ascription of the seraphim of old Isaiah with John's own new threefold title of the past-, present-, and future-coming God.

And at the cue of the living creatures, the twenty-four elders (the church) join in the hymn of praise. Notice that their theme is particularly that of God's glory as *creator* (and thus *Lord*) of all that is. When they sing to Christ the Lamb in the next chapter, their theme, appropriately, will be *redemption*. We would do well to learn both of these songs for ourselves, ready to join in on cue with the rest of the universe.

THE SCROLL

(5:1-5)   Then I saw in the right hand of the One who sat on the throne a scroll,   1
with writing inside and out, and it was sealed up with seven seals. And I   2
saw a mighty angel proclaiming in a loud voice, 'Who is worthy to open
the scroll and to break its seals?' There was no one in heaven or on   3
earth or under the earth able to open the scroll or to look inside it. I   4
was in tears because no one was found who was worthy to open the
scroll or to look inside it. But one of the elders said to me: 'Do not   5
weep; for the Lion from the tribe of Judah, the Scion of David, has
won the right to open the scroll and break its seven seals.'

In his right hand God holds a scroll *which is sealed.* There seems no doubt it represents that part of world history which is sealed from us, namely *the future.* And it is completely understandable that there should be such consternation when it is discovered that no one in heaven or on earth is competent to open and read it.

Where is the world headed? How are things supposed to come out? What is *the end* of it all (and "end" more in the sense of *telos* [purpose] than *finis* [when does it stop])? If the assumption is that history as a whole is a meaningful, directed sequence, then the answer to these questions is important—all important. Of course, if the assumption is that history is *not* a directed sequence, then the questions ought not even be asked; they have no answers. History, in such case, amounts merely to what each generation decides to do with its moment, consists merely in independent moments, each an end in itself.

Neither John nor any Christian can buy this view of things; so for him the questions are crucial; on them, many other questions depend. "Where will it all end?" also becomes "What does it all mean?" and thus "What is the significance of *this* point of time within that total sequence?" and thus "What should be happening in this moment, and what should I be doing?" and thus "Who are we, and who am I?"

If no one can be found to open that scroll, it's all over for the human race; hopeless; we have been plunked down in the middle of a maze with not so much as a sense of direction as to where "out" lies.

And yet, John tells us, there was no one in heaven or on earth or under the earth able to open the scroll. Man—with all his learning, science, and technique—still is too short-lived, too finite, too time-bound to be of any good here. The history he controls is too short a snatch out of the drama as a whole; even our shiny, new computerized science of futurology has difficulty handling decades when our ultimate concern must be with the aeons. Modern man has become a real whiz at manipulating moments; but this has no significance at all in telling us where we should be headed. No more in the twentieth century than in the first can there be found anyone competent to open the scroll. John does well to weep; and we would, too, were we alert enough to realize our situation.

But one of the elders says (and thus the *church* is to proclaim) that there is a *Lion* who *has won* (not "will win," already "has won") the right to open the scroll. And by the way, it will take a "lion" to do it—this symbol of regality and kingship, of courage, strength, and ferocity. Enter, the LION!

THE LAMB

(5:6-14) Then I saw standing in the very middle of the throne, inside the circle 6
of living creatures and the circle of elders, a Lamb with the marks of
slaughter upon him. He had seven horns and seven eyes, the eyes which
are the seven spirits of God sent out over all the world. And the Lamb 7
went up and took the scroll from the right hand of the One who sat on
the throne. When he took it, the four living creatures and the twenty- 8
four elders fell down before the Lamb. Each of the elders had a harp,
and they held golden bowls full of incense, the prayers of God's people,
and they were singing a new song: 9

> 'Thou art worthy to take the scroll and to break its seals, for thou
> wast slain and by thy blood didst purchase for God men of every
> tribe and language, people and nation; thou hast made of them a 10
> royal house, to serve our God as priests; and they shall reign upon
> earth.'

Then as I looked I heard the voices of countless angels. These were 11
all round the throne and the living creatures and the elders. Myriads
upon myriads there were, thousands upon thousands, and they cried 12
aloud:

> 'Worthy is the Lamb, the Lamb that was slain, to receive all power
> and wealth, wisdom and might, honour and glory and praise!'

Then I heard every created thing in heaven and on earth and under the 13
earth and in the sea, all that is in them, crying:

> 'Praise and honour, glory and might, to him who sits on the throne
> and to the Lamb for ever and ever!'

And the four living creatures said, 'Amen', and the elders fell down and 14
worshipped.

Enter, the LION! And look what we get, a little lambkin!

There is nothing wrong with thinking of Revelation as a freaky, far-out book—as long as you spot the freakishness at the right place and the far-outness in the right direction. And *here* is the place, and *this* the direction. It's a freakishness, by the way, not simply of Revelation, but one that lies at the very heart of the Christian gospel; it is just that John presents it more graphically than anyone else. But "freaky"? It's "unearthly"—or better, it's "unworldly," the absolute contrary of what all our knowledge of the world and all our worldly knowledge would lead us to expect. This is one good reason we needed someone bigger than ourselves to open the sealed scroll of the future: our worldly calculation has us headed in precisely the wrong direction.

The Lion is a lamb. John will use that "Lamb" as the controlling symbol of Jesus Christ from here on out; we are up against the heart of the matter. Put "the Lamb" over against "the Lion"—as John certainly invites us to do. They stand for completely opposite things. Over against the characteristics we attributed to the Lion, the Lamb represents meekness, helplessness, defenselessness, and vulnerability. And the situation is compounded when John specifies that this Lamb bears "the marks of slaughter upon him." This Lamb, as lamb, not only looks as though he would be an easy mark, he has proved it in his inability to keep from being slaughtered. How totally vulnerable can a symbol of vulnerability get?

That's the Lamb over against the Lion—which he also is. Now let's try him over against his opponent, his *counter* image, that which he most definitely is not. John obviously intends that these two should be put into conjunctive opposition, in that he calls the one "*Anti*christ," but also in the very words he uses to designate the two.

In the Greek of a sheep-oriented culture, there were many more words for "lamb" than our English language would know what to do with. The one John chooses for his purpose is not the one used regarding Jesus elsewhere in the Bible. He uses *arnion*, which has been translated "lambkin"—a "poor little thing" sort of creature. But his most likely reason for going to this particular term is that he plans to designate Antichrist as *therion*, the *beast*, a great big vicious MONSTER!

So the main bout on the card of history (for the heavyweight championship of the entire created universe) is to be "*Arnion* vs. *Therion*"!

Oh, no, no, no! God wouldn't send that wee, little, slaughtered lambkin up against a monster like that! It isn't fair! He doesn't have a chance!

You're right! It isn't fair; the *arnion* is going to make mince-meat out of that no-good *therion;* the *beast* doesn't have a chance. I can't even give you odds on it, because the fact is the Lamb already has him whipped.

How do you figure that?

Do you see those marks of slaughter upon him? Well, those show that he got himself killed and so won the championship.

Man, you're talking weird!

No, you've got to understand that things aren't what they seem. That Lamb really is a Lion!

Yes, the Lamb is the Lion; and at points in Revelation Christ is presented more like a lamb, at other points more like a lion. But we need to be very careful as to how we handle this alternation. The structure of the present scene makes it plain that John does not mean to say that Jesus switches roles, sometimes taking the role of a lamb and other times that of a lion; that would make for a very undependable, a Jekyll-and-Hyde Christ. But no, the Lamb's very defenselessness *is* his lion-like strength; his suffering death *is* his victory; his *modus operandi* (method of operation) always is that of the Lamb, but the consequences, the results, always are a victory that belongs to the character of the Lion. (So, for example, an allusion such as the Psalm 2 phrase about ruling the nations with an iron rod must be taken as a reference to the fact of his ruling rather than as a description of its method.) John here bonds the Lion and the Lamb as being two sides of one coin; we dare never allow them to be separated or put into tension with each other. Jesus' love, though defenseless, is a ferocious and victorious love.

That the Lamb wins true victory precisely in and through his "lambness" is indicated by the reception given him here upon his appearance in heaven. Remember that heaven is where things are seen for what they really are, regardless of how they appear in the transient actuality of earth. So nobody in this scene finds it strange that the slaughtered Lamb should be heavyweight champion of the universe. Not at all; how else would you ever expect God to do it? That the business strikes *us* as freakish proves only that we are not yet in heaven, that we see things from the perverted worldly perspective which says that monsters are power-ful but lambs are not—this rather than seeing things as they really are. A major purpose of John's book is to help us see on earth as it

already is seen in heaven—not so much to see new realities but to
see the realities of our own history in a new way, from a new
perspective. And only from here can we see that the Lion who
looks and acts like a Lamb is indeed the only one who can open
the sealed scroll of human history, because, in his lion-lambness,
he is the key to that history.

The Lamb appears "in the very middle of the throne" upon
which God already is sitting. That might cause a problem for
simple-minded literalists; but John plainly wants to say that there
is no distinction of dignity between God and the Lamb; both hold
the same position. The Lamb is given attributes in "sevens," the
God number. His eyes are the seven spirits earlier identified as the
Holy Spirit. Literalists, again, will have a hard time with the
Spirit's being flaming torches at one point and Lamb's eyes at
another; but John now wants to suggest how close is the relationship between Christ and the Holy Spirit. Other New Testament
writers do it by referring to the Holy Spirit on occasion as "the
Spirit of Christ."

The hymn the elders sing in praise of the Lamb is a great
statement of what the whole scene is about. There are three main
verbs that form a most interesting pattern. (1) "Thou *art* worthy"
(present tense). As history's Lord, Jesus *even now* is the one
competent to open the scroll and reveal to us who we are and
where we're headed. (2) "Thou *wast* slain" (past tense). His present lordship as the one who opens the scroll was merited by what
he did *in the past* when, like a sheep led to the slaughter, he went
defenselessly to the cross. (3) "They *shall* reign" (future tense). It
is through his lordship that we shall find ours. So the sequence is
this: what Jesus did *in the past* gives him the status *in the present*
that guarantees *our future*. And in this sequence we have what
amounts to an outline of the Christian gospel.

That Christ's act on the cross "didst purchase for God men of
every tribe and language, people and nation" is a *universalistic*
note to put into our collection. It is topped in verse 13, where
"every created thing" is portrayed as voicing the praise of God and
his Christ. We do not demand that a conclusion be drawn even
from this unambiguous a statement; but it must be given due
weight in our final decision.

John's scene, now, opens out in a way the previous description
of God's throne room did not, to include "countless angels" and

"every created thing"—which is about as wide as matters can go. It certainly is not that John desires to ascribe greater honor to Christ than to God. For him, to praise Christ *is* to praise God—as the concluding song indicates. There is no possibility of competition here. But the first scene celebrated God as creator (and thus Lord of the universe). However, when the Lamb is introduced, that celebration inevitably takes on the aspect of *redemption* ("by thy blood thou didst purchase men for God"); and God's lordship is not a total and perfect lordship until it includes redemption as well as creation. It is entirely proper that the scene celebrating creation *plus* redemption open out from that celebrating creation alone. Neither the angels in heaven nor we who live among the created things of earth know God in the fullness of his glory until we know him, not only as Creator, but, through the Lamb, as Redeemer also. "And the four living creatures said, 'Amen,' and the elders fell down and worshipped." Where were you?

6:1–8:1

The End-Time as Seven Seals

The seven seals, of course, are those that bind the closed scroll the Lamb has just been proclaimed worthy to open. This scene builds directly upon and is continuous with what preceded. As each seal is broken, we get more insight into what the future holds—although not necessarily as a chronological sequence of events. Our suggestion is that these seals portray the general character of the End-Time, that is, the period stretching from Christ's death-and-resurrection to his return at the end of the age.

Before John is done, he will present three major series of "sevens"—seven seals, seven trumpets, and seven bowls. Each series is built over an identical and quite sophisticated pattern—which, we will see, in itself suggests that they are meant to be read as parallel descriptions of the same period rather than as a strict sequence of events.

The pattern proceeds as follows: The first four items form a recognizable quartet and come in quick order (not more than one or two verses each). At the close of No. 4, there is a break in the rhythm. No. 5 comes on in a more measured way, and more space is devoted to it. No. 6, then, consistently carries special significance; it marks the intensification of trauma which John, clearly, expects as a prelude of the parousia (see the time-line inside the front cover). No. 6 always steps up the voltage from what it has been during the first five—and No. 7 will come on as the End itself. However, John never moves directly from No. 6 to No. 7. Regularly inserted at this point is an interlude that interrupts and stands outside the sequence that is in progress. The interlude itself falls naturally into two parts (which we shall identify as A and B);

and only then is No. 7 brought in to conclude the whole. John, I think, wants to indicate that No. 7 in no sense is the natural outcome or product of what was described in Nos. 1 through 6; it is rather an *intervention*, a disjuncture that cuts them off. God is the Lord of history; consequently, history's end does not evolve out of the historical process itself but comes as a special act of God which is to be marked off from what has gone before (in John's pattern, by this interlude).

We can sum up the pattern visually:

$$1\text{-}2\text{-}3\text{-}4 \; / \; 5 \; / \; 6 \; / \; \text{Interlude} \; \frac{A}{B} \; / \; 7$$

final   the

intensification   end

SEALS 1-4: THE FOUR HORSEMEN

(6:1-8)   Then I watched as the Lamb broke the first of the seven seals; and I [1] heard one of the four living creatures say in a voice like thunder, 'Come!' And there before my eyes was a white horse, and its rider held [2] a bow. He was given a crown, and he rode forth, conquering and to conquer.

When the Lamb broke the second seal, I heard the second creature [3] say, 'Come!' And out came another horse, all red. To its rider was given [4] power to take peace from the earth and make men slaughter one another; and he was given a great sword.

When he broke the third seal, I heard the third creature say, 'Come!' [5] And there, as I looked, was a black horse; and its rider held in his hand a pair of scales. And I heard what sounded like a voice from the midst [6] of the living creatures, which said, 'A whole day's wage for a quart of flour, a whole day's wage for three quarts of barley-meal! But spare the olive and the vine.'

When he broke the fourth seal, I heard the voice of the fourth [7] creature say, 'Come!' And there, as I looked, was another horse, sickly [8] pale; and its rider's name was Death, and Hades came close behind. To him was given power over a quarter of the earth, with the right to kill by sword and by famine, by pestilence and wild beasts.

The Lamb breaks each of the first four seals in turn; and appropriately enough, each of the four living creatures has a turn at calling out a horseman. Each of these horses and riders has a distinctive (a) color, (b) weapon, and (c) function; these will be important clues in making our interpretation.

It is the first horseman that has given commentators the most
trouble. Admittedly, almost every detail of the description points
toward Christ. In a later scene (Chapter 19), a rider on a white
horse clearly and explicitly is identified as Christ; and even here
the rider wears a crown and is a conqueror. Consequently, many
scholars are ready to say that this horseman *is* Christ.

Yet, to go this way is to violate the Revelator's sense of
symmetry, wreck the finesse of his structure, and foul up his
theology. The other three riders obviously represent forces of Evil;
and John simply could not have Christ riding in conjunction *with*
them, the movement would have to be a *counter* one. However,
there is possible another interpretation which is so appropriate on
every count that it must be correct.

It is not accidental that we here encounter details suggesting
Christ. Remember that John customarily portrays Evil as being a
counterfeit of the Good; and here he is introducing a fake Christ,
the perversion of Christ which is *Antichrist*. True, John does not
portray him under this image at any other place in the book; but
this is very much the "right" point for Antichrist to make his
initial appearance.

For one thing, Christ has just been introduced; and the introduction of Antichrist would serve John's sense of symmetry. For
another, Antichrist immediately would provide the quartet with
its natural leader and make it proper that they charge across the
world in concert. Further, we are at the point in John's story
where Antichrist is called for. Be aware that the scene now is
shifting from heaven to earth and that we are entering the end-
time period. And as John will make abundantly clear, it is precisely *on earth* and during *this period* that Antichrist has his
(apparent) rule. Of course, his mount is actually the Trojan Horse
whitewashed, and his crown nothing but cardboard and tinfoil;
but the world does not know that. He comes on strong; and he is
the *world's* messiah.

Consider that the end-time begins with *the crucifixion of Christ*.
That event carries the weight of "a fact of world history," while
the resurrection is perceived only by eyes of faith. And it is to
Antichrist's interest to keep things so; as long as he can lead the
world to believe that nothing of importance has happened since
Good Friday, he has it made. And look around you; it is rather
evident, is it not, that the Fancy Fake is still riding high and his

act still packing houses everywhere from here to Hellenbac. (I am trying to make one of the Revelator's serious points, that the only real power Evil possesses is that of *seduction.*)

John does give us one solid clue to this reading of the first horseman. Christ already has been introduced as wielder of the two-edged sword; and whenever he appears with a weapon, this is it. But the present rider carries a *bow* (never mentioned in connection with Christ); and it may be relevant to observe that throughout the Old Testament there is some tendency to put the bow and arrow in relation to the *enemies* of Israel. The most significant passage in this regard is Ezekiel 38—39, the account of Gog and his armies. Much later in the book, John will cite Gog by name; but it also is plain that this passage from Ezekiel has had strong influence at many points in John's descriptions—and Ezekiel does attribute the bow to the enemy. Yet stronger than this argument is our observation that the first horseman represents exactly the right place for introducing Antichrist and the right way of doing it: the "arch-deceiver" (2 John 7) comes on, making like a conqueror but bringing nothing but trouble in his train.

His first follower, bloody red and slashing away in splendid slaughter, rather clearly stands for *War.*

With the third horseman, the black of starvation, the scales of the food-seller, and the announcement from price control headquarters—all point toward his being *Famine.*

Bringing up the rear, riding double, comes the duo that, in this world, always and forever catches the stragglers and speaks the last word, *Death and Hades.* (But don't forget who it is that, *we* happen to know, already holds their keys!)

Verse 6, with its "spare the olive and the vine," and verse 8, with its reference to "a *quarter* of the earth," mark a principle of *restraint* and *limitation* upon which we will want to comment in just a bit.

But what history—past, present, or future—does John mean to be characterizing under these figures of the four horsemen? His own day, I am ready to say, the day of the seven hard-put congregations in Asia Minor / and *our* day (it would be no trick to document the contemporary presence of this foursome; any newspaper would serve) / and no telling how many days yet to come (they show no signs of packing up to leave). And this proposal creates the need for an excursus on "trauma in the book of Revelation."

The four horsemen have introduced us into the Revelator's "visions of trauma"; we've got chapters to go before we're through with them. Some general observations may help clarify what we already have seen and save us from having to repeat them at every point ahead. We will talk about *how* to read these visions and then about *what* they mean. First, a picture (see the next page).

This, pictorially, is something like what John does verbally. Now literalists, who think that every picture is meant to be read as though it were a photograph, would have to say, "Well, it's certain we haven't seen anything like this *yet* . . . so it must be something still to come." Actually, Picasso's is a picture of the Basque town of Guernica as it was bombed under the orders of General Franco on April 28, 1937—if it is legitimate to identify this as "a picture of." But notice what Picasso has done; there is nothing in the painting itself that would allow one to say, "Aha! Guernica, Spain, April 28, 1937." With a photograph one could do that—observe the street signs, the clothing styles, the facial characteristics, the car models, etc. What Picasso has done is to decalendarize the event and thus universalize it. Guernica, 1937—yes. But also the war trauma that has wracked the world among all peoples of all times and places.

If he had chosen to do a photograph, think how the artist would have narrowed and tied down the significance of his work. First of all, this would have been to invite in the calendarizers to do their riddle-reading of when, where, and how—thus completely missing the point of what he was trying to do and say. Further, it would invite the viewer to enter the political struggle that was then in progress and take sides: "That's a good picture; it's just what those damned Basques deserved!" Further still, the painting would be just as vulnerable to going out of date as is the event itself. "Nineteen thirty seven? That's over thirty-five years ago— ancient history! And in *Spain*? Who cares?—I've got problems of my own." That's right; the event *is* ancient history. But the painting—ah! the *painting*—it can speak of Guernica *or* those problems of your own, speak at *any* time to *any* man. It will never go out of date—and even less so will Revelation, which led Picasso's work by some 1800 years and, if it needs to, could outlast him by at least as much.

Had Picasso gone toward a photograph, his statement neces-

GUERNICA. By Pablo Picasso (1937, May—early June). Oil on canvas, 11′ 5½″ X 25′ 5¾″. On extended loan to The Museum of Modern Art, New York, from the artist.

sarily would have been confined to the surface of reality, one localized event in a passing moment of history; with his painting, the way is open for making observations of force, depth, and breadth. Yes, in one sense a photograph would give a *truer* picture—if the only sort of truth there is is what we might call "factual truth." But if there is a level of "significative, or meaning, truth," then Picasso's approach is truer than any photograph could be. (For that matter, all the way through, the Bible shows much more interest in this latter sort of truth than in simply reciting outward facts.)

But if a person insists on trying to read *Guernica* as though it were a photograph, he's headed for nothing but trouble. His fascination in trying to sort out and make sense of the details will forever prevent him from feeling the impact or getting the message of the whole. He'll hang up on that bull with the eye underneath its ear until he either invents some wild-eyed theory to "explain" it or else concludes that the whole freaky painting is a bunch of bull.

And certainly in this regard *Guernica* is easy compared to Revelation. It wouldn't take too much of a biological sport to produce a Picassian bull; but in a little while, John will say that "the stars in the sky fell to earth." It is obvious to us that, if even the tiniest of stars moves anywhere close to earth, the earth will give way rather violently. Yet, in John's picture, the earth goes right on (and with people living on it); and in subsequent scenes he again has stars falling to earth. How irrational will Revelation (and *Guernica*) become if one refuses to let the author speak in his own way and instead determines that he has to be a photographer!

What John seems to be saying through his visions of trauma is not entirely unrelated to what Picasso seems to be saying through *Guernica.* Picasso tells us of war's horrors, of the suffering it brings upon people and animals, of the terrible disruption of existence itself. The Revelator says much more than Picasso did: he knows that the picture needs a slaughter-marked lamb in it, along with the cock-eyed bull. The one is the answer for the other.

But the overall thrust of these visions of John seems to say that, as long as the world persists in worshipping the *therion* rather than the *arnion*, chasing the Fancy Fake rather than following the Lamb, it will continue to bring trauma on itself. There is no telling all the forms this trauma might take. War, Famine, and Death are correct enough identifications; falling skies, rolling mountains, and supernatural invaders may constitute more potent descriptions. Just as Picasso had to multiply and exaggerate a wide range of detail in order to express the total horror of war, so must John—faced as he is with the even greater task of expressing the total enormity of world evil.

John makes it plain, too, that the situation is not one that can get itself righted simply through the progress of history. The tendency of evil is to compound itself, so the situation is bound to worsen. It is not necessarily that every symptom of evil goes from bad to worse, but that the overall, long-term drift of history is away from God and his righteousness. Indeed, John is certain that this disintegration is such that it will lead to a time of inconceivably intense trauma immediately preceding the end.

Even so, the nature of John's picture is not such that one can gauge the trauma of the present moment and calculate where that puts us in relation to the coming of the end. It doesn't take much of an eye to see that what John talks about *is happening;* but there is no one who can say which of his descriptions (or how much of his total description) already have taken place, which are in progress, and which are yet to happen when. Part of the difficulty is that our own observations are so subjective. Every generation since John's has had the wherewithal for drawing and documenting the conclusion that things are so bad that the end *must* be at hand. Yet how often it has been the experience of the race that, when things are so bad it seems they cannot get worse, the turn of events demonstrates that they very well *can!* We have no accurate way of measuring the amount of evil in the world and no standard against which to measure it in any case. I think it safe to say that the parousia could happen *now* or could have happened at almost any time in the past—and it still would be the case that John's traumatic prophecies were correct. This, of course, is not to say that things could not get worse than they are now; they could, they are, they most likely will. John's prophecy has been fulfilled; but it can be filled fuller. Who can say what unforeseen calamities might yet occur, and who is to say when is enough? (Answer: God is; and he will say so according to his own plan and wisdom.)

John apparently wants to say that all this trauma is what man has created through his own wrongdoing and brought upon himself. There is no justification for reading these scenes as portrayals of a vicious God sadistically ripping his world to shreds—such would be entirely out of character from what John otherwise tells us of God and the Lamb. Surely we must proceed from the assumption that John intends his picture to be consistent throughout and so recognize our obligation always to try to understand it that way. Punishment—just, legitimate, helpful punishment—properly is central in these visions; cruelty and vindictiveness have no place.

So the trauma bears two different significations. For the Christians (the church) it signifies a *testing;* for the world it signifies *punishment.* Yet the trauma itself catches both groups; John nowhere pictures the Christians as evading or being exempted from it.

Similarly, the trauma is purposed to call forth two different responses: from Christians, *fidelity* and *"the patient endurance of Jesus"*; from the world, *repentance*—in either case, a moving of men toward God. In particular, we will want to note the numerous places where John specifies that the trauma of punishment—even where it is portrayed as being the work of Evil—is intended by God as a motive toward repentance and thus forgiveness. This means—as John himself hints—that the delay of the eschaton, even if it involves a prolongation of the trauma, is a mark of God's grace. He is giving men time for repentance and striving to move them toward it—a repentance which, although won out of trauma, will save them from what is infinitely worse, namely second-order DEATH. Keep ever in mind, then, that John's trauma visions always have a positive side to them.

Further, remember that John already has spent five full chapters establishing with some emphasis that history is being controlled from the throne of God and the Lamb. He does not mean that you should forget the fact now that we turn to earthly scenes where the Fancy Fake rides rampant and everything seems to be going to smash. He inserts two sorts of reminders—and we ought to use them to be reminded. For one, from time to time, even through his end-time descriptions, he intersperses scenes that point toward God, sovereignty, victory, and all such. For the other, right in the midst of scenes of trauma he drops what we have called notes of restraint and limitation, such as "but spare the olive and the vine" or "given power over *a quarter* of the earth." Despite all appearances, Evil has not been given a free rein, is not rampaging unchecked. God is in control; Evil can do no more than he permits it to do; and things will not be allowed to go to total destruction. This still is the world that is destined for redemption.

John's visions of trauma are not any prettier or more pleasant than Picasso's *Guernica;* but John's certainly have something more positive and helpful to say. It is sad that all the world (and most of the church) gives Picasso more credit than it does John.

SEALS 5-6: THE SAINTS AND THE KINGS

(6:9-17)   When he broke the fifth seal, I saw underneath the altar the souls of   9
those who had been slaughtered for God's word and for the testimony
they bore. They gave a great cry: 'How long, sovereign Lord, holy and   10
true, must it be before thou wilt vindicate us and avenge our blood on
the inhabitants of the earth?' Each of them was given a white robe; and   11
they were told to rest a little while longer, until the tally should be
complete of all their brothers in Christ's service who were to be killed
as they had been.

Then I watched as he broke the sixth seal. And there was a violent   12
earthquake; the sun turned black as a funeral pall and the moon all red
as blood; the stars in the sky fell to the earth, like figs shaken down by   13
a gale; the sky vanished, as a scroll is rolled up, and every mountain and   14
island was moved from its place. Then the kings of the earth, magnates   15
and marshals, the rich and the powerful, and all men, slave or free, hid
themselves in caves and mountain crags; and they called out to the   16
mountains and the crags, 'Fall on us and hide us from the face of the
One who sits on the throne and from the vengeance of the Lamb.' For   17
the great day of their vengeance has come, and who will be able to
stand?

It seems evident that Seals 5 and 6 are meant to be played off against each other as part of John's symmetry of Good and Evil. First, the "saints."

"Underneath the altar" is an awkward enough image, but it probably denotes nothing more than a place of particular honor close to the presence of God. The scene, of course, has shifted back to the throne room.

Notice how closely the word *martyria* (testimony) here is associated with being killed for the faith. Now we are speaking of literal martyr-witnesses; and it is plain that John accords them the

highest possible human status in his scheme of things. The fact will
have crucial bearing in our interpretation at a later point.

But the impressive and important thing here is that, although
these people have come through the great ordeal with white robes
unsullied, and even now abide in the direct presence of God, they
are not yet fully content, do not yet count their experience to be
fully consummated. "How long, O Lord?" or as a more literal
translation has it, "Till when?" "How long until justice is done
and things are set right?" In a very real sense, their personal
salvation cannot be complete until the total work of salvation is
complete; that closely do they feel identified with and bound to
"their brothers." "How long, O Lord?" And this, by the way, is
the biblical view of salvation. If all the Christians whose interest in
salvation lies only in getting themselves made secure were to learn
just this one thing from Revelation, John's writing of the book
would have been well worthwhile. Not "Thank God, *I'm* in!" but
"How long, O Lord?" is the prayer of the saved.

Even so, the answer that comes to the martyrs' question is one
of the most penetrating and revolutionary ideas to be found in the
book. As clearly as it can be stated, we are told that *the* human
activity upon which the outcome of history depends, the action
by which progress toward the kingdom is marked, is not the piling
up of good deeds, not our winning of men to Christ, not our
consolidating of power for the Good, not our chasing out and
cleaning up Evil, not our taking over or building up anything. No,
we contribute to the coming of the kingdom by making like the
Lamb, being willing, in love, to *give* ourselves, even to the slaughter. That may seem a rather backward way of overcoming the
world; but John clearly says (and not only here) that this is indeed
the way it must happen. If some Christians are able to pick up this
idea along with the one above, Revelation 6:10-11 could rate
beside anything in Scripture; more than just a play on words was
involved when we called Revelation "the most revealing book of
the Bible."

Seal 5 has given us a picture of the very best of mankind; Seal 6
will show us the very worst—and guess who leads the list. The
martyred saints at the one extreme and *the kings of the earth*
(who did the martyring) at the other.

This, recall, is Seal 6—and thus the final intensification that both completes the end-time and points to No. 7 as being the end itself. Verses 12-13 are intense enough; the imagery is borrowed from Isaiah 34:4—give it a *Guernica*-style reading, please.

The list of people in verse 15 clearly is meant to run from the very worst to the not quite so bad; and the kings of the earth come in just ahead of other military types. Recall that "War" was the first rider in the train of Antichrist, and it becomes evident what the kings represent for John. He knows that the source of Evil lies in apostasy from God; but he spots the most representative manifestation of Evil just where Picasso does.

The "prayer" of these people is perhaps a deliberate counterplay to the "How long?" prayer of the saints. It is taken from Hosea 10:8. Note well that the words are those of the kings, *et alia*, and not those of John or anyone else. What these people well expect and what they know they so richly deserve is "the vengeance of the Lamb"; but this is no proof that what they will in fact receive from the Lamb is "vengeance." Indeed, although they are not smart enough to realize it, "the vengeance of the Lamb" is a rather glaring contradiction in terms—as it would be to speak of "the lovingkindness of the beast." Just as the Lamb is himself a reverse sort of lion, we need to keep alert to the possibility that "the vengeance of the Lamb" might turn out to be something rather strange and wonderful.

Verse 17 makes it quite definite that John understands this scene as standing next to the close of history and looking ahead to Seal 7 as the end itself: "the great day *has come!*"

THE SEAL INTERLUDE: The Church—Below and Above

(7:1-17)

John's pattern, at this point, calls for a two-part interlude to break the sequence between Seals 6 and 7; and that is just what we get. The words "after this," with which the chapter begins, mark the break John intends. Part A and Part B of the interlude are consciously related; together they form a picture of the Christian community which is *the church*. John knows, however, that that church exists in two quite different states. Part A describes the church on earth, the church made up of those who are living. Part B describes the church in heaven; we could say "the church of the dead," but that comes too close to suggesting something like second-order DEATH. Let's call it "the church of those who have died"—they will show up as anything but "dead."

PART A: THE CHURCH OF THE LIVING

1 After this I saw four angels stationed at the four corners of the earth,   (7:1-8)
  holding back the four winds so that no wind should blow on sea or land
2 or on any tree. Then I saw another angel rising out of the east, carrying
  the seal of the living God; and he called aloud to the four angels who
3 had been given the power to ravage land and sea: 'Do no damage to sea
  or land or trees until we have set the seal of our God upon the
4 foreheads of his servants.' And I heard the number of those who had
  received the seal. From all the tribes of Israel there were a hundred and
5 forty-four thousand: twelve thousand from the tribe of Judah, twelve
  thousand from the tribe of Reuben, twelve thousand from the tribe of
6 Gad, twelve thousand from the tribe of Asher, twelve thousand from
  the tribe of Naphtali, twelve thousand from the tribe of Manasseh,
7 twelve thousand from the tribe of Simeon, twelve thousand from the
8 tribe of Levi, twelve thousand from the tribe of Issachar, twelve
  thousand from the tribe of Zebulun, twelve thousand from the tribe of
  Joseph, and twelve thousand from the tribe of Benjamin.

The fore part of this scene makes it evident that the place of the church is right in the midst of the end-time traumas which earlier have been presented as afflicting primarily the apostate men of the world. But John is right; in this world, there is no obvious, easy, outward distinction between believers and unbelievers, no visual differentiation or spatial separation; we are all in it together.

The trauma, in this vision, is portrayed as ravaging winds (tornadoes) to come from the four corners of the earth (thus suggesting the *totality* of their effect). Some scholars have complained that John never gets around to saying whether the winds *did* blow or to describing the event. No problem; end-time trauma obviously does come; it is simply that he uses imageries other than that of winds to describe it. The phrase "sea or land *or trees*"—found in both verses 1 and 2—is an intriguing one. "Sea and land" would seem to cover the matter; so why "trees"? As some sharp thinker has

suggested, trees are where one looks to determine whether or not
the wind is blowing; "not even a tree" is a way of emphasizing
that the winds indeed were being restrained.

The customary note of God's restraining and limiting the depredations of Evil is particularly emphatic in this case; the timing and
extent of end-time horror are in God's hands and not Satan's. At
least one reason for the restraint is stated most explicitly. It is out
of his grace that God is holding things back so that his people will
have time to be prepared for the trial to come; they need to be
given that which will enable them to persevere and manifest the
patient endurance of Jesus. And what is that? It is one's having an
assured knowledge regarding *who he is* and *to whom* he belongs.
John portrays this, appropriately, as a receiving of God's seal on
the forehead (references elsewhere—3:12 and 14:1—indicate that
he thinks of the seal as incorporating the names of God and the
Lamb). Modern experience might incline us to picture it as a
stamp on the back of the hand proving that one is among those
who rightfully belong "in" (and we shortly will suggest that it is
stamped with an invisible, fluorescent ink which can be seen only
in the doorkeeper's black light).

This scene, then, is that of the sealing of the church; and it says
that, in the midst of and out of the wild confusions of the
end-time, there are those who have given themselves, not to the
lord of that madhouse, but to the apparently absent and powerless
Lamb. Consequently, they have been marked as reserved for him;
and although this does not have the effect of taking them out of
the madhouse, it does enable them to keep their wits and hang
through the experience. Several chapters on, John will complete
his symmetry with a counterpart scene in which the beast's people
receive their seals.

Together, these two scenes force an implication which we may
or may not welcome but which John very much intends. For
himself, John is certain that salvation is to be found *only* in Jesus
Christ. Those who accept him as Lord and Savior, who have made
him the central loyalty of their lives, bear his seal. Anyone who
has failed to accept him in this way has some other loyalty at the
center; and because that loyalty—whatever it may be—keeps Christ
from being the center, it is *anti*-Christ, and the person's mark is
that of the beast. There are no more than the two options, and
every person has put (and is putting) himself in the one camp or

the other. Nowhere does John suggest that these seals, even now, are fixed for all eternity; people do have the freedom to switch loyalties; and indeed, one of John's rationales for the end-time trauma is that it can nudge men to get out of the madhouse crowd and come over to the Lamb's people. Nevertheless, at any given moment, one's ultimate loyalty either belongs to Jesus Christ or it belongs somewhere else; you wear the one seal or the other.

But what John's account simply will not allow is the picture many of us would prefer, namely that some people find their salvation in Jesus Christ while others find theirs in other ways. Thus the line is not drawn where John draws it but (whether the thought ever gets made explicit or not) between nice, sincere people on the one hand and "bad" people on the other. Goodness knows, it is impossible enough for us to determine the focus of another man's ultimate loyalty; yet John's distinction is a real and definable one. What this other way actually comes to is that people I like are considered saved and those I don't are considered lost; it turns out to be no line at all. Granted, John's judgment sounds very harsh against all the nice, sincere non-Christians, insisting that they bear the mark of *the beast.* But don't you form such an opinion until you see where John's story comes out; it just could be that his vision is broader and more charitable than that of people who distribute blessing and curses on the basis of their own moral (or immoral) preferences.

It is, of course, obvious that, presently, one cannot tell who are Lamb's people and who are beast's, simply by looking at their foreheads; and I don't believe John means to suggest that this ever will be so. Things just aren't that easy. Christians who claim this sort of sight or who act as if they had it, are an affront to the gospel—whether they try to do it by counting baptismal certificates or by counting those who are willing to stand up and say, "On such-and-such a day, I opened my heart and took Jesus into my life." God and, presumably, the beast do the sealing and thus know who belongs to whom. For the rest, it is better that the seals be kept under our hats and that each person center his attention on taking care of his own loyalty. Yet be clear, this in no way is to suggest that the seals are not real or that they are of little importance. Yours is the most real part of you (or identifies the most real part of you); and upon it hangs your entire destiny. For God's sake, give thought to your seal!

Now a good many scholars will take exception to the entire interpretation above: this can't be a picture of the sealing of the church as a whole; John is speaking explicitly of the twelve tribes of Israel and so *Jews;* these are 144,000 Jews who accept Christianity and are saved.

Our response will be: no, this is another instance of what John does frequently, taking a specific case and then de-calendarizing it so that it can represent the universal and total. But before documenting such a reading, let's look at the difficulties that arise when one proposes the narrower, Jewish interpretation.

In the first place, John's two sealing scenes no longer form a symmetry; we have the sealing of only one special category of the Lamb's people over against that of *all* the beast's. Everything we said about a person's having to bear the one seal or the other falls apart; John has no other scene suggesting when, how, or if Gentile Christians ever get sealed. Likewise, the symmetry between the A and B halves of this interlude is destroyed.

In the second place, in Revelation 14 stands another scene in which a company of 144,000, bearing his seal on their foreheads, appear with the Lamb. There is no hint of their being Jews; the most pointed of their identifications is that they are those who "follow the Lamb wherever he goes" and are "the firstfruits of humanity for God and the Lamb"—plainly an undifferentiating description of Christians as such. Consequently, some commentators propose that John is presenting us with two different groups of 144,000. But that is to break up the book and make it more complicated precisely where the indication is that John wants to tie things together. And the secret of understanding Revelation lies in keeping it tied together as a book rather than letting it fall to pieces as a collection of separate code messages.

Let us turn, then, to the defense of the proposal that this is indeed a picture of the sealing of the church as a whole. We know that the concept "Israel" is a very fluid one for John. There is, of course, the Israel of the Old Testament and Judaism. But the Christian church, the followers of the Lamb, constitute a new Israel—the home of which is to be a "new Jerusalem." John already has as much as named the Christians as being "true Jews." The two groups, then, are distinct; but for John, they are not separate. There is a continuity between them; the one was produced out of the other. Further, John is convinced, the ultimate

destiny of the two Israels is that they become one again. Further
still, John, with Paul, knows that in Christ there is neither Jew nor
Gentile. Putting it all together, John is not inclined to allow the
distinction between the two Israels to carry very much weight in
his picture; at most it marks a momentary and transient detour
within God's total plan for his people. This means, too, that in
John's mind there is no difficulty in using "Israel" as a term to
cover the church as a whole; the fact is, it is a more inclusive term
for what John understands by the church than any other available
to him.

We will give the matter detailed attention in a bit, but the
number 144,000 would not be appropriate *except* as a reference
to the church as a whole; it is a number of *the* church, the
completed, perfect church rather than of any one faction within
it. Yes, John's terminology is meant to suggest that there are Jews
in this church; it is not simply a Gentile church; it is the whole
church.

The listing of the twelve tribes causes the problem; but I think
careful consideration will show that the listing points precisely to
an effort at de-calendarizing the scene rather than calendarizing it.
John is portraying what is essentially an *election* of the people of
God; and he knows that the Old Testament election of Israel
forms his only proper model.

For one thing, John's list does not conform to the way the
tribes are named in the Old Testament lists of land allotment, etc.
If he intended this as any kind of historical reconstruction, it is
faulty. More important, neither for anyone to whom he was
writing (whether Jew, Christian, or pagan), nor for anyone since,
would this business of the twelve tribes make any sense at all. The
tribal divisions had been basic to Israel's life in the period prior to
the establishment of the monarchy more than a thousand years
before John's time. But with Israel's consolidation into a nation-
state, such things as tribal identity, territory, tradition, etc., gradually had dissolved out. Later, a foreign invader captured the
territory which, centuries earlier, had belonged to ten of the
tribes; and the people whose ancestors had made up those tribes
were entirely scattered and their identity destroyed.

At the time of John's writing, then, historical Israel had no
consciousness of tribal identity, no desire to return to a tribal
organization. There had been such complete intermarrying and

such complete obliteration of ten of the twelve tribes that to take contemporary Jews and divide them up as belonging to Judah or Simeon or Issachar or whatever would be an utterly futile and meaningless operation. Besides, there is nothing either in Revelation or the New Testament as a whole to suggest *why* the reconstitution of those twelve tribes would have any significance in a Christian (or even Christian-Jewish) dispensation.

Then John's tribal list has no significance? Only if one insists upon reading it literally, as calling for some sort of impossible historical reconstruction. But let's try it from another angle.

Israel did preserve the number "12"—and John was eager to make use of it—as the number that signifies her own reality. But notice how the "12" normally is handled; it is used to point, not to the individual constituents that went into making up Israel, but to the *sum*, the *totality*, which results from their merger. That Israel is "12" speaks of her *fullness*, her *wholeness;* it says that she has overcome the distinctions and separateness of the twelve individualities, rather than that she exists to preserve the distinctions. (By the way, it is the same with John's ascribing to the Christian church the "12" of "the twelve apostles of the Lamb." This "12," too, points toward the *fullness* of the church and is not at all an invitation for Christians to try to identify themselves as belonging to Peter or James or John—or Judas.)

What, then, is John saying with his tribal list? He is saying that as, in Old Testament times, *that* true, twelve-numbered Israel could be such only by incorporating the totality of all twelve of her tribes, so, in the sealing of the eschatological people of God, the Israel-church must incorporate the fullness of the contributions from each and every one of her constituent parts.

Notice that we have turned the usual reading of this passage on its head—rather, those who insist on the narrow, Judaized reading have turned the true meaning on its head, and we are trying to get it back the way John had it. They have wanted to make it a picture of a partial, factionalized church; John was trying to talk of fullness, balance, and totality. Do a little experiment and substitute the names of some different denominations for the tribes John lists; you will begin to get a glimmer of the idea he is after. This John was an ecumenist (in a way that goes entirely beyond the bureaucratic, organizational efforts we call "the ecumenical movement" today). *The* church is not to be identified

with any part of it—not with any one party or faction or tribe, not
with any one race or culture or theology or creed or ritual, not
with any one period of history or way of reading the Bible. "All
twelve!" John shouts, "All twelve! It takes all twelve! And God
knows, seals, and is going to gather all twelve, *all* those whose
loyalty is to the Lamb—whether the different tribes recognize and
love one another or not. You can't have *God's* Israel without all
twelve!"

One other insight follows. That the church comes out this neat
and beautiful, symmetrical and complete—twelve thousand apiece
from each of the twelve tribes—is proof enough that it is of God's
creation and not man's. No, this is not to deny the freedom of
man or that his is the choice as to which seal he bears. But God's
freedom is great enough that it can incorporate, work in, around,
and through man's freedom without violating it—yet using it to
build this twelve-faceted jewel which is his very own "Israel."

And now, the 144,000—the key to the whole! Rightly understood, it is the capstone to all we have been saying. Wrongly
understood it makes Revelation a mean and crabbed little book. A
hundred and forty-four thousand! The response it customarily
evokes is: "Hear that number; fix it in your mind and count it
through. That's the goal and limit to set your sights on. Only the
top hundred and forty-four thousand make the payoff." Preachers
build an evangelistic appeal around it: "Don't *you* want to be
sealed in that 144,000? You had better get with it and come now.
Remember, the competition is stiff—only 144,000!"

John doesn't use numbers that way; he doesn't know how many
people have or are going to make Jesus the central loyalty of their
lives—that number hangs in abeyance somewhere between the free
choice of man and the persuasive power of God's love. Things have
gotten turned on their heads again. These interpreters make the
number speak of God's salvation as exclusive, elitist, prohibitive,
and impossible; but John wanted the number to speak of the
generosity, expansiveness, and lavishness of that salvation. Let's
look at the number in the way we know John uses numbers.

Even if the number were meant to be taken literally, it would
have had a quite different significance when it was written from
what it does now. Although anything like exact statistics are
impossible to come by, it seems certain that 144,000 would much
more than accommodate all the people in the world who made

any claim to Christianity at that time; for John's readers, this number would not cut people out but invite them in.

Yet that does not get to the heart of the matter. How does John arrive at this number? Not by consulting a crystal ball. Start with a "12"—that is the church's number. In itself it already combines the Jews and the Christians, the twelve tribes and the twelve apostles; it already represents the fullness of God's "Israel"; it is a rather big number to begin with. But we don't stop just with this "12"; we *begin* with this fat "12" and then go: Twelve . . . *times* twelve . . . and that a THOUSAND times over! The number changes its aspect in a hurry when you go at it that way, doesn't it? "There's a wideness in God's mercy like the wideness of the sea!" Indeed there is; and John knew it long before Frederick Faber did.

John pictures the church of the living as great, grand, and glorious, even though it is hidden within the traumas of the end-time. Mark up this one for our count of John's universalistic passages. But then hold your breath as we head for this church's heavenly counterpart, the church of those who have died.

PART B: THE CHURCH OF THOSE WHO HAVE DIED

(7:9-17)   After this I looked and saw a vast throng, which no one could count,   9
from every nation, of all tribes, peoples, and languages, standing in
front of the throne and before the Lamb. They were robed in white and
had palms in their hands, and they shouted together: 10

'Victory to our God who sits on the throne, and to the Lamb!'

And all the angels stood round the throne and the elders and the four   11
living creatures, and they fell on their faces before the throne and
worshipped God, crying: 12

'Amen! Praise and glory and wisdom, thanksgiving and honour,
power and might, be to our God for ever and ever! Amen.'

Then one of the elders turned to me and said, 'These men that are   13
robed in white—who are they and from where do they come?' But I   14
answered, 'My lord, you know, not I.' Then he said to me, 'These are
the men who have passed through the great ordeal; they have washed
their robes and made them white in the blood of the Lamb. That is why   15
they stand before the throne of God and minister to him day and night
in his temple; and he who sits on the throne will dwell with them. They   16

17 shall never again feel hunger or thirst, the sun shall not beat on them
nor any scorching heat, because the Lamb who is at the heart of the
throne will be their shepherd and will guide them to the springs of the
water of life; and God will wipe all tears from their eyes.'

"After this," John says; thus there is a break in the action, and the
scene shifts from earth to heaven—yet it still is the church that is
our focus of interest. Here in heaven the number of people is not
just large, but "impossible to count." And they are people from all
over. Count this among the Revelator's universalistic passages.

The crowd bears the signs of victory, being "robed in white and
with palms in their hands." Their song centers on "victory" as
well. "Victory" is the theme of this church and of these Christians, because their being *here* signifies that, through the patient
endurance of Jesus, they did not apostatize in the end-time trials
but persevered through death and thus to victory. Even so, John is
careful not to portray these people as inhabiting the new Jerusalem and is, in fact, explicit that there is yet more to come in
their experience. The "how long, O Lord?" note is not as prominent nor as plaintive here, but it is present even in the very midst
of victory.

John gives us a wise hint and sets a helpful example in verses
13-14. If, in heaven or any other place, an angelic elder happens
to ask you a factual question, answer as John did—pretending to
know could prove even more embarrassing than admitting you
don't.

The victors of the heavenly church gained their victories by
passing through the great ordeal (not detouring around it); but
verse 14 also emphasizes that they were able to do this only
because of what the Lamb had done for them in giving himself to
be slain; their victory is as much or more *his* as it is theirs.

Beginning in the middle of verse 15, in order to indicate that
these individual victories do not mark the end of the story, John
has to get in front of himself and peek ahead to what is truly the
end, the scene at which he will not properly arrive until Chapter
21. As long as history continues, the church still will have a ways
to go; even the victorious church in heaven has a ways to go—
mainly because we and they are both part of the same church, and
as long as we have a ways to go, so do they. Verses 15-17 are in
the *future* tense.

The first and most basic element in John's description is, "God will dwell with them." This invariably is the primary thing with John, this closeness of personal relationship between man and God. Golden streets and all such business are secondary. May it be so for us as it was for John.

The first fruit of this relationship is the disappearance of all that to which God is opposed; man is now close enough to God that such things as death, tears, hurt, and need can't get in between. The second fruit is simply the other side of the same coin—and perhaps should be considered heads rather than tails. Men shall be guided to "the springs of the water of LIFE." John has not failed to touch upon his great "life" theme; and he is speaking, of course, of second-order rather than first-order life.

It almost goes without saying that the shepherd who gets his sheep to this water is *the Lamb*. The "shepherd" is a "lamb"? (By now we are getting used to the free-flying imagery, and almost didn't notice the literalistic contradictions.)

SEAL 7: THE COMING OF THE END

(8:1)   Now when the Lamb broke the seventh seal, there was silence in heaven   1
          for what seemed half an hour.

John has worked things so as to bring the interlude out at the same point Seal 7 will now represent, namely the end itself. Having portrayed the expansiveness and fullness of the church of the living, the victory of the church of those who have died, and the LIFE of the church that is yet to come, John is ready to return to the seal sequence and complete it with No. 7.

He handles it in very brief compass—one sentence—bringing us *to* the end but not actually describing it. His purpose seems apparent: he is not ready to proceed into the end and beyond it, because he has in mind at this point to double back and present more material regarding the end-time period—in this case under a series of seven *trumpets*. With the seventh seal, then, he is locating the end but not yet exploring it.

"*Silence* for *half an hour*." First, the silence. There is an old Jewish tradition that says God's original creation of the universe was preceded by a period of complete silence. Perhaps it was like the hush that comes over playgoers when the house lights go down and all expectancy is focused on the raising of the curtain which will bring them into a new experience and a new world. Just so, this silence ends the clamor of the end-time and sets the stage for something entirely new and different. Recall, too, that this is the *seventh* seal and that the seventh is *sabbath*, the appropriate time of cessation, quietness, and rest. This deep strand of Jewish tradition also may be in John's mind.

Why "half an hour"? This one is more difficult; but the end-time has been Evil's hour, and we are now moving into God's hour. Perhaps the thought is that God's hour has two halves: a half of expectancy and one of fulfillment, a half of inhalation and one of exhalation, a half of pause and one of action. In any case, this seal has the effect of closing off the old past and putting us on tiptoe for the new future. But John isn't ready to take us in yet; he backs off in order to lead us once more through the end-time.

8:2–11:19
The End-Time
as Seven Trumpets

INTRODUCTION TO THE TRUMPETS

2 Then I looked, and the seven angels that stand in the presence of God (8:2-6) were given seven trumpets.

3   Then another angel came and stood at the altar, holding a golden censer; and he was given a great quantity of incense to offer with the prayers of all God's people upon the golden altar in front of the throne.

4 And from the angel's hand the smoke of the incense went up before
5 God with the prayers of his people. Then the angel took the censer, filled it from the altar fire, and threw it down upon the earth; and there were peals of thunder, lightning, and an earthquake.

6   Then the seven angels that held the seven trumpets prepared to blow them.

The series of trumpets which we are now to examine is structured over the pattern identical to that of the seals. This, plus the similarity in content of the two series, is strong evidence that John still is talking about the end-time rather than proceeding further along the sequence.

There are seven *angels* who are to do the blowing; these are not the seven *spirits* of the Holy Spirit as were mentioned earlier. John very likely has in mind the ancient Jewish tradition of seven archangels—to whom actual names were given: Gabriel, Michael, Raphael, Uriel, Raguel, Saraqael, and Remiel.

Notice that "the prayers of all God's people" are part of the contents of the golden censer, which, upon being thrown to earth, triggers the end-time traumas. In other words, our prayers and cries for the coming of God's justice—our "How long, O Lord, how long?"—have a real part to play in this judgment's very coming about. Perhaps modern Christians would do well to devote more of their energies to this sort of prayer than to the techniques of our own political crusades, trying, on our own, to *make* the world be just and righteous.

TRUMPETS 1-4: THE FOUR PLAGUES

(8:7-12) The first blew his trumpet; and there came hail and fire mingled with blood, and this was hurled upon the earth. A third of the earth was burnt, a third of the trees were burnt, all the green grass was burnt. 7

The second angel blew his trumpet; and what looked like a great blazing mountain was hurled into the sea. A third of the sea was turned to blood, a third of the living creatures in it died, and a third of the ships on it foundered. 8 9

The third angel blew his trumpet; and a great star shot from the sky, flaming like a torch; and it fell on a third of the rivers and springs. The name of the star was Wormwood; and a third of the water turned to wormwood, and men in great numbers died of the water because it had been poisoned. 10 11

The fourth angel blew his trumpet; and a third part of the sun was struck, a third of the moon, and a third of the stars, so that the third part went dark and a third of the light of the day failed, and of the night. 12

The description of the effects of these four trumpets seems to have some parallel with the ten plagues that came upon the Egyptians at the time of the exodus; John uses this frame of reference to draw these trumpets into a true quartet. We have another Picassian portrayal of trauma; that the stars somehow have gotten back into the sky after having fallen to earth earlier should give us no difficulty. Wormwood, by the way, is a plant with a very bitter-tasting root. The note once again of God's restraint and limitation of Evil is made through the reiterated reference to "one third."

TRUMPET 5: THE WARRIOR LOCUSTS
(8:13—9:12)

Then I looked, and I heard an eagle calling with a loud cry as it flew in mid-heaven: 'Woe, woe, woe to the inhabitants of the earth when the trumpets sound which the three last angels must now blow!' 13

1   Then the fifth angel blew his trumpet; and I saw a star that had
fallen from heaven to earth, and the star was given the key of the shaft
2   of the abyss. With this he opened the shaft of the abyss; and from the
shaft smoke rose like smoke from a great furnace, and the sun and the
3   air were darkened by the smoke from the shaft. Then over the earth,
out of the smoke, came locusts, and they were given the powers that
4   earthly scorpions have. They were told to do no injury to the grass or
to any plant or tree, but only to those men who had not received the
5   seal of God on their foreheads. These they were allowed to torment for
five months, with torment like a scorpion's sting; but they were not to
6   kill them. During that time these men will seek death, but they will not
find it; they will long to die, but death will elude them.
7   In appearance the locusts were like horses equipped for battle. On
their heads were what looked like golden crowns; their faces were like
8   human faces and their hair like women's hair; they had teeth like lions'
9   teeth, and wore breastplates like iron; the sound of their wings was like
10   the noise of horses and chariots rushing to battle; they had tails like
scorpions, with stings in them, and in their tails lay their power to
11   plague mankind for five months. They had for their king the angel of
the abyss, whose name, in Hebrew, is Abaddon, and in Greek, Apol-
lyon, or the Destroyer.
12   The first woe has now passed. But there are still two more to come.

The customary break following Item 4 is particularly prominent
here where an angel appears in order to announce that three
"woes" corresponding to the last three trumpets are now to
follow. Trumpet 5 will be an intensification over what has gone
before; but No. 6 will be raised to an even higher power.

A star that is fallen to earth is given a key with which to open a
shaft to the abyss, the underworld. It may be helpful to know
that, in ancient times, stars often were identified as being *angels*. It
probably is this tradition John has in mind; and this particular star
is likely the angel-king named in verse 11.

Portraying a locust plague as though it were an invasion of war
horses had been done earlier by the Old Testament prophet Joel;
John is depending upon him. The details of the description might
suggest that, if you squint your imagination hard enough, you can
see some resemblance between locusts and John's war horses—
their antennae are "like women's hair," and their bodies are plated
with armor. Whether John is thinking of actual locusts or of
super-grotesque locusts the size of horses makes little difference;
we aren't to go out hunting for them in any case. These are locusts
the way Picasso would paint them, a symbol of trauma and

destruction. The "five months" of their assault could represent a "broken" year—thus, an "evil" time—or it could, perhaps more likely, be a traditional way of referring to a fairly long period.

The name of the locusts' king ties them directly into the anti-God world of Evil. Such a spiritual malignity is, in truth, the source of the forces that are chewing up our world.

TRUMPET 6: THE DEMONIC CAVALRY

(9:13-21)   The sixth angel then blew his trumpet; and I heard a voice coming from   13
between the horns of the golden altar that stood in the presence of
God. It said to the sixth angel, who held the trumpet: 'Release the four   14
angels held bound at the great river Euphrates!' So the four angels were   15
let loose, to kill a third of mankind. They had been held ready for this
moment, for this very year and month, day and hour. And their   16
squadrons of cavalry, whose count I heard, numbered two hundred
million.

This was how I saw the horses and their riders in my vision: They   17
wore breastplates, fiery red, blue, and sulphur-yellow; the horses had
heads like lions' heads, and out of their mouths came fire, smoke, and
sulphur. By these three plagues, that is, by the fire, the smoke, and the   18
sulphur that came from their mouths, a third of mankind was killed.
The power of the horses lay in their mouths, and in their tails also; for   19
their tails were like snakes, with heads, and with them too they dealt
injuries.

The rest of mankind who survived these plagues still did not abjure   20
the gods their hands had fashioned, nor cease their worship of devils
and of idols made from gold, silver, bronze, stone, and wood, which
cannot see or hear or walk. Nor did they repent of their murders, their   21
sorcery, their fornication, or their robberies.

Item 6, again, represents the ultimate intensification that brings the trauma to its climax and close—and opens the way for the end. In this instance, the movement is from the *tormenting* of men in Trumpet 5 to the *killing* of them in Trumpet 6.

The restraining power of God is given particular emphasis; the angels of death are "bound at the great river Euphrates." In Old Testament times, almost all the great devastators of historical Israel—Assyrians, Babylonians, and Persians—had come from beyond the Euphrates; so John appropriately takes this eastern territory as the symbolic source of devastation in general. But that the evil angels (and their armies) are *bound*, that they are loosed only at the permitted moment, and that their power extends only over "a third of mankind"—all these indicate that ultimately God and not the angels is running the show.

Except that no bulls are included, the scene is one that would do credit to Picasso.

Verses 20-21 are particularly important in that they make a point we forecasted but have not actually encountered until now. As John tells us, men do not abjure the gods they created for themselves, nor cease the worship of that which is not God, nor repent of wickednesses—certainly this is to say that these things are what they *should* have done, what God wanted them to do and was encouraging them to do. So there is a very positive note hidden right here in the midst of what may be John's most terrible scene. Mankind, through its sin, does bring all sorts of evil and horror upon itself. Yet, in the grace of God, that trauma could have a positive effect and outcome—*if* man would let it work the way God is trying to work it. (And it should be said that you don't have to wait until you see horses of this kind—or even pink elephants—before trauma can have the desired effect. You undoubtedly have enough trauma right now to motivate a real healthy repentance. So why wait? Do it now!)

THE TRUMPET INTERLUDE: The Scroll and Its Contents

(10:1—11:13)

Following Item 6 comes an A-B interlude; and in every case the interlude has to do with the church. The Seal Interlude pictured the *makeup* and *nature* of the church. The Trumpet Interlude now will describe the *fortunes* of the church. And the Bowl Interlude, in its turn, will be an *exhortation* to the church.

In the Trumpet Interlude, Part A will recount an incident regarding a little scroll whose contents are to be divulged; Part B, apparently, represents the contents as they *are* divulged.

PART A: THE EATING OF THE SCROLL

(10:1-11)   Then I saw another mighty angel coming down from heaven. He was   1
wrapped in cloud, with the rainbow round his head; his face shone like
the sun and his legs were like pillars of fire. In his hand he held a little   2
scroll unrolled. His right foot he planted on the sea; and his left on the
land. Then he gave a great shout, like the roar of a lion; and when he   3
shouted, the seven thunders spoke. I was about to write down what the   4
seven thunders had said; but I heard a voice from heaven saying, 'Seal
up what the seven thunders have said; do not write it down.' Then the   5
angel that I saw standing on the sea and the land raised his right hand to
heaven and swore by him who lives for ever and ever, who created   6
heaven and earth and the sea and everything in them: 'There shall be no
more delay; but when the time comes for the seventh angel to sound his   7
trumpet, the hidden purpose of God will have been fulfilled, as he
promised to his servants the prophets.'

Then the voice which I heard from heaven was speaking to me again,   8
and it said, 'Go and take the open scroll in the hand of the angel that
stands on the sea and the land.' So I went to the angel and asked him to   9
give me the little scroll. He said to me, 'Take it, and eat it. It will turn
your stomach sour, although in your mouth it will taste sweet as
honey.' So I took the little scroll from the angel's hand and ate it, and   10
in my mouth it did taste sweet as honey; but when I swallowed it my
stomach turned sour.

Then they said to me, 'Once again you must utter prophecies over   11
peoples and nations and languages and many kings.'

Although John changes a number of details, the main elements of the first part of this vision—the great angel standing above the waters and commanding the sealing of a message—are taken from Daniel 12. The concluding part of the vision—namely the eating of the scroll—is based upon Ezekiel 3.

The speech of the seven thunders which John starts to transcribe and then is prevented from doing is indeed a puzzler. Aside from a desire to be faithful to his Daniel source, it is difficult to see what significance John intends. It would sound as though he were preparing to do another seven-series; but the other one he does do is "bowls" rather than "thunders," and there is no other mention of seven thunders. John does not tell us enough that we even can begin to guess what the thunders might have said; and that he is divinely commanded not to write it down certainly implies that we are not meant to know and so shouldn't try to guess in any case. This is a passage *not* to hang up on.

Just the contrary, the angel's words in verses 6-7 are of utmost importance. Many of the older translations present his first words as: "Time shall be no more!" That way, the concept is most difficult, if not entirely impossible. "Time" is nothing more than a measure of the transpiring of change, action, or movement; and to speak of the absence of time must mean that absolutely nothing is happening. And if anything is clear it is that John has no intention of saying, at this stage of the game, that his story is all over, that any and all activity (of God, man, Evil, or whatever) is ready to come to a dead halt. No, the NEB translation printed here undoubtedly has John's meaning right: "There shall be no more delay!"

As we have said, the holding off of the eschaton is a mark of God's grace, his granting men time for repentance. Nevertheless, John insists, the time *will* come—will *have* to come—when the whistle blows, "Sorry, time has run out; the ball game is over!" John, decidedly, is not one of these moderns who believe that human history never will involve an accounting but will simply run on forever. For John, that would make history as meaningless as a football game without a termination or final score. And the words that follow in verse 7 make it certain that, in this Trumpet Series at least, Item 7 does definitely signify the end.

The "little scroll" appearing in this scene almost certainly is not to be identified with the scroll that the Lamb unsealed; and yet there is at least some connection: the contents of this one, too, represent information about the hidden future—in this case, the immediate future of the church rather than the ultimate future of human history. The prophet's eating a scroll and then speaking out its message may seem a rather strange way for God to communicate his word to man; yet this seems to be what both Ezekiel and John had in mind. Probably the intended effect is to stress both the authority and importance of the message.

Verse 11 likely is meant to point directly to Part B and suggest that it be understood as John's speaking forth the scroll he has just been fed.

PART B: THE FATE OF THE CHURCH

(11:1-13)   I was given a long cane, a kind of measuring-rod, and told: 'Now go and   1
measure the temple of God, the altar, and the number of the worship-
pers. But have nothing to do with the outer court of the temple; do not   2
measure that; for it has been given over to the Gentiles, and they will
trample the Holy City underfoot for forty-two months. And I have two   3
witnesses, whom I will appoint to prophesy, dressed in sackcloth, all
through those twelve hundred and sixty days.' These are the two   4
olive-trees and the two lamps that stand in the presence of the Lord of
the earth. If anyone seeks to do them harm, fire pours from their   5
mouths and consumes their enemies; and thus shall the man die who
seeks to do them harm. These two have the power to shut up the sky,   6
so that no rain may fall during the time of their prophesying; and they
have the power to turn water to blood and to strike the earth at will
with every kind of plague. But when they have completed their testi-   7
mony, the beast that comes up from the abyss will wage war upon them
and will defeat and kill them. Their corpses will lie in the street of the   8
great city, whose name in allegory is Sodom, or Egypt, where also their
Lord was crucified. For three days and a half men from every people   9
and tribe, of every language and nation, gaze upon their corpses and
refuse them burial. All men on earth gloat over them, make merry, and   10
exchange presents; for these two prophets were a torment to the whole
earth. But at the end of the three days and a half the breath of life from   11
God came into them; and they stood up on their feet to the terror of all
who saw it. Then a loud voice was heard speaking to them from heaven,   12
which said, 'Come up here!' And they went up to heaven in a cloud, in
full view of their enemies. At that same moment there was a violent   13
earthquake, and a tenth of the city fell. Seven thousand people were
killed in the earthquake; the rest in terror did homage to the God of
heaven.

The contents of the scroll prove to be a vision of the end-time
fortunes of the church; it is one of the most important passages in
Revelation.

We need to establish first that *the church* is indeed that of
which John is speaking. For one thing, the location of the scene is
Jerusalem, the holy city. With this we come to one of the basic
elements of John's symmetric symbolism. *Jerusalem* (and the *Zion*
hill on which it stands) is, for him, the symbolic home of the
church. I think he never mentions Jerusalem except in connection
with the church. And of course, "the new Jerusalem" is his
designation for the home of the perfected, eschatological church.
This "Jerusalem," then, is to stand over against "Babylon," the

home city of the apostate world. The back-and-forth comparison between the fortunes of "Jerusalem" and "Babylon" will be of utmost significance.

It will be interesting, later, to see how neatly John de-calendarizes (and de-maps) "Babylon"; and although the problem here is a much more tricky one, we will contend that such is precisely what he wants to do with "Jerusalem" as well. There is no good reason why it *should be,* and there is no evidence in the New Testament that it ever *was* the case, that the fate of the Christian church depends upon the fate of a particular plot of ground named Jerusalem. One of the striking things about New Testament Christianity, as over against the Old Testament Judaism out of which it was born, is the way it broke free from any geographical ties, from any theological focus on a particular land, city, culture, or people. And it is inconceivable that so totally *Christian* a thinker as John would move back to tie the outcome of his universal gospel to the fortunes of one particular human city. No, for John, "Jerusalem" identifies an *idea* rather than any specific place.

In this regard, it is probably deliberate that, although it obviously is Jerusalem John here has in mind, he nowhere explicitly names it as such. He calls it "the holy city" in verse 2; but in verse 8—in what would seem to be a conscious effort at "de-mapping"—he calls it "the great city, whose name in allegory is Sodom, or Egypt, where also their Lord was crucified." Jerusalem, yes; but also a Jerusalem that has been freed of any physical, geographical limitations so that it can be located anywhere at any time. Just as Picasso's *Guernica* is, at one and the same time, both Guernica, Spain, 1937, and also any and every other place where war has wreaked its destruction, so John's Jerusalem is the home of the church, thus to be located wherever the church is located. This present scene can and does take place wherever "Jerusalem" happens to be at the time; and finally, as universal, eschatological event, it will happen when, where, and how God chooses to bring it about.

"Jerusalem" is the locale; the central figure (or figures) is, of course, the two "witnesses." That they are *two* creates a problem to which we will need to address ourselves; but for the moment, let's concentrate on their common identity rather than their twoness. Notice, first of all, that although they are cited as two, throughout the scene they act, are acted upon, and are described in complete concert. No distinction is made; they are given no individuality; no significance is attributed to their duality.

That the two are identified as "witnesses" is crucial; this is the same Greek "martyr-witness" word with which John has characterized the church and its Christians since the opening of the book. Further, everything said about them and everything they do fits exactly with what John tells us about the church elsewhere.

But why *two?* Either one witness representing the oneness of the church or twelve witnesses incarnating the church's number would seem more appropriate; but the witnesses are two. One consideration that may have been of decisive weight for John is that much of the imagery of this scene—including the measuring of Jerusalem, the presence of lampstands (although one rather than two), and *two* olive trees who are "the *two* consecrated with oil who attend the Lord of all the earth"—is taken straight from Zechariah 2–4. John is following his source; and this may be all that is involved.

Even so, it is quite possible that John also attributed a meaning of his own to the twoness. In his own experience, John would have been aware of a basic duality of the church to which *our* experience would not alert us. The church of John's day was rather conspicuously divided into congregations of Christians, one group having come out of a Jewish background and the other out of a Gentile background. Although holding a common faith and worshipping a common Lord, their whole style and way of doing things undoubtedly was quite diverse. It seems evident, too, that there was some friction between the two groups. In light of this situation, it may well be that John is using the twoness of these figures to say that the mission of the church wants and needs the witness of both the Jewish and the Gentile Christians. It would be another case of the law of "all twelve," a plea for ecumenicity and the *fullness* of God's church.

The portion of the account dealing with the measuring of the temple probably depends more directly upon Ezekiel 40ff. than upon Zechariah, for the Zechariah vision speaks of measuring "Jerusalem" rather than the temple itself. The contrast between Ezekiel's and John's treatment is instructive, however, and points in the direction of de-literalizing. Ezekiel proceeds to give page after page of actual dimensions and description of the great, new temple he envisions. John shows no interest in this order of reality at all, speaks rather in terms of the people involved, and follows up the theme of "measuring" only long enough to make a point regarding the fate of the church and not the architecture of any temple.

The old Jewish temple consisted of two distinct areas: (a) the inner temple—incorporating the altar and other such sacred apparatuses—which was itself of particular holiness and into which were admitted only devout Jews (those bearing God's seal); and (b) the outer court, much less holy, the site of more secular kinds of activity, and open to the public—including Gentiles (the outsiders). But, we are told, the prophet is to center his attention on the inner temple (the true, loyal church), because the temple itself is to be overrun by the Gentiles (the church by the world) and only the inner temple will be preserved. This situation will last for forty-two months, which is twelve hundred and sixty days, which is three and a half years ("3 1/2" is a broken "7," thus itself the number of Evil and thus, for John, the length of the end-time).

This picture jibes with what John has been telling us all along and what he will continue to tell us. The period of the end-time (from the close of Jesus' earthly career until his parousia) is also the period of the church on earth, the time of her martyr-witness. Her home is "Jerusalem," the holy city; but it is there too "where also her Lord was crucified," a most unholy act. The church does incorporate "an inner temple" which will be preserved through the end-time; but she must also endure the ravaging of her outer courts by the godless world. And of course, John also saw this bipolarity of holiness and unholiness, fidelity and apostasy, witness and deceit, sovereignty and suffering, in the empirical church of the seven congregations of Asia Minor. So he says, "Don't get upset. This tension is part of God's plan for the end-time and is to be expected. But . . . but it is not the whole story of the church; you need to see the outcome!"

And so "Jerusalem" has a very interesting role to play in John's scheme of things. She is the city that obviously belongs on the Good side as over against "Babylon" on the Evil side. But she nevertheless is in the agonizing situation of being the holy city where also her Lord was crucified. She must go through the end-time traumas—and she will not be untouched or uncorrupted by them. Even so, her fate is not at all that of "Babylon," which is to collapse and disappear forever. On the contrary, "Jeru-salem"—in spite of trauma and even *through* trauma—is destined for repentance, resurrection, and redemption until, through God's grace, she is transformed into "the new Jerusalem," the source and center of LIFE.

But during the three and a half years in which she now finds herself, dressed in sackcloth, the symbol of lowliness and humilia-tion (how many churches have you seen lately that give any appearance of being dressed in sackcloth?), the church is called to make her faithful martyr-witness. She is to be an olive tree and a lamp before the Lord. Olive trees bear *fruit*, lamps give *light;* who ever has put the mission of the church any more succinctly? As lamp, we are so to live and act and speak that the truth of who Jesus is and what he does will be illuminated to the world. As olive trees, we are to engage in the same ministry of service and reconciliation that Jesus himself pursued. What else is there to say?

Verse 5 calls for special comment, with its reference to fire pouring from the mouths of the witnesses and consuming their enemies. This *cannot* mean that the church is called to use strong-arm (or even strong-mouth) methods of threat and violence. Such is too out of character with John's total picture and is too directly contrary to the fact that these witnesses even now are on the way to a defenseless martyrdom. John must be wanting to say that God will not allow the witness of these prophets to be cut off before its time. Again it is the principle that the power of Evil is limited and under the restraint of God. The world may be able to bloody the church's head (both through persecution and by seduc-ing her into betraying herself); but the world will never be allowed to stop the church's witness and put her out of the way. "No one takes my life from me, but I lay it down of my own accord."

Verse 6, pursuing the same line of thought, speaks of two powers which apparently the witnesses possess together. Neverthe-less, the power to shut up the rain in the sky points very strongly toward the Old Testament prophet Elijah; and the power of the plagues toward Moses. John very well may have been thinking of Elijah and Moses at this point—and it bothers us not at all. If he is, he is thinking of them as symbols of the church. After all, both are known primarily as leaders of the church (the people of God) who, in situations where they had to stand virtually alone and in

the face of great opposition, were wonderfully preserved by God
and enabled to accomplish their assigned mission and make the
faithful witness. The church *should* follow an Elijah-Moses model.

But for a moment go the other way, as many commentators do,
and put it that, at some time to come, after the Jewish temple is
rebuilt, a reincarnated Elijah and Moses are to appear in the actual
city of Jerusalem, there to be killed and then resurrected in sight
of the citizenry—after which the city will be wracked by an
earthquake. Now even if that should happen, it would be an event
that has nothing to do with me, nothing to say to me; it would be
an event entirely in God's hands and not concerning me one way
or another. John's great work becomes nothing more than data for
speculative gamesmanship. But read it our way and it becomes
God's word *to me*, God's word involving me as much as it did
John's original hearers or it will the generation that happens to
stand at the parousia. And it is a word of God that the remainder
of the New Testament also confirms as being *true!*

When the witnesses have completed their testimony—but not
before; the timing is in the hands of God—the beast will rise from
the abyss to defeat and kill them. This is the first time the beast
(*therion*) has been introduced to us *as beast*. He is Antichrist; and
though we will see much more of him in the beast role, we already
have met him as the first of the four horsemen. The witnesses will
lie dead for three and a half *days*. This period, rather clearly, is the
intensification of trauma that closes off the end-time, corresponding to Item 6 in the various seven-series.

"All men on earth" gloat over the dead witnesses; and verse 9
picks up the very phraseology of universalism that John elsewhere
has used in reference to God and his victory. We have here, then, a
universality of Evil to stand as counterpoint against the universality of the Good. The time comes when apparently Evil has
picked up all the chips. It looked that way on Good Friday; it will
look that way when the witnesses lie dead; it can look very much
that way at any point during the end-time. The difference, of
course, is that this is only an *apparent* universality, at best a
momentary universality. True and lasting universality lies solely
with God.

At the end of the three and a half days, *a breath of life from
God* comes into the witnesses. The word "breath" is the same
Greek word as "spirit"; and it would seem quite proper to read

this as a reference to the Holy Spirit, the Spirit which is always and ever the life-breath of the church. The witnesses stand upon their feet and ascend to join God.

In case any reader is not getting the parallel, John reminds us in verse 8 that all this happens in the great city *where also their Lord was crucified.* Obviously, the experience of the witnesses is to be understood as a reiteration of Jesus' own death and resurrection. The way the church is called to go, the way she is to take through the world of the end-time, is the way Jesus already has gone.

The way of the church is the way of Jesus. John is insistent on this point; he will make it at other places in other ways; he already has made it in the fifth seal when the saints' "How long?" was answered, "When the tally is complete of your brothers also giving themselves to the death in Christ's service." Yet know for a fact that this is not the way the church, in her own wisdom, is inclined to go. The way of the church, as we can observe it, tends more in the direction of organizing for corporate efficiency and power, asserting her own status, mounting crusades, trying to sweep the world off its feet, working to manipulate and dominate society, worrying about her own doctrinal nicety, building more stately mansions. *This*, while our call is to be the faithful witnesses who *give*, who expend themselves and allow themselves to be spent, who eschew dreams of power and aggrandizement in order to love their way relentlessly toward martyrdom. *This*, while the trauma of the times continues to mount and the saints ceaselessly cry, "How long, O Lord? How long?"

How long? It may be that the Lord is waiting for his church, waiting for his church to become the church. Sure as anything, there can't be a resurrection unless someone is willing to die first; if you won't bear the cross, then you can't wear the crown. How long, O Lord? How long?

But in John's picture, with the resurrection of the church, "Jerusalem" goes through her final throes. Many people are lost; but "the rest do homage to the God of heaven." Is that last word meant to suggest *repentance*—and thus the essential difference between "Jerusalem" and "Babylon"? In any case, Jerusalem continues to exist, exists to come back at the end of the story as the *new* Jerusalem. Even though what we said about her above is true—tragically true—the church will come through. John knows that; and we must have the faith to know it with him!

TRUMPET 7: VICTORY TO OUR GOD!

14 The second woe has now passed. But the third is soon to come.   **(11:14-19)**
15   Then the seventh angel blew his trumpet; and voices were heard in heaven shouting:
'The sovereignty of the world has passed to our Lord and his Christ, and he shall reign for ever and ever!'
16 And the twenty-four elders, seated on their thrones before God, fell on
17 their faces and worshipped God, saying:
'We give thee thanks, O Lord God, sovereign over all, who art and who wast, because thou hast taken thy great power into thy hands
18 and entered upon thy reign. The nations raged, but thy day of retribution has come. Now is the time for the dead to be judged; now is the time for recompense to thy servants the prophets, to thy dedicated people, and all who honour thy name, both great and small, the time to destroy those who destroy the earth.'
19   Then God's temple in heaven was laid open, and within the temple was seen the ark of his covenant. There came flashes of lightning and peals of thunder, an earthquake, and a storm of hail.

The interlude vision has brought us through the church's fortunes of the end-time and up to the end itself. Verse 14 now returns us to the trumpets and announces that we are ready for No. 7—which is the end itself. The two lines of action converge very neatly. The final three trumpets earlier had been characterized as "woes" and are again here. No. 7, I guess, is a woe for those who are not part of the scene, but the scene itself is anything but "woeful."

Earlier, in the Seal Series, we found John reluctant to describe the end itself, presumably because he planned to back off and lead up to it again from another angle. Consequently, Seal 7 pictured only the hush before the end. John's same reluctance shows itself another way here; he still does not actually describe the end but jumps over it and pictures the joyful response attending it. He will back off another time or two before showing us the end for real.

The hymn of verse 15 makes a precise statement as to what is the basic significance of that point in history which we have been calling "the end": the sovereignty of the world changes hands. Now, of course, John knows and has sufficiently indicated that *actually* the sovereignty never has been anywhere except with "our Lord and his Christ." Nevertheless, through the end-time it has *appeared* as though the forces of Evil were in control. What happens, then, in the "change of hands" is that the true state of affairs finally is revealed for what it always has been.

There is a neat touch in verse 17. The earlier threefold ascription to God, "thou who art, who wast, and who cometh," now has lost its final term. John sees that it is inappropriate at this point, because the heretofore "coming" God *has* come. The end (which is the parousia of Christ) *is* his coming. There is no need to look for God any longer; we *see* him.

Don't get squeamish over the words in verse 18: "retribution," "judged," "recompense." Above all, hear what John is saying before you decide what those words should imply. In the first place, notice that, most often when John uses words such as these, he is not necessarily talking about *people* but more likely about "the evil ones," the demons, the horsemen, the Evil Trinity—those entities that represent unmitigated evil, nothing but evil. *People*, for John, even "bad" people, come off somewhat differently. Yes, people do get seduced by evil, let themselves be used by it, give themselves over to it, are corrupted by it, are guilty of it. Nevertheless, they still are more the victims of Evil than the source of it—and John portrays God's recompense accordingly.

In the second place, take care not to read implications of cruelty, sadism, and vindictiveness into these terms until John *forces* you to do so. We have a responsibility to interpret each of John's scenes as being consistent with the overall emphasis and character of the book—do this just as long as it is possible to do so.

Finally, it is entirely proper and right for John, at this point, to speak of retribution, judgment, and recompense. In light of the heinous crimes against the church and humanity that John has portrayed, if God now were to ignore what has been going on, he would not be a *good* God, and history itself would turn out a vicious deceit. "Justice" is a godly, Christian value (built into the Bible from beginning to end) and "justice" does and *must* involve "recompense"—not vindictiveness, of course, but "just deserts," Evil's getting what it has asked for, tasting a little of what it has dished out. Jesus himself, the one who was love incarnate, easily can be quoted as supporting this principle; judgment and recompense are not contradictory to love but a necessary aspect of it. Those Christians who would like to improve the New Testament by writing this unpleasant aspect out of it are not—as they are inclined to be credited—superior "lovers"; they are sentimentalists

who have not experienced or faced up to the real nature of life
and the radical character of Evil.

Thus, the concluding line of the passage is very much in place;
there must be a time to destroy those who destroy the earth—
recalling that John has not been identifying the destroyers primarily as *people*. But those four horsemen have got to go—else
John's entire book is a mockery. Yet notice, too, that neither here
nor anywhere in Revelation is there so much as a hint that the
Christians are invited to organize themselves to go out and destroy
the destroyers. The church—the same church that has declined the
martyr-witness role for itself—often has volunteered for the role of
destroyer of the destroyers—and always with the same results.
Like lopping off ripe dandelions, it accomplishes only the scatter-
ing of the evil seed, with the church infesting itself in the process.
"How long, O Lord? How long? For only *your* justice is just, and
only you are great and good enough to undertake the destroying
of those that destroy the earth!"

Verse 19 is interesting. We see God's temple in heaven. But
when we get to the climax of the book and the new Jerusalem, it
will be specified that there is no temple, because mankind is living
in the direct presence of God. Perhaps the temple here is an
indication that, even in heaven, the end-state is not yet achieved;
there is more that must happen.

John still is working at de-literalizing. The ark of the covenant
had been lost in the Babylonian holocaust some six hundred years
before John's time; but the *heavenly* temple has hung onto its
specimen. John himself, of course, is a Christian who has rejected
Jewish temple worship; and it is likely that, at the time he was
writing, the Jerusalem temple itself already had been destroyed.
Also, recall that his previous vision had pictured the desecration of
the temple by the Gentiles. Yet, John wants to affirm, although
the temple has been outmoded by Christianity and actually destroyed by the Romans, its real significance has not been lost and
desecration is not the last word concerning it; it stands in heaven.
Although he is very good at portraying trauma and destruction,
John is a great believer in the idea that the true values of history
will be and are being preserved.

12:1–14:20
The End-Time
in Freehand Sketch

John now is ready to go through an end-time account for the third time; but in this instance he chooses to discard his pattern of the seven-series and do it freehand. We can be glad he does, because it produces what is probably the most meaningful treatment of all. The freehand approach carries a number of advantages. John can let the story make its own way. He will now set the end-time into a somewhat larger perspective, recounting a bit of what preceded the period and what follows it. Also, he will now develop his basic symmetry far beyond what he has done thus far. These chapters constitute a very important portion of Revelation.

THE WOMAN AND HER CHILD

1 Next appeared a great portent in heaven, a woman robed with the sun,   **(12:1-6)**
beneath her feet the moon, and on her head a crown of twelve stars.
2 She was pregnant, and in the anguish of her labour she cried out to be
3 delivered. Then a second portent appeared in heaven: a great red dragon
4 with seven heads and ten horns; on his heads were seven diadems, and
with his tail he swept down a third of the stars in the sky and flung
them to the earth. The dragon stood in front of the woman who was
about to give birth, so that when her child was born he might devour it.
5 She gave birth to a male child, who is destined to rule all nations with
6 an iron rod. But her child was snatched up to God and his throne; and
the woman herself fled into the wilds, where she had a place prepared
for her by God, there to be sustained for twelve hundred and sixty
days.

There appears the woman robed with the sun—a beautiful and glorious figure. She is the *church*—not only her crown of twelve stars but everything else we are told about her makes this plain. Here she is presented specifically as *mother* of the Christ; but John also may intend her later when he describes "the *bride* of Christ"— which also is the church. Normally, of course, for one's mother to be his bride would be the greatest of scandals—but not when John is doing things his way.

Although John never has them meet, this woman, most likely, is meant to be placed in conscious juxtaposition over against the great whore, the woman of *the world*, who enters a few chapters on down the line. Their distinctions are these: this one has *beauty*, that one has *glamor* (there's a difference); this one is pregnant, that one is sterile; this one bears life, that one bears death. John is on target.

We already have seen how fluid is John's concept of the church; and here it is particularly so. The woman who gives birth to the child obviously must be Old Testament Israel, the Jewish people of God. The woman who must then flee into the wilds is just as obviously the Christian, New Testament church. The woman who is the bride of Christ is a Christianity that includes the Jews. Yet all three are the same woman. And by the way, John is correct that it was out of "the anguish of her labor" that Israel brought forth the Christ—that is what the Old Testament story is all about. We seldom think in these terms; but profound insight is involved in the suggestion that God chose Israel to be the bearer of his Son and that Jesus was mothered and brought up in the faith she represents. There is no anti-Semitism in John.

A great red dragon, out to get the child, takes his stand before the woman (and the stars come unglued again). A few verses later, the dragon is specifically named as being Satan, or the Devil. Surely John means to present him as the anti-God and head of the Evil Trinity; we will see a good deal more of him before we are done. (We already have discussed the "iron rod" which the child is to wield. It comes from Psalm 2:9; but in John's mind, it cannot mean simply brutality.)

Satan is well aware that this child is the key to universal history. If he can get the babe, he's got the ball game; if he misses the babe, he loses everything. It is shrewd of John not to have introduced Satan until now; his appearance at this moment pinpoints it as being the most critical of all history. The child is born, and the dragon makes his grab; but he misses, the baby is snatched up to God, and it is all over! The snatching up can be nothing but Jesus' *resurrection*. John has collapsed the entire career of Jesus into his birth and resurrection; but the move is entirely proper in this sort of symbolic presentation.

The scene was so set that, when the dragon missed his grab, it was all over; and in what follows, John will make it plain that this is just what he meant to say. But how can Jesus' resurrection be taken to signify that it is all over, when it leads directly into the end-time where, as John has so graphically portrayed it, things proceed from bad to worse? It is precisely to this paradox John now will speak; and it is precisely the understanding of this paradox that will enable John's original readers (and us) to handle the history that must be lived through. We are at the heart of John's argument.

Although her child has been saved, the woman must flee into the wilds (namely the trials of the end-time), there to spend the three and a half years of Evil's domination.

THE DRAGON THROWN DOWN

7   Then war broke out in heaven. Michael and his angels waged war upon   **(12:7-17)**
8   the dragon. The dragon and his angels fought, but they had not the
9   strength to win, and no foothold was left them in heaven. So the great
    dragon was thrown down, that serpent of old that led the whole world
    astray, whose name is Satan, or the Devil—thrown down to the earth,
    and his angels with him.
10   Then I heard a voice in heaven proclaiming aloud: 'This is the hour
    of victory for our God, the hour of his sovereignty and power, when his
    Christ comes to his rightful rule! For the accuser of our brothers is
11 overthrown, who day and night accused them before our God. By the
    sacrifice of the Lamb they have conquered him, and by the testimony
    which they uttered; for they did not hold their lives too dear to lay
12 them down. Rejoice then, you heavens and you that dwell in them! But
    woe to you, earth and sea, for the Devil has come down to you in great
    fury, knowing that his time is short!'
13   When the dragon found that he had been thrown down to the earth,
    he went in pursuit of the woman who had given birth to the male child.
14 But the woman was given two great eagle's wings, to fly to the place in
    the wilds where for three years and a half she was to be sustained, out
15 of reach of the serpent. From his mouth the serpent spewed a flood of
16 water after the woman to sweep her away with its spate. But the earth

came to her rescue and opened its mouth and swallowed the river which
the dragon spewed from his mouth. At this the dragon grew furious   17
with the woman, and went off to wage war on the rest of her offspring,
that is, on those who keep God's commandments and maintain their
testimony to Jesus.

The scene shifts to heaven, because that perspective is necessary in
order to understand what is happening on earth. Recall what
heaven represents in John's thought; it is the locus of the throne,
the control room from which earthly history is ordered, the place
where the sealed scroll of the future is opened. What we see here
tells us much more about the reality of things than does a look at
the actuality of earthly events. Noting a racing car's fuel gauge
may tell you much more about who is winning the race than to see
who is out front at the moment.

Jesus' resurrection both triggers and decides the war in heaven.
The dragon and his angels are cast out and no foothold is left
them. Thrown out of the control room and with absolutely no
possibility of getting back in, it *is* all over! The matter is decided
once for all; there is no way the dragon can save himself or
anything of his cause.

The first line of the hymn in verse 10 interprets the event
precisely: "*This*, the moment of Jesus' resurrection, is the hour of
victory, the hour of God's kingdom coming in power." These
words come with Jesus' resurrection, which is the beginning of the
end-time. But recall that in the chapter just previous we were given
a scene from the end, at the *close* of the end-time, in which the
hymn read: "The sovereignty of the world has passed to our Lord
and his Christ."

There is no problem; John has his hymnody well in hand. What
was accomplished in Jesus' death-and-resurrection was *the* decisive
victory—none other is necessary. Whatever power and sovereignty
the dragon henceforth may show is illusory. And what the hymn
from the end celebrates is not any new victory but simply the
inevitable working out and being made apparent of the heavenly
victory that had gone before. Both moments are significant, of
course, but only the first is decisive; the second follows from and
is dependent upon it.

But where the cast-out dragon lands is *upon earth*. And he's
mad; he comes down clawing and spitting—ready to fight! Yet his

fight is not that excited by any prospect of winning; he can't win, and he knows it. No, he is moved by the kind of despair that throws all plan or prudence to the wind and is out simply to be mean for meanness' sake—aware that he has nothing to lose (because he's lost it all already). As verse 12 has it, he is in great fury, because he knows his time is short. As those of us realize who have had enough farm experience to have seen it, the most active period of a chicken's life is the first few moments after it is dead; with the cutting off of its head, the body goes into most violent spasms of flopping and lurching around—"like a chicken with its head cut off," as the old phrase so appropriately puts it. John relates that a dragon dies the same way—particularly when it is Jesus who administers the decisive blow.

This tells us something. During the end-time in which we live, as we see the tantrums and traumas growing ever more wild and reckless, it is *not* an indication that Evil is growing in strength and about to take over. Quite the contrary, it is evidence that the dragon already has been decapitated and can't last much longer. This knowledge, of course, does not change the seriousness of his depredations or the reality of the damage he yet can wreak; but it does enable us the better to stand up under them. Through John, the word of God comes to us: "Hang in, fellow! Hang in! You've got it won, just stay in there until the bell!" And the final bell, we are assured, will ring *soon!*

Verse 11—a great one—tells us what hanging-in Christians can and should do to help hasten the demise of the devil. (1) It is by the sacrifice of the Lamb, his death-and-resurrection, and only by this, that the conquest takes place. This is the fundamental and necessary factum. (2) Yet, it is through the testimony, the *martyria Jesu*, Christians make to him that his victory is kept active and the dragon kept confronted with it. (3) And this witness, finally, is full-powered only when it is supported by and includes the willingness "not to hold their lives too dear to lay them down." This victory cost the Lamb everything, and he was willing to give it for our sakes; why do we think it should cost us nothing?

In verses 13ff., the scene shifts from heaven back to earth, where we see the end-time in progress as Evil focuses its attention on the persecution of mother church. God preserves her, although not in any easy, complacent security. The dragon launches his worst at her, but friends come to her aid. The earth itself and the course of history are on the side of the church. Yet notice carefully that nothing is said or hinted about the church's fighting—or even resisting—the dragon. She is to take care of her martyr-witness and let God do the "sustaining."

With verse 17, John apparently distorts his analogy a bit in order to introduce a new idea. Historically it seems correct that persecution against the church first focused on the Jewish Christians; later it moved on to engulf the Gentile Christians (among whom most of John's hearers would be counted). This probably is as much as John has in mind with his reference to "the rest of her offspring"—and would tend to confirm our earlier interpretation of "the two witnesses."

ENTER, THE BEAST

(13:1-10) He took his stand on the sea-shore.   1
 Then out of the sea I saw a beast rising. It had ten horns and seven heads. On its horns were ten diadems, and on each head a blasphemous name. The beast I saw was like a leopard, but its feet were like a bear's   2 and its mouth like a lion's mouth. The dragon conferred upon it his   3 power and rule, and great authority. One of its heads appeared to have received a death-blow; but the mortal wound was healed. The whole world went after the beast in wondering admiration. Men worshipped   4 the dragon because he had conferred his authority upon the beast; they worshipped the beast also, and chanted, 'Who is like the Beast? Who can fight against it?'
 The beast was allowed to mouth bombast and blasphemy, and was   5 given the right to reign for forty-two months. It opened its mouth in   6 blasphemy against God, reviling his name and his heavenly dwelling. It   7 was also allowed to wage war on God's people and to defeat them, and was granted authority over every tribe and people, language and nation. All on earth will worship it, except those whose names the Lamb that   8 was slain keeps in his roll of the living, written there since the world was made.
 Hear, you who have ears to hear! Whoever is to be made prisoner, a   9,10 prisoner he shall be. Whoever takes the sword to kill, by the sword he is bound to be killed. This is where the fortitude and faithfulness of God's people have their place.

The previous scene brought on stage the great, red dragon. It is significant that, in John's book, he lasted a grand total of six verses before he was dead. But from here on out we need always to bear in mind that it is a dead—although quite active, even hyperactive—dragon with whom we have to deal. He now takes his stand by the seashore, in order to introduce to us his colleagues. John, from his Old Testament background, understands the sea as a soupy place of chaos, darkness, and monstrosity. It is as if this new character stuck his head up out of a garbage can.

This is *therion*, the beast, the Fancy Fake in a different get-up—or perhaps the Fancy Fake seen for who he really is. Yet notice that virtually every detail we are told about him suggests a counter comparison with *arnion*, the Lamb; Fancy Fake he still very much is.

John constructs the forepart of this beastly description out of the four beasts described in Daniel 7. But then, "the dragon conferred upon it his power"—as God had upon the Lamb. The beast, although living, bears a mark of slaughter upon him—as does the Lamb. The beast leads the world to worship the dragon—as the Lamb leads the church to worship God. The beast has the right to reign (in appearance) for the three and a half years of the end-time—as the Lamb will (in reality) for the thousand years of the millennium. And finally, the beast commands a pseudo-universality that corresponds to the true universality of the Lamb.

Verse 8, then, confirms the point we argued earlier: a person's loyalty belongs either to the Lamb or to the beast—there is no other option. The urgency and cruciality of this choice—plus the fact that the vote seems currently to be going for the beast—moves John to close off the scene with an exhortation: "Be very clear! If you go with the beast, you go *with* the beast. What he stands for, you stand for; what he gets, you get! God's people had better be ready to stand by and hang in at all costs!" And note that the Lamb's people are identified as "those whose names appear in his roll *of the living.*" Here, again, is the basic distinction: those who are in the Lamb have LIFE; outside of him, all is DEATH.

AND ANOTHER, THE UNHOLY SPIRIT

11 Then I saw another beast, which came up out of the earth; it had two **(13:11-18)**
12 horns like a lamb's, but spoke like a dragon. It wielded all the authority of the first beast in its presence, and made the earth and its inhabitants

worship this first beast, whose mortal wound had been healed. It   13
worked great miracles, even making fire come down from heaven to
earth before men's eyes. By the miracles it was allowed to perform in   14
the presence of the beast it deluded the inhabitants of the earth, and
made them erect an image in honour of the beast that had been
wounded by the sword and yet lived. It was allowed to give breath to   15
the image of the beast, so that it could speak, and could cause all who
would not worship the image to be put to death. Moreover, it caused   16
everyone, great and small, rich and poor, slave and free, to be branded
with a mark on his right hand or forehead, and no one was allowed to   17
buy or sell unless he bore this beast's mark, either name or number.
(Here is the key; and anyone who has intelligence may work out the   18
number of the beast. The number represents a man's name, and the
numerical value of its letters is six hundred and sixty-six.)

The dragon made his entrance out of the *air* (accidentally, as it
were, falling on his tail from heaven). *Therion* arose out of the
garbage-can *sea*. Number Three now comes out of the *ground* (he's
the dirty one); and his, obviously, is intended as a counter description
of the Holy Spirit.

This Unholy Spirit is called "another *beast.*" That could make
for confusion; but whenever John talks about "*the* beast" it seems
evident that he has in mind the Antichrist. Elsewhere he calls this
third member of the Evil Trinity "the false prophet"; inasmuch as
the Holy Spirit acts primarily as teacher and communicator in
behalf of God and Christ, so does this one serve *his* colleagues—
although, of course, in a false way. That he has "horns like a
lamb's" establishes his relationship to Antichrist, who is a fake
lamb. That he "spoke like a dragon" establishes the relationship in
that direction.

This beast wields the authority of the first beast and leads men
to him—as the Holy Spirit does with Christ. He performs
miracles—as does the Holy Spirit (and the coming down of fire
could be a reference to the Pentecost miracle of the Holy Spirit's
coming in tongues as of fire). Catch the implication; the sheer
occurrence of miracle is no proof that the Holy Spirit is at work;
the Unholy Spirit can fake that sort of thing. Through his miracles
he wins men, leads them into the worship of Antichrist, and even
breathes life (false life) into that worship—as the Holy Spirit wins
men for Christ, leads them to worship him, and inspires (breathes
into them) their spiritual life.

Verse 16, then, brings John to the counterpart of his earlier scene, namely the sealing of the Lamb's people. Again the implication is plain that every person bears one seal or the other; he carries the brand of either *arnion* or *therion;* none is unclaimed.

With the observation that "no one was allowed to buy or sell unless he bore this beast's mark," John may be saying something quite profound. "Buying and selling," the whole business of *economics*, is, of course, one of the central activities of this world; John knows this and will make that knowledge explicit at a later point. "Buying and selling" is the world's big operation; the world has set up the game, defined its rules, and is running the tables; and never forget, *the beast* is lord of "this world." You won't get very far at these tables, then, John is saying, unless you can show proof that the boss has okayed you. You'll never win at this game unless you're willing to play according to the way of the world.

Now I am confident that John does not mean to say that, if you so much as go to the supermarket, you have sold out to the beast. He probably does not even mean to say that the fact that a person has chanced to amass some worldly riches necessarily is *proof* that he wears the mark of the beast. Nevertheless, John's observation is true, and we need to be greatly alerted by it: "buying and selling" is the world's game, and you can't go far in it without selling your soul to the boss who runs it.

The parenthesis of verse 18—and it is significant that the translators have understood it as being a parenthesis—is one of the most difficult passages in Revelation. It is a riddle which, quite plainly, goes along with some similar material in Chapter 17. We can be more effective if we handle the two passages together; let's hold this verse in abeyance for now and come back to it then. Such a procedure will not affect our understanding of the present scene.

THE LAMB AND HIS HUNDRED FORTY-FOUR THOUSAND

1 Then I looked, and on Mount Zion stood the Lamb, and with him were   (14:1-5)
   a hundred and forty-four thousand who had his name and the name of
2 his Father written on their foreheads. I heard a sound from heaven like
   the noise of rushing water and the deep roar of thunder; it was the
3 sound of harpers playing on their harps. There before the throne, and

the four living creatures and the elders, they were singing a new song.
That song no one could learn except the hundred and forty-four
thousand, who alone from the whole world had been ransomed. These   4
are men who did not defile themselves with women, for they have kept
themselves chaste, and they follow the Lamb wherever he goes. They
have been ransomed as the firstfruits of humanity for God and the
Lamb. No lie was found in their lips; they are faultless.   5

John's introduction of the hierarchy of Evil closed with the
picture of those who were sealed into that company. The matter
immediately recalls those who had been sealed the other way.
John moves, then, to the positive side of his counter play. In the
process, this move will take us beyond the end-time (which belongs to the side of Evil) and into the end (which is a transition
into the Good). We stand now at what would be the spot between
Items 6 and 7, if this account were one of the seven-series.

The scene opens upon the hundred forty-four thousand whom
we met earlier; they stand upon Mount Zion (Jerusalem), which is
their proper location, the home of the church. With them stands
the Lamb. This is most significant, being the first time he has
appeared on earth since John undertook to portray the end-time.
With that, another very interesting thing happens: the scene shifts
to heaven—but *without any sense of a shift.* What is happening is
that the line between heaven and earth is beginning to dissolve—
which is what occurs as Evil disappears. The church on earth and
the church in heaven show signs of coming together. That the
church—the united church—now sings "a new song" indicates that
something is taking place that never has happened before.

By now it is becoming clear that John's "interludes" are not
interludes at all, in the sense of being a break in the action for the
sake of a break; they are an integral part of his sequence. Think
back: In the Seal Series, Part A of the "Interlude" was a picture of
the church *on earth*, the sealing of the 144,000; Part B was a
picture of the church *in heaven*, the numberless throng of those
who had washed their robes in the blood of the Lamb. The two
churches were presented in juxtaposition but as being quite distinct from each other. The "Interlude" of the Trumpet Series,
then, gave us a picture of the church on earth being martyred and
then resurrected and called up to heaven. The church *in* heaven
was not mentioned, but certainly something was beginning to
happen in their relationship.

The Freehand Sketch which we presently are treating, although it is not structured as a series of seven, follows the same sequence of action as the others. The dragon's fall from heaven, his chasing of the woman, and the descriptions of the works of Antichrist and the Unholy Spirit, all correlate with the earlier accounts of the traumas of the end-time. Indeed, the sealing of the beast's people and their domination of the world may be meant as corresponding to the final intensification normally presented as Item 6. The present scene of the church on earth "blending into" the church in heaven comes, then, at the proper spot for the "Interlude." And notice that John's interludes are making progress each time they are repeated; the two churches are moving into convergence—and we will have more to say on that point in a moment. From here, then, we move directly into the two events that consistently characterize the end (normally Item 7): the collapse of Evil's kingdom, Babylon, and the parousia of Christ.

John has been moving the earthly church toward the heavenly church until now the 144,000 stand on Mount Zion. From heaven is heard a song; and behold, it is a *new* song, the song of the 144,000 alone.

The way John has led up to and now performs this dissolution of the line between earth and heaven tells us a great deal about his concept of the two. He has never understood the basic distinction between them as being a space gap, heaven being up there and earth down here. Rather, "earth" is the historical situation *as it actually is;* and given the presence of some of the characters we have just met, that means the situation inevitably has a consider-able degree of "wrongness" about it. "Heaven," on the other hand, represents *the rightness that is coming to be.* So, of course, any development toward the elimination of Evil can be portrayed as earth's moving into heaven or a dissolving of the line between them. And this happens, John tells us, through the church.

Yet it is important to note—as we have done previously—that even heaven itself does not represent final perfection, the absolute end of God's work. It represents that which is *coming to be* rather than the firm *accomplishment* of that perfect state. Heaven is sufficiently with earth that, as long as earth is wrong, heaven cannot be entirely right (just as we observed earlier that, as long as any of my brothers are still lost, I cannot be saved to the uttermost; there is too much of me that is of a part with them).

And thus John's heaven still has a temple, a symbol of mediation and thus distance between God and man (11:19); it still has saints crying, "How long, O Lord?" (6:10); it still has talk about what God must yet do for his people (7:15-17).

When, then, at the close of his book, John does present the final perfection that is the end of God's work, it is not simply "heaven." It is "the new Jerusalem," the city *come down from* heaven. It cannot be identified directly with either heaven or earth, although it includes something of both. It is neither simply earth redeemed nor heaven completed. It is a *new* work of God which catches up both of these and yet is a new thing. The new Jerusalem is "rightness" in the situation of an "actually now is." Yet this new Jerusalem is also a "12"-numbered city and a "Jerusalem," the home of the church. It is in and through *the church* that all this is to happen. Of course, we are not at that point in our story yet; but when the line between earth and heaven begins to go, things are moving in the right direction.

In verses 4-5, we are given a definition of the church of which we speak. What we are told fits completely with what we have been told of the church all along; but this is probably John's most succinct and penetrating statement. At first blush it seems way off the mark—male chauvinism raised to the power of blasphemy. Not only is the Lamb's church exclusively male, but these are men "who did not defile themselves with women"—both sexual intercourse and women themselves are directly equated with evil. But this reading cannot be allowed to stand; if it is, the whole book of Revelation is compromised, in that it would then contradict the gospel which clearly proclaims that "there is no such thing as male and female; for you are all one person in Christ Jesus."

To this point we have seen nothing indicating that John shared the mentality seemingly betrayed here. Sex distinctions would seem to have been the farthest thing from his mind; he has presented people simply as people.

Almost certainly, then, John now is harking back to the very familiar Old Testament model in which idolatry and other forms of apostasy are portrayed as sexual promiscuity. But no, the church is the virgin bride of Christ, a bride who never has had and never wants any other Lover (except that in this passage—contrary to what we find elsewhere—the church is *male;* it just goes to show how oblivious John is to sex distinctions). Indeed, John may have it in mind, here, that the particular woman with which the church does not defile itself is the great world whore, to be introduced a few chapters on. In any case, John is speaking of "fidelity" rather than "sex."

Such an interpretation is virtually assured by the next line, which specifies that the 144,000 "follow the Lamb wherever he goes"—which is what "fidelity" means. Also, it goes without saying that the "way" the Lamb goes is that of the self-giving martyr-witness which leads even to death and resurrection. This is the quality and content of the loyalty that typifies the church of the Lamb.

And then, in a new and mind-boggling note, we are told that this church is "the firstfruits of humanity for God and the Lamb." We need to know, first, what a "firstfruit" is; it is a basic biblical concept. With apples or any other crop, it is not the case that one night every fruit is still green and the next morning every one is ripe. No, some naturally will ripen a little ahead of the rest. This first-ripe fruit is the "firstfruit"; and it is very precious in the eye of the farmer, because it is as much as a guarantee that he is going to get a crop. The firstfruit is considered as bringing the entire harvest in its train. Further, in Old Testament practice, this fruit-fruit was dedicated to the Lord as a "thank offering" and an expression that the harvest as a whole was his doing and belonged to him.

This little phrase, then, tells us that the church is not merely that community out of the world which is moving toward heaven—and, with heaven, toward the new Jerusalem. Not at all; the church also is the vehicle by which God means to move "humanity," the world itself, along that course; the church's experience is also the sign of what the experience of mankind is to be. Put these words into the collection of John's universalistic references.

It later will become evident that the primary way in which the church acts as vehicle, the means by which the world is brought along, is by the church's incorporating men into herself; the world is saved by becoming church. Nevertheless, the church dare never act as though she exists only for her own sake, as though her only goal were to get herself saved. Her need to be faithful is a double one, because humanity itself, and not simply her own salvation, is dependent upon it—the firstfruits determine the harvest.

In all this, of course, we are talking more precisely about what the Lamb is doing and will do through the church than about what the church can or will do on her own. Yet this in no way lessens the church's responsibility to be his faithful instrument. And so, as verse 5 has it, she must be the church *of truth;* the gospel—and never any lie—must be found on her lips; the fate of humanity hangs on it.

THE COLLAPSE OF EVIL'S KINGDOM

(14:6-13)   Then I saw an angel flying in mid-heaven, with an eternal gospel to   6
proclaim to those on earth, to every nation and tribe, language and
people. He cried in a loud voice, 'Fear God and pay him homage; for   7
the hour of his judgement has come! Worship him who made heaven
and earth, the sea and the water-springs!'

Then another angel, a second, followed, and he cried, 'Fallen, fallen   8
is Babylon the great, she who has made all nations drink the fierce wine
of her fornication!'

Yet a third angel followed, crying out loud, 'Whoever worships the   9
beast and its image and receives its mark on his forehead or hand, he   10
shall drink the wine of God's wrath, poured undiluted into the cup of
his vengeance. He shall be tormented in sulphurous flames before the
holy angels and before the Lamb. The smoke of their torment will rise   11
for ever and ever, and there will be no respite day or night for those
who worship the beast and its image or receive the mark of its name.'
This is where the fortitude of God's people has its place—in keeping   12
God's commands and remaining loyal to Jesus.

Moreover, I heard a voice from heaven, saying, 'Write this: "Happy   13
are the dead who die in the faith of Christ! Henceforth", says the
Spirit, "they may rest from their labours; for they take with them the
record of their deeds." '

We come now to John's first description of the events of the end itself; recall that, in both the Seal and the Trumpet Series, he backed off from or jumped over the spot without actually describing it. As the time-line in the front of the book indicates, the end is signaled by two different events: (1) the collapse of Evil's kingdom and (2) the parousia of Christ. The present scene portrays the first of these. In the scene just previous, we saw at least the beginning of a movement of the church (the Lamb's people) toward heaven. Now in what is probably a deliberate counter play, we see a movement of the beast's crowd in a different direction.

It is highly significant that the scene opens as it does with "an eternal gospel (good news)" being proclaimed *universally* "to those on earth." The good news, obviously, is the possibility of repentance: "Even if you have been part of this evil kingdom right up until now, to the very point of its collapse, you don't have to go down with it. It is not too late; turn to God and be saved!" Yes, the proclamation does have an urgency about it and does itself call for action on the part of the hearer; but if it isn't *good* news for those to whom it is addressed, I don't know what would be. Ask yourself, also, whether it would be accurate for John to term this possibility of repentance an "*eternal* gospel" if he has in mind that the invitation will terminate the next moment in the fall of Babylon. The eternal gospel proclaimed to the whole earth belongs in our collection of universalistic texts.

A second angel follows the first, proclaiming that Babylon, the great whore who symbolizes promiscuity (as opposed to fidelity), has fallen. As a much more detailed scene will establish later, Babylon is the city of this world, of "worldliness," and thus the very capital of *therion*'s realm. Babylon *falls*—but notice carefully that neither here nor anywhere else is there a hint that she was attacked by outsiders. There are no armies from heaven, not even a thunderbolt. More significant, there is no suggestion that the Christians had been working to subvert her, that they had plotted a revolution designed to overthrow the regime of Evil, not even that they had huffed and puffed in an effort to blow the house down with their railing.

John's book customarily is classified as *apocalyptic*. Likewise, the mood of the revolutionist, liberationist movements that have swept both society and the church in our own day customarily has been identified as apocalyptic. Yet if that connection has any validity at all, it obviously does not hold on this most central point: our modern movements organize to overthrow wicked regimes; John stands by to watch them collapse.

John's picture here fits in beautifully with his earlier scene of the dragon's fall from heaven. A headless chicken can't sustain its frenzy for very long—and inevitably that whirl is going to end in total collapse. Just so, structures built upon evil cannot stand for very long; they have no foundations. In our own history, we have

seen the relatively weak and insignificant communities of God's
people—both Jewish and Christian—outlast the imposing edifices
and impressive power alignments of regime after regime, civilization (so-called) after civilization. Yes, "Fallen, fallen is Babylon
the great!" And we do not simply have to take John's word for it
that this will happen in a grand smash at the end of history; we
have seen Babylon fall time and again. And that being the case,
John makes it plain that the Christian's call is to be doing the
self-giving service and making the self-giving witness that moves
the church toward heaven and *makes it the firstfruits of humanity*—this, rather than being out trying to engineer things in
Babylon itself.

The third angel comes with a message which, both in its placement and basic content, clearly is appropriate and as much as
inevitable. The word of warning must be heard: "You people who
have chosen to build your pleasant homes in Babylon, who have
found the life of the world so attractive and convenient, who
either through deliberate choice or carelessness have let yourselves
be marked for the beast—you must know that, when Babylon
goes, you go. The situation is of utmost seriousness; please, please
give some thought to it!"

That much certainly is in place—and even part of the *good*
news. It is a favor to a person to warn him of a danger he has not
seen. But even so, most of us will feel that John has overdone it
when he talks about "the wine of God's wrath," "the cup of his
vengeance," "tormented in sulphurous flames before the Lamb,"
"the smoke of their torment will rise for ever and ever." The issue
no longer has to do simply with whether punishment is a proper
and necessary part of justice and how much and what kind of
punishment is enough. Now it becomes a question of the basic
character of God and the Lamb; the language is the sort that has
been associated with the dragon and beast up to this point.

I do not at all claim to have a neat solution for this problem; I
will try to offer what help I can.

(1) The easy move—and one a number of scholars are inclined
to take—is to suggest that John did not write this passage; someone else stuck it in. I do not feel it justified to go such a route in
this case. In the first place, regarding the overall structure of
John's thought, this entire scene of the fall of Babylon is just too
"right" to suggest that he did not have it here. In the second place,

the three angelic messages together—and even the basic idea behind the third message—are so much a part of one another and so
typically "John" that it is hard to believe they are not all original.

(2) Whoever wrote these words, we must not let them determine our own understanding of God and Christ; the whole thrust
of the Bible is too much the other way.

(3) We dare not even allow these verses (and a few others yet to
come) determine what we will accept as being *John's* understanding of God and Christ. The book of Revelation, in and of itself,
has too much evidence pointing another direction—evidence that
includes our entire collection of "universalistic" texts, plus much
other material. Both in amount and emphasis, that material far
outweighs anything of the tenor of what we find here.

(4) Although we must take care to be honest about the actual
wording that appears, it also is incumbent upon us to do everything we can to interpret the words so as to make them as
consistent with the rest of John's thought as is possible. In relation
to any speaker, it is we who have the control of our own bias as to
what construction we will put upon his words; try your best, now,
to hear John as a teacher of the Christian gospel—which we have
abundant proof he is.

(5) In this regard, even if the passage carries implications we
cannot accept, we dare not allow them to turn us off to the truth
that is present.

(6) At any number of places, the Bible speaks about "the wrath
of God." Scholars have given a great deal of attention to the
phrase and come to the conclusion that it should not be read as
carrying the implications we normally give to the word "wrath."
When applied to God, "wrath" does not describe an emotional
state with overtones of rage, irrationality, self-assertion, and de-
structiveness. God's "wrath" is rather an aspect of his deep sense
of justice. His concern is wholly that things be made right; but he
also knows that the only way this can happen is to let evildoers
feel the "wrath" they have created for themselves. If God did not
let men know that he has this concern and feels this way about
evil, they could never know what love is represented in his efforts
at saving them from that evil. Even a very small child, found
playing in the street, catches on that the consequent parental
"wrath"—including even a swat or two—is the expression of a love
that cannot stand to see the child destroyed. This consideration is

not adequate entirely to resolve the difficulty of this passage; but use it as far as it will go.

(7) In verse 11, the phrase "for ever and ever" should be translated "for the aeons of the aeons"; it does not *necessarily* denote endlessness. If the torment has the possibility of an end, it can be understood as redemptive in character. If it has no possibility of an end, then, of course, there is no way it can be understood as redemptive.

(8) This passage will need to be put alongside some others yet to come suggesting that even punishment after death has a redemptive purpose behind it.

(9) Verse 12 shows us where John wants the main thrust of this passage to come. His primary purpose is not in giving us the satisfaction of seeing bad people fry (and we ought not try to deny that there is in us that which does take satisfaction in such a scene). Many of the people who would be most upset over this passage from Revelation are quite willing to use a rather similar sort of language in regard to this or that public official or some other favorite target of their own "righteous indignation." But John is not indulging such feelings; he is warning God's people of what can happen if they relax in their endurance and lose their loyalty to Jesus.

(10) It may be that John's language has distorted his thought—and to whom has this not occurred? In such case, let's go with his thought!

The third angel spoke of what is in store for those who bear the beast's mark. In verse 13, a voice from heaven appropriately winds up the scene with a beatitude regarding those who belong to Christ. Another translation, just as true to the Greek as the one given here, may be preferable: "Happy are the dead who die in the faith of Christ henceforth [i.e., since faith in Christ was made possible through his death and resurrection]!" the Spirit says. "They may rest. . . ." They have nothing to fear from all the punishment now taking place; their forehead-seals attest that they have accepted the lordship of Christ and lived in loyalty to him.

14   Then as I looked there appeared a white cloud, and on the cloud sat **(14:14-20)**
one like a son of man. He had on his head a crown of gold and in his
15   hand a sharp sickle. Another angel came out of the temple and called in
a loud voice to him who sat on the cloud: 'Stretch out your sickle and
16   reap; for harvest-time has come, and earth's crop is over-ripe.' So he
who sat on the cloud put his sickle to the earth and its harvest was
reaped.
17   Then another angel came out of the heavenly temple, and he also had
18   a sharp sickle. Then from the altar came yet another, the angel who has
authority over fire, and he shouted to the one with the sharp sickle:
'Stretch out your sickle, and gather in earth's grape-harvest, for its
19   clusters are ripe.' So the angel put his sickle to the earth and gathered
in its grapes, and threw them into the great winepress of God's wrath.
20   The winepress was trodden outside the city, and for two hundred miles
around blood flowed from the press to the height of the horses' bridles.

The fall of Babylon is the first event of the end; the parousia of
Christ is the second; we are now at the second. It is presented here
as a *harvest* (a most appropriate figure), based upon a suggestion
from Joel 3:13 and with much of the imagery taken from Isaiah
63. It is a double harvest: a positive *grain* harvest of blessing and a
negative *grape* (wine) harvest of "wrath."

In the first instance, the harvester is "one like a son of man"
(the phrase from Daniel which John already has used as identifying Christ); he wears "a crown of gold"; and it is, by the way,
appropriate that he uses a "sickle" rather than his two-edged
sword (this is a harvest and not a battle scene; judgment is not
involved). There would seem to be no doubt at all that John
intends this as an account of *the parousia*. That an angel must
come from the heavenly temple to give the signal may be John's
way of affirming what Jesus himself had said, that not even the
Son knows the day and hour but only the Father.

Particularly in light of the previous scene, it is important to
note that John very explicitly dissociates Christ from the grape
harvest of wrath; a mere angel is the harvester here. Yes, the wrath
is a proper and necessary aspect of God's plan; but it is not the
proper work of Jesus Christ; he is to be preserved as the symbol of
forgiveness and redemption. This is somewhat different than people being tortured by fire before the Lamb.

The wine that flows from this winepress is, of course, human blood; people are being killed. Yet we need to realize that "getting killed" does not have quite the same significance for John as it does for us. We tend to see death as signifying finality. But "dead *and gone*" was never John's phrase; he paints on a canvas large enough that he can include characters who would be off the edge for other artists.

With John, the dead go on playing their roles almost as though nothing had happened. We already have seen this regarding the saints of the earth-and-heaven church; but we will see it regarding bad people as well. For John, death (first-order death) is a transition of comparatively minor theological significance. Certainly John intends the bloody winepress as a symbol of punishment; but just as certainly, it is not for him a symbol of annihilation.

For calendarizers who might be interested, I can report that some clever head has figured out the amount of blood that could be squeezed from an average human being and divided that into the volume of a puddle two hundred miles in radius and as deep as a horse's bridle. His conclusion is that, even if everyone went through the press of wrath, the cumulative population of the world still has not been nearly enough to provide the juice. It's a bloody shame!

Introduction to the Bowls 15:1—16:1
Bowls 1-5: The Worst Plagues of All 16:2-11
Bowls 6 (Interlude) and 7: Collapse at Armageddon 16:12-21

15:1–16:21
The End-Time Intensification as Seven Bowls

Having completed the freehand sketch that ran from the child's being born of the woman to his return as harvester, John now is ready to give the end-time a final go. Indeed, with this series, he does not even propose to describe the end-time as a whole. Although he will again make use of the familiar rhythm of a seven-series, he makes it clear that he is treating only that interval running from Item 6 on through the end, namely the final intensification of trauma, the rescue of the church, and the end itself. This compression means also that he will noticeably quicken the pace of the series as a whole; he deliberately is building to a climax.

INTRODUCTION TO THE BOWLS

1   Then I saw another great and astonishing portent in heaven: seven   (15:1
angels with seven plagues, the last plagues of all, for with them the   —16:1)
wrath of God is consummated.

2   I saw what seemed a sea of glass shot with fire, and beside the sea of glass, holding the harps which God had given them, were those who had won the victory over the beast and its image and the number of its name.

3   They were singing the song of Moses, the servant of God, and the song of the Lamb, as they chanted:
'Great and marvellous are thy deeds, O Lord God, sovereign over all;

4   just and true are thy ways, thou king of the ages. Who shall not revere thee, Lord, and do homage to thy name? For thou alone art holy. All nations shall come and worship in thy presence, for thy just dealings stand revealed.'

> After this, as I looked, the sanctuary of the heavenly Tent of 5
> Testimony was thrown open, and out of it came the seven angels with 6
> the seven plagues. They were robed in fine linen, clean and shining, and
> had golden girdles round their breasts. Then one of the four living 7
> creatures gave the seven angels seven golden bowls full of the wrath of
> God who lives for ever and ever; and the sanctuary was filled with 8
> smoke from the glory of God and his power, so that no one could enter
> it until the seven plagues of the seven angels were completed.
>
> Then from the sanctuary I heard a loud voice, and it said to the seven 1
> angels, 'Go and pour out the seven bowls of God's wrath on the earth.'

Unlike the earlier series, John gives this one a comparatively lengthy introduction and a very positive one. The bowls will be full of terrible things, and perhaps John wants to make us aware of the positive side of things in order to help carry us through the negative.

Within this scene are enough reminiscences of the Old Testament account of the exodus from Egypt to indicate that John most likely intends it as a conscious model. The exodus was a journey through trauma to liberation; and just so is the church's experience of the end-time. The important thing is not to become so overwhelmed by the trauma as to forget that it is liberation that is taking place.

Verse 1 tells us that the bowls represent the final intensification, "the last plagues of all." That the scene opens beside "the sea of glass" recalls the exodus scene of victory that took place on the far side of the Sea of Reeds (the Red Sea). The singers are "those who had won the victory over the beast"; the account in 12:11 already has told us how this was accomplished—by the sacrifice of the Lamb, by their testimony to that act, and by their willingness to put their lives where he had put his.

The song they sing is that "of Moses" and "of the Lamb"—and it is but *one* song. As Moses led that people of God out of the bondage of slavery in Egypt, so the Lamb leads the new people of God out of their slavery to Evil and this world; the Lamb is a new and greater Moses. The song is a hymn of praise to God for the wonder of his deeds, the justice, truth, and holiness of his ways. The note of universalism in verse 4 belongs in our growing collection of such passages.

Because this scene is built on exodus motifs, the old Tent of Testimony, the tabernacle, makes a more appropriate setting than the temple used heretofore. That no one can enter the sanctuary until the plagues are over may be recognition that, although necessary, the "wrath" of God is not his true work of holiness; as long as the bowl plagues are in progress, the "sanctuary" is not a completely appropriate location.

BOWLS 1-5: THE WORST PLAGUES OF ALL

2   So the first angel went and poured his bowl on the earth; and foul   **(16:2-11)**
malignant sores appeared on those men that wore the mark of the beast
and worshipped its image.

3   The second angel poured his bowl on the sea, and it turned to blood
like the blood from a corpse; and every living thing in the sea died.

4   The third angel poured his bowl on the rivers and springs, and they
turned to blood.

5   Then I heard the angel of the waters say, 'Just art thou in these thy
6   judgements, thou Holy One who art and wast; for they shed the blood
of thy people and of thy prophets, and thou hast given them blood to
7   drink. They have their deserts!' And I heard the altar cry, 'Yes, Lord
God, sovereign over all, true and just are thy judgements!'

8   The fourth angel poured his bowl on the sun; and it was allowed to
9   burn men with its flames. They were fearfully burned; but they only
cursed the name of God who had the power to inflict such plagues, and
they refused to repent or do him homage.

10   The fifth angel poured his bowl on the throne of the beast; and its
kingdom was plunged in darkness. Men gnawed their tongues in agony,
11   but they only cursed the God of heaven for their sores and pains, and
would not repent of what they had done.

Following up the exodus theme, these bowl plagues show perhaps even more dependence upon the Old Testament account of the Egyptian plagues than those of the Trumpet Series did. Note that here the elements of restraint and limitation which marked the earlier end-time descriptions have all disappeared; verse 3 even specifies that "*every* living thing in the sea died." We are right at the end now; and John is intensifying the trauma with all stops out.

The break that normally comes after the fourth item, in this instance follows the third, for no clear reason. The content of that break (verses 5-7) includes important insights. The threefold ascription to God again has lost its final "who cometh" term; we are

close enough to the end that John considers that God has arrived.
The thrust of the words from heaven is the assurance that, no
matter how severe these punishments appear, they are *just*—in true
proportion to the evil that infests the earth and the crime committed. The measure of that crime is specified as being the world's
treatment of the church. The world crucified Jesus in the first
place and has continued that enormity by slaughtering his saints,
the very people who have most lovingly given themselves in service
and witness for the world. The "altar" that cries in verse 7 may
intend the saints underneath the altar who, in 6:9-10, cried, "How
long, O Lord?"; the cry does celebrate the answering of that
prayer.

In both verses 9 and 11—Bowls 4 and 5—there are references to
the possibility of repentance. Even at this late point, no man's fate
is finally fixed; the purpose behind even these terrible bowls is to
move men to change their ways so that they can be saved; no one
has to suffer these bowls if he chooses not to.

BOWLS 6 (INTERLUDE) AND 7: COLLAPSE AT ARMAGEDDON

(16:12-21) The sixth angel poured his bowl on the great river Euphrates; and its   12
water was dried up, to prepare the way for the kings from the east.

Then I saw coming from the mouth of the dragon, the mouth of the   13
beast, and the mouth of the false prophet, three foul spirits like frogs.
These spirits were devils, with power to work miracles. They were sent   14
out to muster all the kings of the world for the great day of battle of
God the sovereign Lord. ('That is the day when I come like a thief!   15
Happy the man who stays awake and keeps on his clothes, so that he
will not have to go naked and ashamed for all to see!') So they   16
assembled the kings at the place called in Hebrew Armageddon.

Then the seventh angel poured his bowl on the air; and out of the   17
sanctuary came a loud voice from the throne, which said, 'It is over!'
And there followed flashes of lightning and peals of thunder, and a   18
violent earthquake, like none before it in human history, so violent it
was. The great city was split in three; the cities of the world fell in ruin;   19
and God did not forget Babylon the great, but made her drink the cup
which was filled with the fierce wine of his vengeance. Every island   20
vanished; there was not a mountain to be seen. Huge hailstones,   21
weighing perhaps a hundredweight, fell on men from the sky; and they
cursed God for the plague of hail, because that plague was so severe.

Evidently verses 12-14 and 16 constitute Bowl 6, and the parenthesis of verse 15 is the A-B Interlude. That the interlude is just a
little out of place in this instance may be deliberate; it is important that Bowls 6 and 7 be read in continuity rather than as
independent scenes.

Let us review how John handled this sequence in his freehand
sketch and see its relationship to what he does here. There the Evil
Trinity were introduced to seal their people with the beast's mark
and give them domination over the commerce of the world; here,
in Bowl 6, the Evil Trinity musters a great army from all over the
world—at least something of a parallel. There, then, the Lamb and
his people appeared on Mount Zion and sang a duet with heaven;
here, in the interlude, the Lamb calls upon his people to be ready
for his imminent coming to them—at least something of a parallel.
There, finally, an angel proclaimed that Babylon had fallen; here,
in Bowl 7, there is a fall of cities of somewhat wider scope than
before, although Babylon is mentioned specifically and in language
almost identical with that used in the previous scene—a very
definite parallel.

The important thing to notice is that there is here no more of a
war or an attack upon Babylon than there was previously.
Granted, it looks for a while as though there will be, what with
Evil's gathering its great army for battle; but the battle does not
come off. John's picture still supports the view that Jesus' death-
and-resurrection, the battle that got the dragon kicked out of the
control room, was sufficient to do the job.

Let's look first at verse 15, the Interlude, so that we then can be
free to treat Bowls 6 and 7 as a unit. The two sentences can be
understood as the customary Parts A and B. John will not *describe*
the parousia in connection with the Bowl Series; but here it is
specified that that parousia is coordinate with the fall of Babylon,
which *is* being described. Jesus' statement implies most strongly
that Christians do not know and are not supposed to know ahead
of time about the "when" of the end; the plea is rather for what
we have been calling "perpetual expectancy."

Now to Bowl 6. Verse 12 indicates that Evil's big, last try is to
be launched from beyond the Euphrates—where Babylon also is
located, by the way—the traditional source for depredations
against God's people. In verse 13, for the first time, John lists the

three bosses of Evil as a definite trio—as much as positive proof that he intends them as a conscious counterpart of the Trinity. Their appearing together at this time indicates something of the importance of this scene.

Look who form the first rank of Evil's armies! The kings of the earth—wouldn't you know?—very much in character! We haven't seen this crew for a while; but they will be very much with us from here on out.

The name of the place where the muster takes place is "Armageddon." When John makes a deliberate effort to tell us that the word is *Hebrew*, he is as much as pointing us to an Old Testament source; but the reference is a real puzzle. The name combines two Hebrew terms—the first meaning "Mount" and the other being the place name "Megiddo" or "Megiddon." In the Old Testament, "Megiddo" is the name both of a plain and a city located on it. Two important battles did take place on this plain (one of which Israel won and one she lost), so the assumption is made that the spot was seen as a traditional site for battles fought in defense of Israel. But the biblical support for this view is very slight indeed. The term "Megiddo/Megiddon" occurs in the Old Testament a total of eight times. None of these has the remotest connection with a mountain; indeed, two of them refer to Megiddo as a "vale," or "valley." Only three of the eight references have to do with battle or war.

Mathias Rissi has proposed an entirely different interpretation of "Armageddon." He sees it as a reference to Isaiah 14:12-15. The passage is speaking about "the king of Babylon" (14:4) which, in John's terminology, would be an apt title for Antichrist. It reads:

How you have fallen from heaven, bright morning star,
felled to the earth, sprawling helpless across the nations!
    You thought in your own mind,
        I will scale the heavens;
I will set my throne high above the stars of God,
    I will sit on the mountain where the gods meet in the far recesses
    of the north.
    I will rise high above the cloud-banks and make myself like the
    Most High.
    Yet you shall be brought down to Sheol, to the depths of the
    abyss.

Elsewhere (22:16) John has Jesus refer to himself as "the bright
morning star"; and according to his principle of symmetry, he
easily could take Isaiah's as being a reference to the *fake* morning
star, Antichrist. Isaiah's scene itself fits perfectly into what John is
doing here; it is a picture of Evil strutting and vaunting itself
against God, attempting even to set itself up over him. Yet the
effort has no chance of success; it will eventuate (or has eventu-
ated) only in grand and total collapse. "How you have fallen!"

In the sixth line of the Isaiah quotation, where are found the
words "the mountain where the gods meet," the wording, more
literally, is "the mount of assembly." And if just one letter of that
Hebrew phrase is changed, it will read "Armageddon." Rissi's
theory is that John wrote "mount of assembly" but that an early
copyist misunderstood the reference and so put it down to make
the best sense he could understand, namely "Armageddon."

Realize, first of all, that the matter is not a crucial one—except
for calendarizers who may want to sell seats and thus need to
know just where the scene is to transpire. Otherwise, John's basic
picture is not affected by one's interpretation of "Armageddon."
But we have the choice of sticking with the text as it has come to
us, even though it results in a rather meaningless puzzle—or of
being forced to change one letter, but getting a reading filled with
the kind of symbolic significance for which John is noted. Personally, I am not inclined to push the matter; but I do find Rissi's
argument quite convincing.

But here they are. The forces of Evil, like a bunch of street
brawlers, have gathered under the drunken notion that they can
"call out" God himself and take him on his own ground ("I will sit
on the mountain where the gods meet [i.e., Armaggedon].... I
will rise high above the cloud-banks and make myself like the Most
High"). Evil has been getting along so well on earth that the
dragon has forgotten he can't even *get to* God any longer ("No
foothold was left them in heaven"). But then, I suppose it must be
difficult to remember anything after your head has been cut off!

With Bowl 7, then—since frequently it is the only action re-
quired to break up so ill-conceived a venture—there comes an
authoritative voice from the speaker on the squad car, "All right,
boys, the party's over!" And it is! There isn't any fight; there
doesn't have to be. The whole challenge simply collapses. As verse

20 has it, "there was not a mountain to be seen"; the mount of assembly has become a hole in the ground. "How you have fallen, fake morning star!"

Verse 19 says that *the great city* was split in three." Earlier, in 11:8, John had used that phrase to designate "Jerusalem"; later, in 17:18, he will use it in reference to "Babylon." However, because Babylon is here named in series with "the great city," it makes sense to take it as intending Jerusalem. In that earlier scene where Jerusalem was called "the great city," after the two witnesses had been resurrected and called up to God, Jerusalem did take a terrific blow—which resulted in some repentance, you will recall. Although "Jerusalem" is the home of the church, she also has been sufficiently invaded by the world and involved with the world that she cannot escape its holocaust unscathed. Yet she is only split in three and will survive to become the new Jerusalem; it later will become clear that Babylon's destruction is total and final.

17:1–20:3
The Events
of the End

With the completion of the Bowl Series, John now is finally ready to leave the end-time period. As was suggested earlier, it likely is because he knows that this is the time in which his readers actually must make their decisions and live out their Christian lives that he has given it so much space and attention. Certainly his treatment has been relevant to *our* problems regarding the relationship of Good and Evil, the nature of the church and the Christian life, the meaning of the time in which we live.

Recall how that Bowl Series concluded—with a picture of the collapse of Evil's kingdom and a note that this also is the time of Christ's parousia ("That is the day when I come like a thief!"). The parousia itself, however, was not described. Now John will back up once more—although not very far. He will describe the collapse in greater detail than before, proceed into an account of the parousia, and then keep on going. The book is a straight shot, a direct sequence, from here on out (or almost so).

THE GREAT WHORE, BABYLON

1   Then one of the seven angels that held the seven bowls came and spoke   (17:1-6)
     to me and said, 'Come, and I will show you the judgement on the great
2   whore, enthroned above the ocean. The kings of the earth have com-
     mitted fornication with her, and on the wine of her fornication men all
3   over the world have made themselves drunk.' In the Spirit he carried me
     away into the wilds, and there I saw a woman mounted on a scarlet
     beast which was covered with blasphemous names and had seven heads

153

and ten horns. The woman was clothed in purple and scarlet and   4
bedizened with gold and jewels and pearls. In her hand she held a gold
cup, full of obscenities and the foulness of her fornication; and written   5
on her forehead was a name with a secret meaning: 'Babylon the great,
the mother of whores and of every obscenity on earth.' The woman, I   6
saw, was drunk with the blood of God's people and with the blood of
those who had borne their testimony to Jesus.

That it is one of the bowl-angels who introduces this scene is a
way of tying it to the one that just concluded. That scene closed
with a reference to Babylon and her fall; now we are to get a
closer look at the event.

The phrase in verse 1 that has the whore "enthroned above the
ocean" is a poor translation and a misleading one. Literally, it
reads "sitting on many waters" and seems to be a direct reference
to Jeremiah 51:13, "O opulent city, standing beside great waters."
In Jeremiah, the city being characterized is *Babylon* and the "great
waters" are those of the Euphrates River upon which the city was
located. But when the translation is made "ocean," the reference
has to leave Babylon and is most likely to land on *Rome.* And this
is a crucial point. Almost all commentators on Revelation assume
that when John talks about "Babylon" he means "Rome." In
other words, they take for granted that John intended a calendarizing of this symbol: "Babylon" is a symbolic name which is to be
understood as a reference to the actual city of Rome. We are going
to challenge this customary interpretation and not allow a
"Rome" reading until there is compelling evidence for doing so.
And this present phrase is not to be allowed among that evidence;
it is all "Babylon."

The explanation usually given as to why John says "Babylon"
when he means "Rome" is that he wants to hide his true meaning
from the eyes of Roman police so that he will not be accused of
subversion. But if every would-be scholar who has read the book
can decide in an instant that "Babylon" means "Rome"—even
when he is as far as we are from the first-century situation—then
surely the Roman police would have been able to see the truth as
well.

We already have more than enough evidence to indicate that
John uses symbols as a means of communicating his message, not
obfuscating it. Now if someone were to have asked John which
city of his day was most Babylon-like, the chances are that he

would have answered, "Rome!" But this is not at all the same
thing as suggesting that he wrote his book as a prediction that, at
the end of history, the fate of the world would be determined
there. Rather, as a de-calendarized (de-mapped) symbol, "Babylon" is the perfect choice. Historically, in John's own Old Testament tradition, Babylon did represent everything he attributes to
her. But at the time John wrote (and ever since) there was no
Babylon; that city was long gone. And thus was the symbol freed
from calendarizing implications.

So make "Babylon" Babylon; John's picture is accurate—it fell!
Make "Babylon" Rome; right again—it fell! Make "Babylon" New
York or Washington or Las Vegas or Hollywood (or a combination
of all of them); still right—they will fall, you can depend upon it!
And in the end, worldliness will fall finally and completely.
Where? In "Babylon," of course; but how and when and where
John doesn't presume to tell us—that is in God's hands, where it
belongs!

But this Babylon is a great whore—and with that, John intends
to say a great deal. (And recall that she is to be seen in contrast to
the woman clothed with the sun.) She seduces people into promiscuity, into giving their love and attention to things other than
Jesus Christ. And who is first in line among her customers? The
kings of the earth, again. Undoubtedly what they love in her is
power, authority, and glory; they are continually drunk on the
stuff.

(In verse 3, John tells us that he was taken "into the wilds" to
see this woman—a reference that is entirely appropriate for Babylon but not at all for Rome. The beast she rides, it later will be
made plain, is *therion*, the Antichrist.)

Her garb speaks of wealth, luxury, glamor, sophistication, and
culture. She also seduces men with and to these values.

She is a sex-hungry drunkard; pleasure, sensuality, and wanton-
ness are other of her attractions.

Finally, the wine she drinks is made from the blood of God's
people. The whore is an opponent, subverter, and persecutor of
the church, hating what the church stands for.

An important implication follows from what we have found
here. Certainly, in her dalliance with the kings, it is suggested that
the symbol of the whore includes something of that which we
commonly associate with government, or *the state*. But just as

certainly, it would be much too narrow to take the whore as signifying merely the state—and least of all, merely the state of first-century Rome. If the whore is given the full significance John implies, it is not nearly as easy to dissociate oneself from her and stand over against her as some contemporary leftist movements would propose. Those groups frequently have latched onto these passages of Revelation as their rationale. However, although their exegesis obviously has considerable truth in it, it is too narrow and oversimplified to do justice to John's concept. John's is a more complex picture and thus calls for a much more radical response— not merely mounting worldly opposition to the state and forming a counter*culture* but building the only truly counter*whore* community, which is the church of Jesus Christ.

THE WHORE AND BEAST EXPLAINED

(17:7-8
&18)

As I looked at her I was greatly astonished. But the angel said to me, 7 'Why are you so astonished? I will tell you the secret of the woman and of the beast she rides, with the seven heads and the ten horns. The beast 8 you have seen is he who once was alive, and is alive no longer, but has yet to ascend out of the abyss before going to perdition. Those on earth whose names have not been inscribed in the roll of the living ever since the world was made will all be astonished to see the beast; for he once was alive, and is alive no longer, and has still to appear. . . .

The woman you saw is the great city that holds sway over the kings of 18 the earth.'

You will notice that the text as it is printed here skips from verse 8 to verse 18 of this seventeenth chapter. We are going to suggest that the intervening material was not part of the original version of Revelation. Please try not to make any evaluation of that proposition until we have had opportunity to examine it in detail. The only thing to note now is how logical and well constructed the passage is *without* verses 9-17. In verse 7, the angel indicates that he will explain the secret "of the woman and of the beast she rides." In verse 8, he gives a brief explanation of "the beast you have seen." In verse 18, he gives a brief explanation of "the woman you saw." As easy as that!

In verse 8, the occurrences of the word "alive" at the beginning

of the verse and at the end should not be there; there is nothing in
the Greek to correspond to them. The more accurate reading in
the early instance is "he who once was, and is no longer, but has
yet to ascend out of the abyss" and in the later, "he once was, and
is not, and will be present." John may have "death" in mind; but
we need to be careful not to read in more than he actually says.

The issue involved is that this wording *can* be read as a reference
to the Nero Myth (which we will discuss presently). Our concern is
to show that it does not *necessarily* betray any knowledge of that
myth and probably does not refer to it; it makes perfectly good
sense on its own.

Recall John's penchant for symmetric counterpart and that it is
Antichrist who is here being portrayed. Christ, of course, has a
death-and-resurrection as a prominent aspect of his being. The
Antichrist already has been noted as bearing the mark of having
had a head cut off, a parallel to the Lamb's mark of slaughter.
Now John apparently wants to comment upon the beast's equivalent of death-and-resurrection. It cannot be precisely equivalent,
of course, for "resurrection" (graduation into second-order LIFE)
is one of John's most precious terms and one he could in no way
grant to the beast. (As we noted, John does not use the word
"life" or "alive" in this passage.) The beast's, then, is *fake* resurrection which takes the form of disappearance and reappearance.
But note carefully that it is the men of the world who are
"astonished" at the beast's reappearance and explicitly not the
Christians, who are ready for it. This is the opposite of what we
would expect, seeing that the men of the world are the beast's
own people. Also, as we will learn, the Nero Myth was a product
of the world rather than the church. If this myth, then, were what
John had in mind, it should not be the *world* that is surprised at
the beast's reappearance.

I take John to be saying that there have been and will be times
when things seem to be running quite smoothly and men of the
world are able to convince themselves that they have engineered
the "beastliness" out of history. "Yes, there were a lot of bad
things in the past; but we have outgrown all that; this is a new
generation, a new and much more humane and civilized breed!"
Christians, however, from the many warnings in their New Testament, know that the world does not change its fundamental
character. Any disappearance of the beast is only an illusion; he

can be back in full fury in no time at all. And how often has it happened that—with the beginning of a war, an economic recession, a drought or plague, the disclosure of scandal, or whatever—a society's veneer of civilization suddenly has dropped away. The world always is surprised to discover such beastliness in itself; the Christian has known that it was lurking there beneath the surface all along. It does not require recourse to a Nero Myth to explain John's "explanation of the beast."

The woman, on the other hand, we are told in verse 18, is a symbol for the city of worldliness. The passage, verses 9-17, is not essential to the structure of the scene as a whole.

This seems the place to comment on the relationship between the whore and the beast. John, obviously, sees them as very closely related; the whore rides the beast. But does he see any distinction between them? Perhaps they are two symbols for the same thing. Not precisely, I would suggest. I see the Babylon-whore as representing more the outward, empirical manifestations of worldliness. She actually is visible; one can see her (or at least her footprints) in our cities, our activities, our newspapers, our movies, anywhere. The beast, on the other hand, I see as representing more the spiritual power that lies behind worldliness. Our analysis is too shallow if we think of worldliness consisting only in the sum total of all the worldly things people do. No, "the world" also denotes a particular philosophy or faith, a demonic spirit. Worldliness has the function of a religion and is indwelt by a power, a motive, a tendency, a directive of its own. Men not only do worldly things; their loyalty is captured by "the prince of this world." This, I think, is who John is calling "Antichrist." And we, for our part, are headed for trouble if we try to deal with the world simply as "whore" and fail to recognize the reality of the "beast" she rides.

THE NERO CIPHERS

(13:18)   (Here is the key; and anyone who has intelligence may work out the   18
number of the beast. The number represents a man's name, and the
numerical value of its letters is six hundred and sixty-six.)

(17:9-17)   'But here is the clue for those who can interpret it. The seven heads are   9

10   seven hills on which the woman sits. They represent also seven kings, of whom five have already fallen, one is now reigning, and the other has yet to come; and when he does come he is only to last for a little while.
11   As for the beast that once was alive and is alive no longer, he is an
12   eighth—and yet he is one of the seven, and he is going to perdition. The ten horns you saw are ten kings who have not yet begun to reign, but who for one hour are to share with the beast the exercise of royal
13   authority; for they have but a single purpose among them and will
14   confer their power and authority upon the beast. They will wage war upon the Lamb, but the Lamb will defeat them, for he is Lord of lords and King of kings, and his victory will be shared by his followers, called and chosen and faithful.'
15   Then he said to me, 'The ocean you saw, where the great whore sat,
16   is an ocean of peoples and populations, nations and languages. As for the ten horns you saw, they together with the beast will come to hate the whore; they will strip her naked and leave her desolate, they will
17   batten on her flesh and burn her to ashes. For God has put it into their heads to carry out his purpose, by making common cause and conferring their sovereignty upon the beast until all that God has spoken is fulfilled.

We have come to a most crucial point in our treatment; I invite you to give me a very open mind and very close attention. Two different passages are quoted above. The one, which we skipped over at the time, is from the scene of the beast's people being sealed and given control of the commerce of the world. The second comes from within the explanation of the beast and the whore just examined. The two passages belong with each other and together represent a sort of material much different from anything else in Revelation. They are riddles, ciphers, code puzzles, whatever they might be called, which the reader is challenged to unravel and solve. They can represent nothing other than sheer calendarizing, an effort to hook the Revelation account to localized events involving historically known personages at a predictable time.

The greater number of scholars decipher the passages as referring to the Roman Emperor Nero, even though getting to that solution by somewhat different routes. The interpretation here owes most to Mathias Rissi, although Rissi himself also makes use of earlier scholarship. Our final conclusion will be that these passages are not by John and were not part of the original edition of Revelation. Rather, they were inserted some years later by an unknown person whom we will call "the Interpolator." He, clearly, was a person of calendarizing mentality who read Revelation as being crystal-ball type prediction and sincerely felt he could improve the book by making it point specifically to the date he was confident would bring the end of the age. However, before examining the evidence regarding this interpolator, we need to work on the ciphers themselves.

In the first cipher we are told that the number 666 can be made to produce a man's name. The most obvious way to go at this is by a mode of calculation that was very familiar to the ancient world. The letters of the alphabet are given numerical values—the first letter being a 1, the second letter a 2, and so on through 10; the eleventh letter is then a 20, and so on through 100; the twentieth letter is then 200, etc. By this method, the name "Nero Caesar," if written *in Hebrew* (not Greek or Latin), will add up to 666. Of course, Revelation itself is in Greek and the cipher has absolutely no Old Testament connections that would point the decipherer to Hebrew; so the solution seems somewhat fantastic. And of course, many other names—including Hitler's—can be made to produce 666; the trick must lie in making the solution to this cipher fit the second cipher as well.

However, there is a totally different approach to the problem which produces what strikes me as a much more likely solution. It uses another mathematical game familiar to the ancients, that of *triangular numbers*. The diagram shows how it works.

Rank		Total No. of Dots
1	•	1
2	• •	3
3	• • •	6
4	• • • •	10
5	• • • • •	15

According to this method of calculation, any number of dots that forms a perfect triangle is a triangular number; and in a triangular number, the total number of dots and the number of the rank are taken as equivalents. Now if the diagram above were extended until it comprised a total of 666 dots, this would be discovered to be a triangular number of the rank 36; so 666 = 36. However, 36 dots also form a triangle—this to the rank 8; so 36 = 8. And things equal to the same thing are equal to each other; so 666 = 8. And the second cipher makes it entirely clear that Antichrist is an *eighth;* 8 is the secret number that identifies him. The first cipher is meant to point us directly to the second.

Thus far the scholars have taken us; but I now intend to show you that I can do a thing or two on my own, too. What follows is "scholarship"—and I did it by my very own self. If you make a triangle to the total of 8 dots, it comes out at the rank 3 1/2—how about *that?* Seriously, I don't think partial triangles are allowed by the rules; and it probably is just an accident that things work out that way; but I couldn't let the opportunity pass.

The second cipher is more complicated than the first but produces a much more assured solution; it will confirm the first, rather than the other way around. But before we even look at it, we need to be aware of what we have been calling "the Nero Myth," the Roman tradition regarding Nero *redivivus* (come back to life). Be clear that this is a story of Roman, not Christian, origin; first-century Christians would have become aware of it, of course, but it did not start with them.

All our historical information indicates that the Emperor Nero— whom the chart below shows as having reigned A.D. 54-68—was decidedly out of the ordinary. A real maniac who murdered both his mother and his wife, he was deeply feared and hated by his own people, let alone the Christians on whom he loosed persecution. So despicable was he that the memory lived on after him. Following his death, the folk myth arose that, in time to come, he would come back from the underworld, raise an army among the hated Parthian kingdoms of the east, and move to sack and destroy Rome. It seems clear that our cipher is built over this myth.

Verse 9, in mentioning that the whore sits on "seven hills," immediately tells us that the cipher has to do with Rome; for centuries already before this time, Rome was known as "the City of Seven Hills." Yet note that it is *only* here in the cipher that "Babylon" is tied specifically to Rome. In the lament over Babylon in the next chapter, John will have sea-captains and sailors watching the fall of the city and bemoaning it—a detail that does not accord very well with historical Babylon. However, in the passage it is evident that John is depending very heavily upon Ezekiel 27, which is a description of the fall of *Tyre*. Only in the cipher is "Babylon" calendarized directly and inevitably as Rome.

When the very same symbol that signifies the seven hills of Rome also is specified as representing "seven kings," there is little place else to look but to the sequence of Roman emperors. And when contemporary calendarizers start with these "kings" and stretch the reading to mean "kingdoms" and then stretch "kingdoms" to include modern nation-states with no monarchial tradition at all and then build an arbitrary chronology of world history divided into a neat sequence of "kingdoms"—when they do this, they are playing games with the very scripture for which they profess such great reverence.

The accompanying chart gives us the chronology of Roman emperors and the means for reading the cipher.

Although there had been many Roman rulers before the time of Augustus, he was the first upon whom the Senate conferred the title "Emperor"; and secular history, right down to the present day, identifies him as the founder of "the Roman Empire" as such. From a Christian point of view, the additional fact that he was the ruler under whom Jesus was born also would mark him as No. 1. There would seem little grounds for doubting that the Interpolator intends that his sequence begin with Augustus.

The five kings who "have already fallen," then, would take us through Nero. Notice the three names that appear on the chart at that point; they are claimants who tried for the throne but who—as their dates would indicate—got themselves killed off as fast as they could get there. It seems clear that the tradition even of that day would not have considered these men as true emperors but rather explain the situation as an "interregnum," an interval of confusion between reigns. Vespasian, then, would be No. 6, "who is now reigning." Be clear as to what this implies. The Interpolator is writing some time after Revelation was composed, but he wants his insertion to be taken as part of the original; thus "now reigning" should apply to the time of John's original composition of the book. Our theory would suggest, then, that the Interpolator had knowledge that the book originally had come out during the

CHRONOLOGY OF THE ROMAN EMPERORS

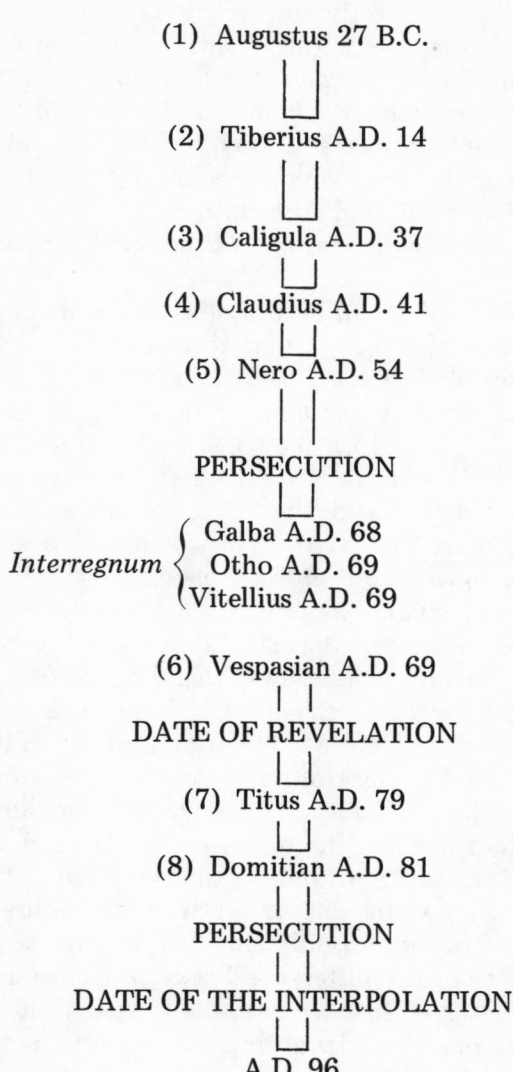

(1) Augustus 27 B.C.

(2) Tiberius A.D. 14

(3) Caligula A.D. 37

(4) Claudius A.D. 41

(5) Nero A.D. 54

PERSECUTION

Interregnum { Galba A.D. 68
Otho A.D. 69
Vitellius A.D. 69

(6) Vespasian A.D. 69

DATE OF REVELATION

(7) Titus A.D. 79

(8) Domitian A.D. 81

PERSECUTION

DATE OF THE INTERPOLATION

A.D. 96

reign of Vespasian; and this is our best evidence for dating Revelation—some time between A.D. 69 and 79.

No. 7, Titus, then is to come and "to last only for a little while"—three years, as the chart indicates. But remember that, although the Interpolator writes as though it were John making a prediction, the Interpolator himself actually is looking *back* on the reign of Titus, knowing exactly how long it had been.

These, then, are the "seven kings"; but the point of it all is that the beast himself, Antichrist, will appear as "an *eighth*" (666 = 8; 8 is his special code number). John already has told us that the beast disappears and reappears, although without giving any evidence that he had the Nero Myth in mind. But the Interpolator now picks up that detail and uses it to suggest that, wonder of wonders, this eighth king is also one of the earlier seven. Who but Nero *redivivus?*

Yes, as per the Nero Myth, he will amass an army out of other kingdoms. By the way, although John regularly has had "the kings of the earth" associated with the beast, it is only here in the cipher that they are calendarized into a particular group of "*ten* kings"; the Interpolator has tried to make specific what John used simply as a general symbol. And yes, verse 16 indicates, as per the Nero Myth, that No. 8 with his kingly following will attack and devastate Babylon-Rome. The Nero Myth would seem the only possible key for making sense out of this cipher

According to the chart, Emperor No. 8 turns out to be Domitian (A.D. 81-96). We know that Domitian was a "bad" emperor with traces of insanity about him, that he exacted "emperor worship" in a stricter way than ever before, and that, consequently, widespread and severe persecution came upon the church during his reign. At the onset of these troubles, then, the Interpolator would have had at least as good grounds for thinking that Domitian was the beast and the last days were at hand as contemporary calendarizers have in thinking that they are at hand *now*. Both probably act out of sincere motives, the desire to make Revelation speak directly, urgently, and helpfully to the readers of their own day. The only difference between them (and I don't mean to minimize it) is that, whereas the moderns add to Revelation a great deal of calendarizing interpretation to support their time-prediction, the Interpolator was willing to add a bit of *text* to support his.

This has been our attempt to break and solve the two ciphers; now let's look at evidence indicating that neither were they written by John nor were they part of the original version of Revelation.

(1) We have seen that neither of the ciphers is essential to nor integral with the scenes in which they appear; they display a *parenthetical* character.

(2) They *demand* a calendarizing type of interpretation which is not indulged—and is, in fact, resisted—in the remainder of the book.

(3) The ciphers are introduced with sentences that are most unlike John; they sound like formulas. In the first case, 13:18 reads literally: *"Here* is *wisdom* for him who has the *mind* to calculate. . . ."* In the second case, 17:9 reads literally, *"Here* is the place for the *mind* that has *wisdom."*

Now we know that in the course of time there grew up a version of Christianity which saw the faith as centering in a secret knowledge of the things of God, which secrets were made known only to initiates, the "insiders" who had been granted special powers of esoteric understanding. These formula-sentences would be most congenial to this sort of "gnostic" mentality; but there is no evidence that John was such a person or thought in such terms. He does not use this sort of phraseology anywhere else.

(4) Looking at the second cipher in particular, the device in verse 9 of giving one symbol two different referents is something John nowhere does.

(5) In verse 14, the cipher says, "They will wage war upon the Lamb, but the Lamb will defeat them." We have not yet come to John's last word on this subject (in Chapter 19); but we have seen that he studiously *avoids* saying the very thing that is said here. To suggest that it is necessary for the Lamb to defeat the beast *again* inevitably is to imply that the victory he won the first time—in his death-and-resurrection, booting the dragon out of heaven—was not adequate for the job. It is hard to envision John writing this line.

(6) Verse 16, with its description of the beast and his kings turning against the whore to attack and destroy her, fits the Nero Myth very well but runs counter to everything we find outside the cipher. Indeed, just ten verses beyond this point we find the statement: "The kings of the earth who committed fornication with her and wallowed in her luxury will weep and wail over her, as they see the smoke of her conflagration." That hardly jibes with what the cipher says.

We have looked at the evidence and at the theory that attempts to account for it; what are our options in making a final decision?

(a) What we have called the "ciphers" clearly are riddles we explicitly are invited to solve. I have never seen any proposal other than one using the Nero Myth that even begins to provide a convincing explanation of the clues contained in the ciphers.

(b) If we both accept the Nero Myth solution to the ciphers *and* maintain that John is the author of them, we've got ourselves big problems. The entire view of Revelation we have been presenting goes down the tube; it becomes clear that John *is* a calendarizer and his purpose is to tell us the when, how, and who of the end—and we should try to read him that way throughout. But what is worse, he is a *mistaken* calendarizer. He said that the Emperor Domitian was to be the beast who would destroy Rome and signal the end of history. That, of course, turned out not to be true; Domitian was only another bad Roman emperor. Yet, if John wrote Revelation primarily to predict matters of last things, and if his predictions were manifestly wrong, then there is no good reason for us to give attention or weight to Revelation at all. If the book is wrong regarding its fundamental purpose, it hardly can be rated as Scripture on other counts.

 (c) Many people, as a matter of principle, cannot even entertain the idea of an interpolator; they can't believe that God would allow anyone to add material to the original text of a book of the Bible (although, in our theory, the Interpolator would have done his adding *before* Revelation had come to be considered a biblical book). I don't know *how* these people envision God as preventing this—whether by instantly striking dead anyone who threatens to take a pen to the sacred script or by giving subsequent readers the power immediately to recognize the added passages as false. But never mind; I do respect the position.

Many such people, then, will insist that John *must* have written the ciphers along with the remainder of the book—but for the rest, they simply deny that they have any idea as to what the cipher passages may mean. And this is a solution I can buy! "No, John was not a *mistaken* calendarizer; he was not speaking of Nero and Domitian. Beyond that, I don't know what he was talking about. I don't know that he was calendarizing; I simply don't know what he was doing. I certainly am not going to try to use these cipher-passages to make predictions of my own. I am not going to use them to draw *any* conclusions about either John or Revelation; I simply don't know what they mean."

The position is an honest one. In effect, it brackets out the cipher passages as being sheer mystery; yet it lets the rest of Revelation stand as it is, leaves the interpretation open for the sort of noncalendarizing, perpetual-expectancy approach the New Testament itself calls for.

(d) Personally, the suggestion of an interpolator makes good sense to me and does not threaten my view of the Bible's being the inspired word of God. In addition, it has the advantage of explaining some things which, I guess, I simply cannot be content to leave as sheer mystery. My hope, however, is that those who cannot conscientiously accept the interpolator theory will nevertheless understand that those who do accept it are motivated, not by any desire to destroy Scripture, but precisely by the desire to preserve it and allow it to speak most meaningfully and truly. And that is the most important consideration—whether one takes the "mystery" route *or* the "interpolator" route for getting there!

THE FALL OF BABYLON

1 After this I saw another angel coming down from heaven; he came with　　**(18:1-8)**
2 great authority and the earth was lit up with his splendour. Then in a mighty voice he proclaimed, 'Fallen, fallen is Babylon the great! She has become a dwelling for demons, a haunt for every unclean spirit, for
3 every vile and loathsome bird. For all nations have drunk deep of the fierce wine of her fornication; the kings of the earth have committed fornication with her, and merchants the world over have grown rich on her bloated wealth.'
4 Then I heard another voice from heaven that said: 'Come out of her,
5 my people, lest you take part in her sins and share in her plagues. For her sins are piled high as heaven, and God has not forgotten her crimes.
6 Pay her back in her own coin, repay her twice over for her deeds!
7 Double for her the strength of the potion she mixed! Mete out grief and torment to match her voluptuous pomp! She says in her heart, "I am a queen on my throne! No mourning for me, no widow's weeds!"
8 Because of this her plagues shall strike her in a single day—pestilence, bereavement, famine, and burning—for mighty is the Lord God who has pronounced her doom!'

From the complicated contortions of the ciphers we come into some of the best of John's writing; a welcome relief. Not so much from a theological point of view, but from a *literary* standpoint, this description of the fall of Babylon—and particularly the lament that follows—marks a climax. John's graphic realism and poetic force come through in a great way; this chapter really calls for a dramatic actor to read it aloud.

The theme of the whole is powerfully expressed in the opening proclamation: "Fallen, fallen is Babylon the great! She has become a dwelling for demons, a haunt for every unclean spirit, for every foul and loathsome bird." Plainly, one aspect of Babylon's fall is nothing more than the stripping away of her glamor so that she can be seen for what she truly is; her outward state now reflects what her inner being always has been, a haunt for every foul and loathsome bird.

In verse 3, "the kings of the earth" are mentioned again—but, along with them, "merchants the world over." Part of Babylon's evil centers in "the state," in its making of war and its pretension of power. But just as much it centers in "commerce" and everything that involves. Indeed, the latter gets the major attention throughout this scene. There is, of course, no point in trying to separate and proportion these different aspects of worldliness; but we do need to keep in mind that all are involved. Certainly, one of the purposes behind John's description is to help us spot and contemplate our own involvement in worldliness. (Notice, again, that neither here nor elsewhere is there evidence indicating that mandatory Caesar-worship was a major concern at the time of John's writing.)

Verse 4 presents the command that, in itself, states the primary lesson of the scene: "Come out of her, my people!" There is nothing to suggest that John was recommending either to his original readers or to us that Christians should pack up, move away from the cities of this world, and go out somewhere to form monasteries, communes, or holy communities of our own. Even so, we need to keep alert to the possibility that historical situations might arise or the time of the end may be such that God *will* call his people to do the very thing of separating themselves physically from the world. Nevertheless, the major thrust of the command is that Christians take care not to become involved in the sin of the world, not to drift into an acceptance of its values and ends. The warning carries real weight: if you "take part in her sins" you are bound to "share in her plagues."

In verse 4, the angelic voice clearly is speaking *to* God's people; but by verse 6 it would seem that this is no longer so. There probably is not intended any suggestion that the Christians are being invited to take matters into their own hands and pay Babylon back in her own coin. Rather, the lines likely should be understood more in the nature of a prayer: "May she be repaid!" Certainly the thrust of John's thought has been to leave the work of punishment in the hands of God. As soon as human beings take it upon themselves to act as God's agents of wrath, they are sure to bungle the matter. To apply punishment in a truly just and helpful way is a very delicate operation at best; and we human beings are ourselves too sinful and too emotionally involved to do it right. This *must* be God's work.

Also, here where the language of retribution is getting pretty strong, we need to be reminded that the subject of it all is "worldliness." Now John, of course, would not try to deny that "people" are involved and do get hurt in the fall of Babylon—that is inevitable. Nevertheless, read carefully and it becomes plain that his account is focused, not upon the hurting of people, but upon the destroying of evil—a somewhat different thing. Of course, it is not possible to make a neat and clear separation between evil and the people who give themselves to it; yet for John to call down all sorts of retribution upon the whore Babylon is not at all the same thing as his asking God to torment other human beings. And as his book proceeds, we will see that John (and God) takes a much different stance toward even wicked people from what he does toward the powers of Evil itself.

LAMENT OVER BABYLON

9 The kings of the earth who committed fornication with her and   **(18:9-24)**
   wallowed in her luxury will weep and wail over her, as they see the
10 smoke of her conflagration. They will stand at a distance, for horror at
   her torment, and will say, 'Alas, alas for the great city, the mighty city
   of Babylon! In a single hour your doom has struck!'
11   The merchants of the earth also will weep and mourn for her,
12 because no one any longer buys their cargoes, cargoes of gold and silver,

jewels and pearls, cloths of purple and scarlet, silks and fine linens; all
kinds of scented woods, ivories, and every sort of thing made of costly
woods, bronze, iron, or marble; cinnamon and spice, incense, perfumes   13
and frankincense; wine, oil, flour and wheat, sheep and cattle, horses,
chariots, slaves, and the lives of men. 'The fruit you longed for', they   14
will say, 'is gone from you; all the glitter and the glamour are lost, never
to be yours again!' The traders in all these wares, who gained their   15
wealth from her, will stand at a distance for horror at her torment,
weeping and mourning and saying, 'Alas, alas for the great city, that   16
was clothed in fine linen and purple and scarlet, bedizened with gold
and jewels and pearls! Alas that in one hour so much wealth should be   17
laid waste!'

Then all the sea-captains and voyagers, the sailors and those who
traded by sea, stood at a distance and cried out as they saw the smoke   18
of her conflagration: 'Was there ever a city like the great city?' They   19
threw dust on their heads, weeping and mourning and saying, 'Alas, alas
for the great city, where all who had ships at sea grew rich on her
wealth! Alas that in a single hour she should be laid waste!'

But let heaven exult over her; exult, apostles and prophets and   20
people of God; for in the judgement against her he has vindicated your
cause!

Then a mighty angel took up a stone like a great millstone and hurled   21
it into the sea and said, 'Thus shall Babylon, the great city, be sent
hurtling down, never to be seen again! No more shall the sound of   22
harpers and minstrels, of flute-players and trumpeters, be heard in you;
no more shall craftsmen of any trade be found in you; no more shall
the sound of the mill be heard in you; no more shall the light of the   23
lamp be seen in you; no more shall the voice of the bride and
bridegroom be heard in you! Your traders were once the merchant
princes of the world, and with your sorcery you deceived all the
nations.'

For the blood of the prophets and of God's people was found in her,   24
the blood of all who had been done to death on earth.

As was mentioned earlier, the basic pattern for this segment of
John's work is taken from the lament over Tyre in Ezekiel 26–27;
but John far outstrips his predecessor. This passage is one of the
masterpieces of world literature in its evocation of pathos and
poignancy.

And from a theological standpoint, also, we can be grateful for
this passage. The emphasis and mood of John's treatment of evil
thus far has been one of condemnation and the cry that justice be
done; he has anticipated the fall of evil and exulted in that
expectation. All that is quite proper, of course; but now comes a

new note: in spite of the propriety of evil's collapse, the event itself nevertheless carries overtones of tragedy. It is not that anything good goes down in the fall of Babylon; for John, "Babylon" is itself the symbol of that which is sheer and unrelieved evil. It will yet become apparent that one of John's ground principles is that God redeems whatever is redeemable; he does not destroy anything of good. So the tragedy of Babylon is not that anything good is lost but rather the dissipation of all that might have been good, the human investment, the energy and resources that had been poured into Babylon. Not "How sad to see Babylon go!" but "How sad to realize now how much Babylon has wasted and ruined!" The consequence of this pathos is not sympathy for Babylon nor will it prove any inhibition to the celebration of her demise; but it does contribute an important insight into John's mind and an important aspect of the Christian relationship to the world.

The listing of "cargoes" in verses 12-13 is very effective. More than any accusation could do, it manifests the opulence, display, luxury, comfort, and pride of ownership that lie at the heart of the world's standard of values. And you can be sure it is not accidental on John's part that "slaves and the lives of men" come at the bottom of the list, following "sheep and cattle, horses, chariots." This is accurate; the world does not value persons, it uses them; it consumes, exploits, and manipulates people for the sake of the "higher values" of gold and silver, jewels and pearls. The splendor of the world customarily is bought at the expense of the *people* of the world. How right and just and necessary, then, that "all the glitter and the glamor be lost, never to be yours again!"—how right and yet how sad!

How sad!—and yet verse 20 is correct, too! How can the mood be anything other than exultation when wrong is being made right, when falsehood is being revealed, its power and threat being taken from it, when the truth is being justified?

But then, back on the other side, the "no more" passage returns to pathos—perhaps the most moving segment of the entire scene. Yet, again, in response comes the conclusion of verse 24: in truth, the judgment is altogether just, for both the most accurate and most damning thing that can be said about Babylon is that she eats *people*—that is the wrong that cannot be allowed to stand; it must be countered and put to an end.

EXULTATION AND THE PROMISE OF THE WEDDING SUPPER

(19:1-10)   After this I heard what sounded like the roar of a vast throng in heaven;   1
and they were shouting:

> 'Alleluia! Victory and glory and power belong to our God, for true   2
> and just are his judgements! He has condemned the great whore who
> corrupted the earth with her fornication, and has avenged upon her
> the blood of his servants.'

Then once more they shouted: 3

> 'Alleluia! The smoke goes up from her for ever and ever!'

And the twenty-four elders and the four living creatures fell down and   4
worshipped God as he sat on the throne, and they too cried:

> 'Amen! Alleluia!'

Then a voice came from the throne which said: 'Praise our God, all you   5
his servants, you that fear him, both great and small!'

> Again I heard what sounded like a vast crowd, like the noise of   6
> rushing water and deep roars of thunder, and they cried:

> 'Alleluia! The Lord our God, sovereign over all, has entered on his
> reign! Exult and shout for joy and do him homage, for the wedding-   7
> day of the Lamb has come! His bride has made herself ready, and for   8
> her dress she has been given fine linen, clean and shining.'

(Now the fine linen signifies the righteous deeds of God's people.)

> Then the angel said to me, 'Write this: "Happy are those who are   9
> invited to the wedding-supper of the Lamb!" ' And he added, 'These
> are the very words of God.' At this I fell at his feet to worship him. But   10
> he said to me, 'No, not that! I am but a fellow-servant with you and
> your brothers who bear their testimony to Jesus. It is God you must
> worship. Those who bear testimony to Jesus are inspired like the
> prophets.'

The direct counter-scene to the lament sung by the whore's lovers on earth is the hymn of victory sung by the hosts of heaven. They exult in God's just judgment of the whore; there is no suggestion here of some people exulting over the calamity come upon other people. The theme-word of this scene is "Alleluia!" The word—a transliteration of the Hebrew for "Praise God!"—although familiar from the Psalms of the Old Testament, is found only in this passage within the whole of the New Testament.

Verse 7 introduces the idea of the wedding of the Lamb and the great supper that attends it. Neither of these events gets picked up for more than passing reference by John; but there is no mystery about what they represent. The "bride of Christ," it will be made explicit, is *the church*—and by that token *could* be taken as "the woman clothed with the sun," although John does not himself

draw the connection. However, he does seem to intend a deliberate counter-comparison between, on the one hand, *therion* and
his whorish lover-rider who wind up together in the ditch and, on
the other, *arnion* and his virgin bride who proceed to the glory of
wedding and feast. In his reference to "the wedding-supper," John
may very well have in mind the Lord's supper of the church's
practice, which the New Testament Christians understood as itself
being a preview and sign of the great eschatological banquet which
marks the final reunion of God with his people. Verse 9 makes it
clear that the real purpose behind the passage is to encourage
readers to make themselves part of the scene; *you* are invited!

Verse 10 may indicate that John was aware of a tendency of
some of his intended readers to indulge in angel-worship; he took
the opportunity to combat it. In the concluding sentence, although it is not absolutely clear, the angel probably means to say,
"I, the angel, like you, John, the prophet, have significance only in
the testimony I bear to Jesus; so let's keep our attention on that
martyria Jesu rather than upon the bearers of it!"

THE PAROUSIA OF THE RIDER

11 Then I saw heaven wide open, and there before me was a white horse;   (19:11—
and its rider's name was Faithful and True, for he is just in judgement   20:3)
12 and just in war. His eyes flamed like fire, and on his head were many
13 diadems. Written upon him was a name known to none but himself, and
he was robed in a garment drenched in blood. He was called the Word
14 of God, and the armies of heaven followed him on white horses,
15 clothed in fine linen, clean and shining. From his mouth there went a
sharp sword with which to smite the nations; for he it is who shall rule
them with an iron rod, and tread the winepress of the wrath and
16 retribution of God the sovereign Lord. And on his robe and on his thigh
there was written the name: 'King of kings and Lord of lords.'
17 Then I saw an angel standing in the sun, and he cried aloud to all the
18 birds flying in mid-heaven: 'Come and gather for God's great supper, to
eat the flesh of kings and commanders and fighting men, the flesh of
horses and their riders, the flesh of all men, slave and free, great and
19 small!' Then I saw the beast and the kings of the earth and their armies
20 mustered to do battle with the Rider and his army. The beast was taken
prisoner, and so those that had received the mark of the beast and
worshipped its image. The two of them were thrown alive into the lake
21 of fire with its sulphurous flames. The rest were killed by the sword

which went out of the Rider's mouth; and all the birds gorged themselves on their flesh.

Then I saw an angel coming down from heaven with the key of the   1
abyss and a great chain in his hands. He seized the dragon, that serpent   2
of old, the Devil or Satan, and chained him up for a thousand years; he   3
threw him into the abyss, shutting and sealing it over him, so that he
might seduce the nations no more till the thousand years were over.
After that he must be let loose for a short while.

We are now come to one of the key scenes of the book, John's
central treatment of the parousia of Christ. Let us recall the ways
in which he has handled it earlier, with a particular view to
establishing the relationship between it and the fall of Babylon.

At the conclusion of the Freehand Sketch, in Chapter 14, an
angel first announces that Babylon has fallen (though the event is
not portrayed) and then the parousia is described under the image
of Christ as harvester. At the conclusion of the Bowl Series, in
Chapter 16, Bowl 6 shows the forces of Evil gathering for the
battle at Armageddon. Christ does not appear in that scene,
although the Interlude specifies, "That is the day when I come like
a thief!" Bowl 7, then, recounts the fall of Babylon. In the present
case, of course, the fall of Babylon is described at length, and then
we move to an event that is very like that of Armageddon *except
that* Christ appears on the scene in his parousia.

It might seem as though we have a chronological problem, but I
think that is not the case. John is not concerned with fine details
of sequence; he wants to say that the fall of Babylon and the
parousia of Christ are, in effect, simultaneous. The end consists in
both events, and it would be fruitless to try to separate them,
whether chronologically or in any other way. In particular, they
are not arranged so as to make either one dependent upon the
other. It does not take the parousia, an attack by Christ, to bring
down Babylon; the momentum of his previous death-and-
resurrection action is sufficient to do that. But neither, on the
other hand, dare it be assumed that it is the course of world
history that controls the time of Christ's return. No, the chronology of both these events and of the entire situation lies solely in
the hands of God; it is not for us to try to calculate either of them
or from one of them to the other.

It seems correct to assume that this scene is meant to take the
same spot and play the same role as the earlier Armageddon scene,

even though, in detail, the two are quite different. Because John does not mean to present a photographic, calendarized picture in either case, there is no difficulty (but indeed, considerable advantage) in using variant imageries and scenarios for making the same point. Only calendarizers will feel the need to argue about which way it actually is going to happen.

In the earlier instance, the Evil Trinity took the initiative in mustering the kings of the earth and their armies at Armageddon, for an attack upon God. However, the entire effort collapsed without Christ or any opposing army even putting in an appearance. In the present instance, conversely, Christ and his armies come from heaven and take their stand on an undesignated battlefield. The Evil Trinity, with the kings of the earth, then muster their forces in response—and promptly collapse! "Take it either way," John seems to be saying, "it comes to the same thing"— although, as usual, John's repetitions add insight and depth to the earlier references.

John regularly has pictured Christ and referred to him as "the Lamb"—"the Lamb with the marks of slaughter upon him"—and this image has been made very rich in theological content regarding his gracious, loving, longsuffering, self-giving character. Yet recall that, at the time John first introduced the Lamb, he was able also to describe him as "the Lion"—and without in any way compromising his lamblike character. Now, in the present scene, he pictures Christ as "the Rider," a warrior king. But if anything is certain, it is that, in doing so, John has no intention of deserting or betraying all his careful efforts in establishing Jesus as the Lamb. This Rider *is* the Lamb, just as the Lion was earlier; and just as the Lamb image took priority and controlled the Lion image there, so must the Lamb control the Rider image here. This scene can be interpreted in consistent "lamb" terms; and we have an obligation to do so.

Recall that, clear back with the opening of the first seal on the scroll of the hidden future, John introduced the period of the end-time with the appearance of a crowned rider on a white horse. Here, to introduce a new period, is another. In fact, the new Rider will now face down the first one—although, truth to tell, that first one does not present a very kingly picture in this scene. The two riders, clearly, are meant to show some parallels; but it is their contrasts that are telling. The first one carried a *bow;* this one carries (and uses) a sharp *sword.* The first one brought in his train War, Famine, and Death—and all the trauma of the end-time. This one brings justice, righteousness, and redemption. The first one actually was *therion,* the beast; this one actually is *arnion,* the Lamb. The first one has had his time; this one's time is yet to come. The first one *we* named "the Fancy Fake"; this one *John* names "Faithful and True."

"Faithful and True"; recall that, at the opening of his book, the very first title John gave to Jesus was "the *faithful* witness." And the name John gives him now is as important as anything that can be said concerning him. So much of the picture to this point has been dominated by falsehood, deceit, corruption, and seduction. But the parousia of Jesus marks also the parousia of *truth.* With him present, things become "trued" in a way that simply was not possible before his coming.

Verse 12 indicates that he is wearing "a name known to none but himself." John has referred to this name several times previously, as a suggestion that, in our time, we cannot yet know Jesus fully, cannot know him for all he is and represents. But here, in the parousia, that name is written for all to see; here, in the climax and completion of his work, we can begin to comprehend him in his "fullness."

He is robed in "a garment drenched with blood"—here is the key line of the entire scene (if not the entire book). This description usually is taken as just one more bloody detail out of the whole gruesome scene; but it deserves closer attention than that. Notice several things concerning it:

(1) The Rider's garment is bloodied as soon as he appears. The blood cannot come as a result of the present engagement; no enemy has arrived on the scene; he doesn't even get mustered until verse 19.

(2) At no earlier point in Revelation has there been described an engagement in which the Rider's robe could have been bloodied. In a previous account of the parousia, a crowned figure appeared in order to conduct the grain harvest, the gathering of the saints; but he very explicitly was dissociated from the grape harvest with its blood to the depth of a horse's bridle—perhaps John's deliberate move to preserve the symbolism of *this* scene. No, the one and only time John has put Jesus in direct contact with Evil or any representative of it was when the dragon stood by

to snatch the child—an event that took place some time before John's own story opened.

(3) So let's look at that event. This Rider is the Lamb, remember. The Lamb is one with the marks of slaughter upon him. It might be expected that blood from the slaughter would be on his robe. John knows all of this about the Lamb; he does use symbolism just this carefully and skillfully; and there is every reason to believe this is the way he is using it here. The blood on the Rider's robe is that which he shed on Calvary. It is true, as John elsewhere has told us, that the saints wash their robes *white* in the blood of the Lamb; but that his own robe retains the stain is most vital to John's story; we shall see how in a moment.

In verse 14, the description of the Rider continues with details which, for the most part, already are familiar to us. There are the white robes of the saints. There is the sharp sword of judgment in his mouth. There is the Psalm 2 reference to ruling with an iron rod—with which we have wrestled several times already. There is "the wrath and retribution of God," concerning which we already have said all we know to say.

The Rider and his armies now have taken the field and been presented. Verses 17-18 form an interlude before the opposing armies are introduced. The content of the interlude is an invitation (or perhaps an anti-invitation) to another eschatological supper, a post-battle banquet that almost certainly is intended as a counter comparison to the wedding supper of the Lamb, for which invitations were extended just a few verses earlier. You have your choice; either you can go to the Lamb's supper as *guests*, friends of the bride (better, *members* of the bride), or you can go to this other supper as part of the *menu*, food for the vultures. I really believe John set it up that way as a means of urging people to accept the *Lamb's* invitation.

Now in this post-battle supper (which happens, then, in verse 21) it is plain that those who get eaten are not, in this case, the supernatural representatives of Evil, but "people." Specifically, it is those kings of the earth (who always turn up right where we have come to expect them), along with their militarist sidekicks and all such types—listed, by the way, in almost the identical fashion they were in Seal 6, when they wanted the mountains to hide them from the vengeance of the Lamb.

But although being eaten by vultures is, I would guess, a

somewhat discomposing experience (and is meant to be), as "the vengeance of the Lamb" it is very mild indeed. The picture is much more that of cleaning up litter than it is of torturing people. The kings and their cronies are not thrown into the lake of fire (at this point); neither does their being eaten take them out of the action; and the Lamb is not through with them yet—not by a long shot!

But talking about this supper has us ahead of the action; verse 19 is where we must pick it up again. The combatants are lined up in readiness; but by the time we get to verse 20, it's all over, the prisoners are being carted off, and the hungry crew of vultures already is at work. There just isn't any battle; and since we already have witnessed the Armageddon scene dissolve in almost the same way, it would seem that John is being anticlimactic on purpose.

But why no battle, when everything was all set for one? We have suggested the reason before: John is convinced that Jesus, in his death-and-resurrection, did all that needed to be done, won the only victory that needs to be won in order to take care of Evil once and for all. To portray Jesus in another battle necessarily would be to say that his first victory wasn't good enough; and this, of course, John will by no means say.

Yet, if there wasn't a battle, what *did* happen here? I think John means it something like this: Recall the memory problems of a dragon with its head cut off. He, the Deceiver, has deceived himself into thinking that his successes *in the world* indicate that he is ready to take on anybody. He's not afraid of any "armies of heaven." He leads his force onto the field . . . and who should be the first person he lays eyes upon but a rider "robed in a garment drenched in blood." Memories begin to awaken—and his tail begins to throb in consequence. He'd seen that blood before! Oh, yes, that was the day and that the way in which he had gotten "thrown down to earth, and his angels with him." There is no sense in even trying it with *that* one again! "Forget it, troops; we're *dead!*"

And so they were—and had been all along; it is just that it took a parousia of the Truth to make the fact of the matter clear to them and everyone else! Christ's "victory" here is simply the revelation of the one sufficient victory he already has won over death, the world, and the devil.

Without any "fight" at all, then, the Evil Trinity is taken prisoner and their dead armies "go to supper." The beast (Anti-

christ) and the false prophet (the Unholy Spirit) are thrown into
the lake of fire; and when any one of the supernatural representatives of Evil goes into the lake of fire, it is the end of him, he will
not be seen or heard from again. The dragon (Satan) is preserved
from that fate—at least for the moment. This is not because the
Lamb's power is not yet complete or because the dragon himself
still has a chance of reversing his situation. No, as 20:3 indicates,
he simply has been put into storage so he can appear in a
particular role a bit later. But for all practical purposes, the
parousia of Christ marks the end of the threat and power of Evil;
from here on out, it's God all the way!

20:4-15

The Apportioning
of Mankind

To this point, John has been very careful and thorough regarding every event he has described; indeed, there may not be one he has not *repeated* a number of times in the effort to give us fuller insight and elucidation. But now—at least until he gets to the new Jerusalem (which is only one chapter away)—he rushes along at such a pace that seemingly very important matters get glossed over and serious questions are raised which he shows no interest in answering. Part of his reason may be that he sees these as events which are not particularly pertinent to the present lives and decisions of his readers. The maintaining of faithfulness through the end-time and the decision as to which supper we want to attend at the parousia—yes, these very much involve us; but with the parousia, our decisions have been made and matters are out of our hands, so to speak. Nothing is to be gained by curiosity and argument concerning this post-parousia period. Consequently, John treats it rather casually and encourages us to do the same.

Nevertheless, his major purpose and intent in this chapter seems quite evident; and it *is* important. In parallel scenes of the millennium and the final sentencing, he wants to portray the post-parousia fate of the Lamb's people on the one hand and the beast's people on the other. None but the Lamb's people appear in the millennial scene; none but beast's people in the sentencing scene. John's interest is focused entirely upon the destiny of these two groups; it is only toward matters of physical and chronological detail that he is casual. He is no more interested in doing a photographic study here than he was earlier. So recall Picasso's *Guernica* and consider that a painting can communicate great

181

truth even when the literal details are quite discrepant—indeed, can focus upon a deeper level of truth by deliberately making the details discrepant. The very presence of discrepancy is a signal to quit fussing with details and look to the central truth involved.

LIFE: THE MILLENNIAL RESURRECTION

(20:4-10) Then I saw thrones, and upon them sat those to whom judgement was 4
committed. I could see the souls of those who had been beheaded for
the sake of God's word and their testimony to Jesus, those who had not
worshipped the beast and its image or received its mark on forehead or
hand. These came to life again and reigned with Christ for a thousand
years, though the rest of the dead did not come to life until the 5
thousand years were over. This is the first resurrection. Happy indeed, 6
and one of God's own people, is the man who shares in this first
resurrection! Upon such the second death has no claim; but they shall
be priests of God and of Christ, and shall reign with him for the
thousand years.

   When the thousand years are over, Satan will be let loose from his 7
dungeon; and he will come out to seduce the nations in the four 8
quarters of the earth and to muster them for battle, yes, the hosts of
Gog and Magog, countless as the sands of the sea. So they marched over 9
the breadth of the land and laid siege to the camp of God's people and
the city that he loves. But fire came down on them from heaven and
consumed them; and the Devil, their seducer, was flung into the lake of 10
fire and sulphur, where the beast and the false prophet had been flung,
there to be tormented day and night for ever.

That John spent about twice as many *chapters* describing the three and a half years of the end-time as he does *verses* describing the *thousand* years of the millennium indicates the order of speed-up that has occurred.

Because we now are to focus upon the fate of "mankind," it would be helpful to review how John has handled the matter thus far. He consistently has seen humanity as divided into two—and only two—major categories: all men are marked as belonging either to *arnion* or to *therion;* there is no third alternative. But further, John has shown no real interest in establishing distinctions *within* either of the groups; he is content to speak simply in terms of the groups as such. Thus, for instance, he has told us nothing about the beast's people who have died, where they are or what their situation might be; bad people, living or dead, he has treated simply as a unit.

And thus, for another and more critical instance, although John began by recognizing the distinction between the church of the living (on earth) and the church of those who have died (in heaven), he proceeded to rather wipe out the line between them— but without making it completely clear as to just how this takes place. Now, in this millennial scene, he has lost the distinction entirely; and that creates a real problem in logistics—if one insists on reading John photographically.

The account clearly intends to deal with the Lamb's people en masse. The scene obviously takes place on earth—and yet everyone in it seems to have come from heaven, for they are those who have died, and everybody in sight gets resurrected. "But certainly there will be *living* Christians on earth at the time of the parousia; where do they come in? Can a person be resurrected if he hasn't even died yet?" Questions, questions, no end of questions! And I rather think John would answer them by saying, "Oh, please don't hang up on trifles! God can and will take care of details like that; and there is no reason why you need to know *how* he will do it. No, please hear what I am trying to say, that the Lamb's people will all be graduated into second-order LIFE!"

While we are looking at problems, let's consider the other big one; it arises out of verses 7-10. The scene, with its reference to "the hosts of Gog and Magog," is based directly upon Ezekiel 38–39; there is no mystery in that respect. But recall the situation at this point: "Babylon"—all the power and seduction of worldli-ness—is gone and completely out of the picture. Both Antichrist and the Unholy Spirit, with all their deceitful wiles, are also lost and gone forever; and the Dragon himself has been off the scene for a thousand years. The parousia account implied that all the human supporters of the Evil Trinity had been eaten by the vultures. It is hard to conceive what representatives of Evil might have been around during the millennium and how they could have maintained themselves; and indeed, the text of the millennial scene gives no hint of their presence.

But then, what power can Satan possibly control for this untimely effort of verses 7-10? Where do these supporters come from, the hosts of Gog and Magog? Has Satan any chance at all of seducing these saints who already "have passed through the great ordeal and washed their robes white in the blood of the Lamb," who already have won the victory which, we have been told, makes them immune to the second death? Does John here mean to reopen the door he spent nineteen chapters getting closed? Is he undoing what Jesus has done and putting the fate of the world back into doubt? Is he implying that, even with his death-and-resurrection *and parousia*, Jesus has not yet done enough entirely to eliminate the threat of Evil?

Although a literal reading of this passage would make such implications as much as inevitable, I am confident that they are not at all what John intends. For one thing, if he had seen this as a serious—and even critical—juncture in his story, he would know that it requires much more than four short verses to deal with it. *Four verses* in which to describe a new and sudden outburst of Evil that overcomes its defeat in the parousia to mount a new threat to the world, seducing the saints, and even laying siege to the church (Jerusalem, "the city that God loves") before God can find the wherewithal for winning a victory that must be counted even greater than Jesus' parousia? No, that John can do it in four verses indicates that he must have something much less crucial and decisive in mind.

To me, the evidence suggests, rather, that this last stand of Satan is used as a somewhat arbitrary symbol for marking the conclusion of the millennium. What demarcates the millennium from the events preceding and following it? Well, it begins with Satan being taken prisoner at the parousia and ends with his being dumped into the lake of fire. (It is noteworthy that John does not see Satan's final fling to be significant enough even to call for the presence of Jesus in the scene.) So let this incident play its role as a boundary marker of the millennium. But when we try to go beyond that, I think John would say, "You're trying to make it say much more than I ever intended it should."

"But," the next question comes, "why do we need this millennium at all? It has created nothing but problems. Wouldn't both the plot line and the theology go much more smoothly if John were to move from the parousia directly to the new Jerusalem—or at least to the final sentencing?"

In one sense, John almost does this. He does not move *directly* from the parousia to the new Jerusalem; but he does move *quickly* (one brief chapter). We need to keep this proportioning in mind.

Even though a time period of *a thousand years* intervenes, John clearly wants to establish that the coming of the new Jerusalem is a direct consequence of Jesus' parousia—this is the essential sequence. Yet we will see that John could not have included the final sentencing *without* including the millennial scene as well; the resurrection of the saints is necessary to establish that they are not involved in the sentencing. But even to omit the two scenes together would destroy the structure of John's theology; he needs to establish the situations of both the Lamb's and the beast's people before his new Jerusalem scene can say what he wants it to.

In the present millennial scene, it would seem that John is more interested in the "resurrection" aspect than in the "thousand years" aspect; but let us begin with the thousand years and then move to the resurrection. I see two primary reasons why this thousand-year period is a "must" in John's thought. Look at the time-line diagram inside the front cover. The symmetrical counterpoint of John's approach is very important to him—and not simply for aesthetic reasons; it is a means by which he affirms the justice and glory of God. The beast and his people got a three-and-a-half-year period on earth when they pretty much had things their own way, while the Lamb and his people had to take it in the neck (the Lamb in his crucifixion, his people in their faithful martyr-witnesses). Yet, even with the Lamb's eventual victory, that period cannot be allowed to stand unanswered; history would not have come out "right," full justice would not have been done, and "the very truth of things" would not have been manifested. The Lamb and his people deserve a thousand years (a large, full, complete number as over against the broken "3 1/2") of reign *on earth*—to put that end-time nightmare into proper perspective, if for no other reason. Our tendency (living in the time we do) is to think of history as constituted solely of nightmare. Not so, says John, this world-history of ours belongs to God; and, for every three-and-a-half-year nightmare, it includes a thousand-year reign with Christ.

But the millennium also serves another purpose for John. As we have observed, he does not make many distinctions between person and person within the total body of the Lamb's people; for instance, he doesn't particularly care whether you are a living Christian or one who has died. Yet there is one distinction that is important to him—and he has indicated so previously.

Some Christians were called upon to make a faithful witness of an order that involved actually laying down their lives for the sake of Christ and the brethren; these are the *martyrs*, in the strict sense of that term. Many more Christians, although faithful to their own call, won their crowns without having to make this greatest act of commitment. The distinction is not an ultimate one, John knows; both types of Christians finally come out indistinguishable. Nevertheless, he feels that the martyr-saints do deserve some special recognition and honor; and the millennium affords an opportunity for this.

Verses 4-5, unfortunately, are not crystal clear; but we will do the best we can with them. First, in identifying the martyrs, John does call them the "beheaded"; but he probably means this in the general sense of "executed" rather than specifying for honor only those who met death in the one particular way. The original Greek does have an "and" preceding the phrase "those who had not worshipped the beast." If we insert it and understand the sentence as identifying two groups rather than one, the entire passage will render better sense. The first group, then, consists of those Christians who lost their lives for the sake of God's word and their *martyria Jesu*. The second group consists of the rest of the Christians, who had not worshipped the beast or worn his image but who had not been martyred, either.

Apparently John means to say that the first group comes to life at the beginning of the millennium. "Coming to life," or "resurrection," means, now, graduating into second-order LIFE, the quality of life that will characterize the new Jerusalem, the ultimate of human experience which, we are told, is forever immune to anything of death. John never uses these terms in any other way. "The rest of the dead," who come to life after the thousand years are over, surely must intend the second group of Christians; the dead among the *beast's* people certainly are not eligible for "resurrection" (the next scene will find them still very much "dead"), and they are not even in John's picture at this point. But with the raising of the second group, any distinction between the two is lost; their history proceeds as that of the *one* church. The martyrs' recognition was that of receiving their prizes a little ahead of the others; their final status is in no way different.

In fact, perhaps as a means of emphasizing that no ultimate distinction is involved, John apparently groups both raisings to-

gether as constituting "the first resurrection." The millennial experience is that of one resurrection in two stages—and all Christians
are included in either one stage or the other. There is nothing to
indicate nor any way of conceiving that any of God's people has
been left out. The church as a whole has graduated into LIFE. At
this juncture, then, the distinction between the Lamb's people and
the beast's is easy and obvious: the Lamb's people are all in
second-order LIFE, the beast's all in first-order *death*.

John here chooses a very intriguing phrase; let's give it careful
notice. He calls this scene "the *first* resurrection." That word
"first" carries with it some implications—just as surely as if I were
to refer to "my first wife." There is no sense in referring to an
item as "first" unless it is one of a series, unless there is at least a
"second" to follow. It is true that John nowhere speaks of a
"second resurrection"; however, there is a spot where there is
room for it and where John may be hinting that it takes place. Of
course, we are not yet in position to make any decision in this
regard; but do keep in mind that explicitly (in two different
sentences) John has called this millennial experience "the *first*
resurrection."

We present here a chart designed to give graphic representation
to what we have been saying—and what we have yet to say. Let us
examine the appropriate portion of it now.

The Destiny of Mankind–

according to the book of Revelation

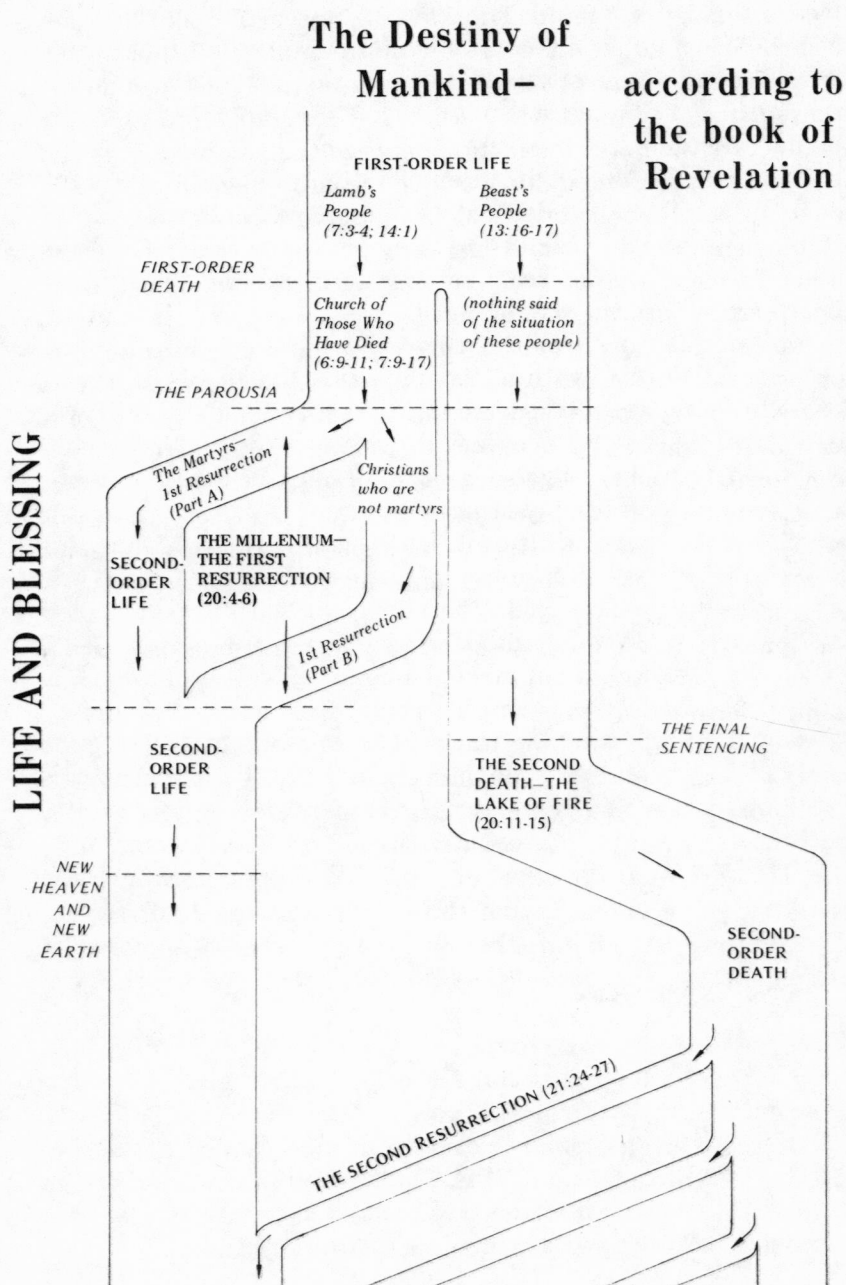

FIRST-ORDER LIFE

Lamb's People (7:3-4; 14:1)

Beast's People (13:16-17)

FIRST-ORDER DEATH

Church of Those Who Have Died (6:9-11; 7:9-17)

(nothing said of the situation of these people)

THE PAROUSIA

The Martyrs— 1st Resurrection (Part A)

Christians who are not martyrs

SECOND-ORDER LIFE

THE MILLENIUM— THE FIRST RESURRECTION (20:4-6)

1st Resurrection (Part B)

SECOND-ORDER LIFE

THE FINAL SENTENCING

THE SECOND DEATH—THE LAKE OF FIRE (20:11-15)

NEW HEAVEN AND NEW EARTH

SECOND-ORDER DEATH

THE SECOND RESURRECTION (21:24-27)

LIFE AND BLESSING

DEATH AND PUNISHMENT

The chart portrays the destinies only of "mankind"; to have tried to include those of the various supernatural personages would have made it too complicated. It is a flow chart that moves downward through history. A turn to the left marks a move toward Life and Blessing; a turn to the right, a move toward Death and Punishment.

At the top, all men begin together in first-order life. It is here that their fates first are decided, and the division takes place as they accept the seal either of the Lamb or of the beast. However, in first-order life, those seals are invisible and the two groups inextricably mixed.

A real complication in the charting is that all men do not experience first-order death at the same time; some are already in first-order death while others are still in first-order life—and this is true of both the Lamb's people and the beast's. John handles this complication mainly by ignoring it; and the chart does the same. Surely there is some kind of separation between the two groups at death; but John makes little of it. He has shown us, in heaven, the saints who have died; but he has mentioned not a word about the beast's people who have died. The important thing to note is that John does not agree at all with the idea most people seem to hold on the subject. He does not make the moment of first-order death a critical juncture. The Lamb's people do not, at that point, automatically jump into the finale of second-order LIFE; consequently, John's pictures of the saints in heaven still carry elements of incompleteness and more yet to come. Likewise, the beast's people do not, at that point, automatically proceed into second-order DEATH and the lake of fire. John does not show us individuals going, at individual times, to individual destinies; he has us waiting for one another and then proceeding as groups. (And by the way, the rest of the New Testament agrees with John on this point.)

With the dead of both groups being in a "holding pattern," it is the parousia of Christ that truly puts things into motion for the first time. With that parousia comes "the first resurrection," graduating the Lamb's people clear over to the lefthand side of the chart and into second-order LIFE. That resurrection takes place in two stages, including first the martyrs and later the rest of the Christians. The two stages together span the millennium.

With the saints safely "home," we turn our attention now to the beast's people, who have been waiting patiently all this time in "hold."

DEATH: THE FINAL SENTENCING TO THE LAKE OF FIRE

(20:11-15) Then I saw a great white throne, and the One who sat upon it; from his presence earth and heaven vanished away, and no place was left for them. I could see the dead, great and small, standing before the throne; and books were opened. Then another book was opened, the roll of the living. From what was written in these books the dead were judged upon the record of their deeds. The sea gave up its dead, and Death and Hades gave up the dead in their keeping; they were judged, each man on the record of his deeds. Then Death and Hades were flung into the lake of fire. This lake of fire is the second death; and into it were flung any whose names were not to be found in the roll of the living.   11 12 13 14 15

In the previous scene, the Lamb's people went to their destiny; now, in its counterpart, the beast's people go to theirs. This scene usually is referred to as "The Last Judgment"; I have changed that wording for a very particular reason. A "judgment" usually is thought of as a situation in which the guilt or innocence of the defendants has not yet been determined, in which the meeting takes place for that very purpose, in which there is just as much opportunity for the defendants to be found innocent as guilty.

But none of that is the case here; and I have changed the wording to reflect the fact. That these people are here and are dead is proof enough that they belong to the beast and thus are guilty. Plainly, none of the Lamb's people is anywhere around; none of them is dead, having all graduated into second-order LIFE and by that act been guaranteed that "the second death has no claim upon them." No, even before anything like "judgment" takes place, it is evident that everyone present is guilty; they are gathered here only for the handing down of sentence.

The scene transpires before "a great white throne," but John does not specify whether it is God or Christ upon it—probably not Christ, because John has shown some tendency to keep him out of such scenes. Notice that the defendants consistently are described as being "dead"; they do not need to be resurrected or brought back to life in order to act their roles; and John would not be willing to use such terms in their connection. The record books are produced not on the chance that some of them might be found innocent but simply to prove to them that their sentences are just. Their very desire to justify themselves "upon the record of their deeds" is a mark against them; and of course, their deeds will show them to have been minions of the beast. Obviously, their names will not appear in "the roll of the living"; if their names were there, they wouldn't be here, they even now would be "living"— living the second-order LIFE of the saints.

All of the dead—which is to say, all the beast's people—are involved. The sea, that garbage can from which the beast originally came, gives up its dead; Death and Hades give up all they have been holding. "Death and Hades," that ghastly pair for whom, at the very outset, Jesus told us he was holding the keys and who rode across the earth on the pale horse—they get tossed into the lake of fire. With this jettisoning of Death and Hades, every one of the supernatural representatives of Evil has disappeared for good. Things can't be anything but very, very different from now on.

But the beast's *people*, too, now go into the lake of fire; what does it represent in their case? Well, don't jump to the conclusion that it necessarily means the same thing for them as for the "supernaturals"; there is a difference! The "supernaturals" are symbols of pure (if that's the right word) evil. The "people," although gone bad, are nevertheless persons who were created in the image of God, whom "God so loved," who are "brothers for whom Christ died."

Recall, however, that to this point John has not described any special punishment for them. Yes, they had to endure the end-time traumas—but so did the Christians! Yes, they have suffered first-order death—but so have the Christians! Yes, some of their deaths were quite gruesome (being eaten by vultures)—but so were the deaths of some of the martyrs! But now John wants to say (taking a word from Paul): "The wages of sin is death!" Mere first-order death will not fill the bill in that statement; saints die first-order deaths just as sinners do. But no, to reject the Lamb is to reject LIFE; and outside of LIFE there is only DEATH. Through sin, natural death leads on to death to the second power; the person kills himself *spiritually*, becomes not merely a dead person but a supporter and promoter of DEATH. John, here, is not speaking in terms of any exaggerated retribution, vindictiveness, or cruelty; he does not use the sort of language that earlier was directed against the "supernaturals." He simply is stating a law of the universe: to reject the way to LIFE is to take the way of death; and the *way* of death can lead nowhere but to DEATH.

21:1–22:21
The New Heaven
and the New Earth

John has completed his rush from the parousia and, in one chapter, now has made it to the new Jerusalem, the climax, goal, and finis of his work. Being here, he will settle down to his normal way of doing things, taking a more leisurely look and even using his familiar device of repetition. He will give us a quick scan of the scene in 21:1-8, and then will double back to spend the remainder of the book going through the same scene at greater length, even following the same order of scan.

Let us refer to the chart on page 188 to make sure we have our alignments right for this new picture. All the supernatural forces of Evil are gone for good; they no longer figure in the account. Mankind exists in just two groups, as regularly has been the case in John's thought—although now the distinction and separation between the two are at a maximum. The Christians (i.e., the church) have been resurrected into the ultimate of second-order LIFE and await only the opening of the urban renewal project just being completed. The beast's people have gone from death to death, into the ultimate second-order DEATH of the lake of fire. Thus, in the present scene, just as there are only two groups of people, there are only two locations, the new Jerusalem and the lake of fire. John shows no knowledge of any people apart from these two groups or any territory except these two locations.

This fact explains an important feature of John's final scene. Clearly, he is basing it upon a similar picture from the concluding chapters of Ezekiel. Ezekiel's dream of eschatological redemption centers upon a magnificent new temple (man's link with God), which itself sits in the center of a new Jerusalem (redeemed

193

Israel), which is itself the center of a new landscape (the redeemed world). John tries to follow this pattern but discovers that his Christianity won't let him do it. The points at which John is forced to modify Ezekiel's picture are the most theologically instructive.

Ezekiel found it natural and right to make a distinction among the redeemed. Even though both may be fully redeemed, a Jew is still a Jew and a Gentile a Gentile; nothing can change the fact, because the faith itself is premised upon this ethnic distinction. A new Jerusalem, *outside of which* lies a new world, is the proper way for Ezekiel to draw his picture.

But John can't do it, because he knows that Christianity recognizes no distinctions, ethnic or otherwise. With Christianity, redemption is based solely upon faith in Jesus Christ—and anyone who so believes is just as much a Christian as anyone else. There is no way of recognizing or delineating two spheres of redemption. John tries to follow Ezekiel in speaking of the church and the world (the redeemed world); but he realizes that these come to the same thing. The only alternative is to make them coextensive—just as the City of San Francisco and the County of San Francisco occupy precisely the same territory and claim precisely the same citizenry. We will find evidence to indicate that John has in mind this very solution.

INTRODUCTORY OVERVIEW

(21:1-8)   Then I saw a new heaven and a new earth, for the first heaven and the   1
first earth had vanished, and there was no longer any sea. I saw the holy   2
city, new Jerusalem, coming down out of heaven from God, made
ready like a bride adorned for her husband. I heard a loud voice   3
proclaiming from the throne: 'Now at last God has his dwelling among
men! He will dwell among them and they shall be his people, and God
himself will be with them. He will wipe every tear from their eyes; there   4
shall be an end to death, and to mourning and crying and pain; for the
old order has passed away!'

Then he who sat on the throne said, 'Behold! I am making all things   5
new!' (And he said to me, 'Write this down; for these words are
trustworthy and true. Indeed they are already fulfilled.') 'I am the   6
Alpha and the Omega, the beginning and the end. A draught from the
water-springs of life will be my free gift to the thirsty. All this is the   7
victor's heritage; and I will be his God and he shall be my son. But as   8

for the cowardly, the faithless, and the vile, murderers, fornicators, sorcerers, idolaters, and liars of every.kind, their lot will be the second death, in the lake that burns with sulphurous flames.'

This scene is organized into three parts—which three we also will locate as we go through it again later. The first part, verses 1-4, describes the new Jerusalem, the redeemed church. The second part, verse 5, is at least an attempt to speak of the redeemed world. The third part, verses 6-8, consists of exhortations to the reader.

The keynote of everything John will show us is its "newness"; and plainly, the distinction that defines it as "new" is the total absence of anything that is less than perfectly good and right. Evil, with all its consequences, implications, and overtones, is gone. So, too, is anything like separation, alienation, distance between God and man, between man and man. And what sort of newness could be conceived that would be more strikingly "new" to human experience? New architecture, new flora and fauna, new technologies would be only as new as the same old stuff we've seen in science-fiction movies since H. G. Wells. But this newness will go far beyond that.

John talks of a *new heaven* and a *new earth*. Yet it is significant that he speaks of a new *heaven and earth* rather than a completely different "something else," a "somewhere else" totally divorced from what had gone before. In short, although John wants to speak of newness, he also wants to affirm a continuity with what had been previously. Certainly there is a continuity of the people involved—though also a rather radical discontinuity in their having been resurrected. Just so, John knows that, in spite of what happened to it consequently, God's original creation was "very good"—and God is not about to act now in a way that would deny the fact. Why, even the new holy city is still "Jerusalem"— very different from the old one, of course, but Jerusalem nonetheless. God will make "all things new"—not "all new things."

The newness of God is properly the *consummation* of history— not a junking of history in order to start over with something entirely different. Yes, Evil has been junked; but history was more than that. God is Redeemer as well as Creator; and his newness is as much or more that of redemption as of creation. Whatever is redeemable, God will redeem.

John talks of a new heaven *and* a new earth; but when the new

Jerusalem comes *down* from *heaven*, the distinction between the
two is lost—and thus another element of radical newness is introduced. From here on, the picture will include elements of heaven-
liness and elements of earthliness—with absolutely no way of
extricating the two. Recall our previous suggestion: earth was that
which *actually is* but with inevitable aspects of *wrongness* about it;
heaven was *rightness* but still in process of *coming to be*; what we
have now is the union representing a *rightness* which *actually
is*—and that is something new!

The new Jerusalem comes down "like a bride adorned for her
husband." The language recalls John's earlier references to "the
wedding of the Lamb"; the likelihood is that he means to spot it
at this point. After all, just as "Jerusalem" was the city of the old
church, "the new Jerusalem" is the city of the resurrected church;
so the scene here does portray the church coming into a new
relationship of special intimacy with God and the Lamb.

Verses 3-4 describe the new situation in terms almost identical
to those in which John had predicted it in 7:15-17. The emphasis
is completely in terms of personal relationship between man and
God and the disappearance of everything that earlier had hamp-
ered such relationship. Note well that John gave us two descriptions of this sort before he breathed so much as a word about
pearly gates and golden streets—we should let our own expectations be formed accordingly.

Verse 5 attempts to expand the newness—as if there were
anywhere else to go with it! John is reaching beyond the new
Jerusalem to a new world. But perhaps there *is* somewhere else to
go with it. Is it quite accurate for God to say, "Behold! I am
making *all things* new," if, in fact, nothing is changed in the lake
of fire? I only ask the question; but this line could point toward
something like, say, the *second* resurrection. We still are not ready
to make a decision; but by all means put this verse into the
"universalism" collection.

Verses 6-8 turn away from the scene and address the reader in
order to spell out the implications of what he has witnessed: The
picture can be taken as trustworthy and true; there is no doubt of
its reality. Indeed, it can be taken as "already fulfilled." How so? I
think John means to say that God's promise and commitment—
and his having already accomplished the pivotal event in Jesus'
death-and-resurrection—make this new heaven and earth as sure as

if we already were living there. That God is the End of history just as truly as he is its Beginning makes the outcome a certainty. And the basic promise behind it all is that of LIFE. This the victor can count upon, life the quality of a father's life in and with his son. (Undoubtedly it is deliberate that John here is picking up ideas he introduced clear back in the letters to the Christians of the seven churches. He wants to show that his entire story has been dealing with them—he has not wandered off into some imaginative "other world." This new heaven and earth is *for them*.)

However, in verse 8, he comes down hard to insist that it is for them only if they are and remain "in Jesus." Whoever chooses rather to be "in the beast"—his place is the lake of fire and not the new heaven and earth. Let's be careful at this point. That the new Jerusalem includes no people of the sort John describes is obvious; the only people there are those who belong to the Lamb rather than the beast. However, John neither says nor implies that, once a person has been cowardly, faithless, or whatever, he is condemned to be so forever. That plainly is not the case: John has allowed for (and urged) the possibility of repentance, of a person's changing his loyalty from the beast to the Lamb. Further, we have not seen one word to indicate that John understands this possibility to be closed off with the moment of first-order death. Granted, this verse does not suggest the continued possibility of repentance; and we are not arguing that it does. Our point is only that this verse cannot be used as proof that damnation is eternal. The question must be left open and settled on other grounds.

THE NEW JERUSALEM IN DETAIL

9   Then one of the seven angels that held the seven bowls full of the seven   (21:9-27)
    last plagues came and spoke to me and said, 'Come, and I will show you
10 the bride, the wife of the Lamb.' So in the Spirit he carried me away to
    a great high mountain, and showed me the holy city of Jerusalem
11 coming down out of heaven from God. It shone with the glory of God;
    it had the radiance of some priceless jewel, like a jasper, clear as crystal.
12 It had a great high wall, with twelve gates, at which were twelve angels;
    and on the gates were inscribed the names of the twelve tribes of Israel.
13 There were three gates to the east, three to the north, three to the
14 south, and three to the west. The city wall had twelve foundation-

stones, and on them were the names of the twelve apostles of the Lamb.

The angel who spoke with me carried a gold measuring-rod, to   15
measure the city, its wall, and its gates. The city was built as a square,   16
and was as wide as it was long. It measured by his rod twelve thousand
furlongs, its length and breadth and height being equal. Its wall was one   17
hundred and forty-four cubits high, that is, by human measurements,
which the angel was using. The wall was built of jasper, while the city   18
itself was of pure gold, bright as clear glass. The foundations of the city   19
wall were adorned with jewels of every kind, the first of the founda-
tion-stones being jasper, the second lapis lazuli, the third chalcedony,
the fourth emerald, the fifth sardonyx, the sixth cornelian, the seventh   20
chrysolite, the eighth beryl, the ninth topaz, the tenth chrysoprase, the
eleventh turquoise, and the twelfth amethyst. The twelve gates were   21
twelve pearls, each gate being made from a single pearl. The streets of
the city were of pure gold, like translucent glass.

I saw no temple in the city; for its temple was the sovereign Lord   22
God and the Lamb. And the city had no need of sun or moon to shine   23
upon it; for the glory of God gave it light, and its lamp was the Lamb.
By its light shall the nations walk, and the kings of the earth shall bring   24
into it all their splendour. The gates of the city shall never be shut by   25
day—and there will be no night. The wealth and splendour of the   26
nations shall be brought into it; but nothing unclean shall enter, nor   27
anyone whose ways are false or foul, but only those who are inscribed
in the Lamb's roll of the living.

Now John doubles back upon his brief overview to repeat the scene in more detail. This passage corresponds to 21:1-4, the appearance of the new Jerusalem. Verse 9 makes it even clearer that this event also represents the wedding of the Lamb. The business of measuring a magnificent structure comes straight out of Ezekiel. However, Ezekiel's efforts were focused on the measuring of the temple. John doesn't have a temple (for reasons we shall discover in a bit), so he measures the city!

John seems to have two main purposes behind this scene. One is to highlight the *beauty* of the redeemed church. He resorts to the most impressive physical imagery he knows to describe a reality and a glory that are far more than and quite different from the sheerly physical. Therefore, no one is to get literal and start asking questions like: "Who'd want to live in that kind of a city?" or, "Would pure gold even stand up as a construction material?" What John is saying here is, "Beautiful, beautiful, beautiful!"

John's second purpose in the measuring is to show us that this entire city is built on *twelves* (the same "12" as that of the

twenty-four elders; the 144,000; the stars in the crown of the
woman clothed with the sun). Here is *continuity*. Granted, this
new Jerusalem doesn't look much like any church we have known;
but all those twelves are meant to ring a bell. If you belong to the
church of Jesus Christ, then this is *your* church; this is what God
will make of the church as he gets the twelves to come right!
Every measurement given in this passage is related to twelve. (Be
careful with some of the Bible translations that try to put these
references into modern measurements and, in the process, accomplish nothing except to lose the twelves. John isn't trying to tell us
how big the city is; he is describing its character.)

Two of the twelves call for particular attention. The gates, the
instruments of "entering," bear the names of the twelve tribes of
Israel. The foundation stones, the instruments of "upholding,"
bear those of the twelve apostles of the Lamb. John has not told
us when and how it happens, but these details confirm his earlier
indications that Israel is to become an integral part of the bride of
the Lamb. The city "foursquare" is an *inclusive* city—and we
haven't seen the half of it yet!

With verse 22, John leaves his beauty-measurement theme and
his dependence upon Ezekiel, and things begin to get interesting.
In direct contradiction to Ezekiel he says, "I saw *no* temple in the
city." Why so great a "no"? Partly because John is a Christian and
so has moved beyond need of the mediatory services of temple,
cult, and priest; Jesus Christ is the one mediator between God and
man. But more, John likely sees that the temple is actually a poor
symbol to include in the present scene; what sense does a symbol
of mediation have, when the entire point is that man and God
have now come into face-to-face intimacy? When the sovereign
Lord God and the Lamb are right there, the last thing you need is
a temple; they can be their own temple.

Out of the biblical tradition of eschatological vision which had
come to John, two themes always had been strong: light and life.
The "light" theme John picks up here; he will get to "life" in just
a bit. But light? Don't talk about suns and moons and stars and
novas; we have God and the Lamb—and with them is the light that
is truth, clarity, and illumination with nothing of darkness about
it.

"By its light shall the nations walk, and the kings of the earth
shall bring into it all their splendor. . . . The wealth and splendor

of the nations shall be brought in." Now, honestly, aren't those the very last people you ever expected to see here—and the wealth and splendor of the nations the last merchandise you would have thought could be allowed in? After all, the last we saw of those kings, they were a feast for buzzards (and leading candidates for the lake of fire); and the wealth and splendor of the nations went down with Babylon!

Both of these—"the kings of the earth" and "the wealth and splendor of the nations"—are terms John has used often enough, consistently enough, and with enough of pointed overtone, that it simply is inconceivable that he could have written them this time offhandedly, carelessly, without thinking of what he was doing. In fact, that he did know what he was doing is indicated by verse 27, where he turns quickly to assure us that "nothing unclean shall be entering." (This, by the way, is a more exact translation than NEB's "shall enter"; the Greek verb definitely suggests *continuing* traffic into the city.) In other words, "Yes, I did say 'kings of the earth,' but I still insist 'nothing unclean.' In that lake of fire something has happened to these kings that makes them entirely different people, gives them an entirely different significance than they had before. If the kings of the earth are here (as I, John, say they are), it can be only because their names now are to be found 'in the Lamb's roll of the living.' "

When John deliberately puts "the kings of the earth" and "the wealth and splendor of the nations" right onto the streets of the new Jerusalem, there would seem no alternative but that he also is talking of a continued possibility of repentance and redemption, of a "*second* resurrection." And if that is a possibility for the kings of the earth—whom John, clearly, has considered as the worst of all people—then it is a possibility for anyone.

There is another detail that reinforces our interpretation. In verse 25, John makes it emphatic that the new Jerusalem is an *open-gated* city; its gates are never closed. John plainly has something in mind with his symbol; what could it be? Walled cities were, of course, as common to his experience as they are uncommon to ours. The walls (and more particularly, the gates) are for one purpose only: to let wanted people in and keep unwanted people out. They normally are kept open during the day when those entering can be watched; at night, when bad people are intent on wickedness, they are closed. Because there is no night in the new Jerusalem (it isn't like the old earth where the "light" sinks below the horizon just when it's getting dark and you really need it), the gates are always and forever open.

Open gates have no meaning at all unless there is traffic to use them. Rather certainly, there is no out traffic from the new Jerusalem: Why would anyone want to leave?—and where is there to go, except to the lake of fire? The gates must be "open" for the sake of *incoming* traffic. John says as much in verses 24, 26, and 27: "shall bring into it," "shall be brought into it," "shall enter." Yet there is no place for any traffic to come from *except the lake of fire*. What other interpretation possibly can be given to John's emphasis upon the open-gatedness of the city?

So, the chart on page 188 is designed to show the possibility of a continuing traffic from the lake of fire into the new Jerusalem. It can only be labeled as a "resurrection"; for the lake of fire is second-order DEATH and the new Jerusalem second-order LIFE, and by what conceivable means could a person get from one to the other except by "resurrection"? This passage—both for its reference to "the kings of the earth" and to the open-gatedness of the city—must rate as Exhibit #1 in our "universalism" collection.

THE NEW WORLD ATTEMPTED

1   Then he showed me the river of the water of life, sparkling like crystal,   (22:1-5)
2   flowing from the throne of God and of the Lamb down the middle of
    the city's street. On either side of the river stood a tree of life, which
    yields twelve crops of fruit, one for each month of the year; the leaves
3   of the trees serve for the healing of the nations. Every accursed thing
    shall disappear. The throne of God and of the Lamb will be there, and
4   his servants shall worship him; they shall see him face to face, and bear
5   his name on their foreheads. There shall be no more night, nor will they
    need the light of lamp or sun, for the Lord God will give them light;
    and they shall reign for evermore.

This passage corresponds to 21:5 in the introductory overview and is again John's attempt to follow Ezekiel in describing a new, redeemed world. He does stick close to the Old Testament model; but it gives him trouble.

The theme, now, is "life"—and as with Ezekiel, "water" is taken as its symbol. Anyone who has lived in arid country that requires irrigation instinctively will feel the force of the symbol. Ezekiel's vision had "the water of life" come from a spring in the temple, flow through the city and out one of the gates to become an ever growing blessing that ran on to irrigate the world. John tries; but he doesn't have a temple, so the river starts from beneath "the throne of God" (a theological improvement over Ezekiel). The river then flows down "the middle of the city's street." The picture is a little awkward perhaps; but John has no alternative. There can't be a sphere of blessing and redemption outside the city, because redemption is in Jesus Christ—and that redemption is what the city itself stands for. The world is the city, and the city is the world. But despite the difficulty, John says all that Ezekiel had said: God redeems and blesses everything in sight, everything redeemable.

The *river* of life irrigates the *tree* of life; the tree man lost when he was driven out of Eden is his once more. Life, now, is nourishment as well as irrigation. Ezekiel, apparently, had thought simply of an orchard that bore fruit the year around, whereas John envisions a special kind of tree that bears a different variety of fruit each month. The leaves of John's trees, we are told, make poultices effective for "the *healing* of the nations." Further, "every accursed thing shall disappear." But surely, there is no "accursed thing" in the new Jerusalem nor anything that needs "healing." John's language has again pointed us to something like "continued redemption" and a traffic into the city from out the lake of fire. This verse constitutes another specimen for our "universalism" bag—the contents of which we will examine in just a moment.

Verses 3-4 close John's description of the new heaven and earth as it opened—with an emphasis on the direct presence of God and man to each other, the intimacy and completeness of their relationship. The seal on each person's forehead—originally so dim as to be invisible—now shines in brilliance: "I belong to God and the Lamb!" And verse 5 ends the scene with a burst of eternal light.

AN EXCURSUS ON UNIVERSALISM

All told, we have found in Revelation quite a number of references that are "universalistic" in thrust, either directly or by implication. We have not tried to hang a theological argument upon any one of them alone. Of course, they are of differing weights and values and point to differing aspects of what could be called "universalism." But now, looking not at any one of them in itself, what does the collection as a whole amount to, what does it tell us?

First, *if* John does teach a universalism (and we are still holding that question open), it is a universalism of a somewhat rare type—one that avoids most of the objections usually raised against the doctrine. He, obviously, is not proposing the possibility of salvation apart from faith in Jesus Christ. His is not the picture of a God who says, "Oh, shucks, you were all fairly nice people (in your own ways); come on in! All that bit in the New Testament about the necessity of accepting Jesus Christ—I didn't really mean that. So come on in!" John cannot be accused of any sort of deviation from the rest of the New Testament on this score.

Neither can John be accused of underestimating the power of evil and the pervasiveness of its influence among men. He does not show us a world that every day in every way is getting better and better—until one fine morning we wake up to discover that we are all saved people and wasn't that nice! If John exaggerated the truth about the world's condition, it wasn't in this direction.

Likewise, John is fully aware of the *seriousness* of sin. It is not something that can simply be ignored or brushed aside. God does *forgive* sin, but that is something quite different from saying that it doesn't matter. John knows that to reject the Lamb and go after the beast is to bring great calamity upon oneself and others; the way of sin is the way to second-order DEATH and a lake of fire.

John knows, too, that God's love cannot be true unless it includes *justice;* he understands the propriety and rightness of *punishment.* His is not the sort of universalism that would ask God simply to forget wrong rather than insist that it be made right.

And finally, John never could be accused of the sort of universalism that undercuts the evangelistic *urgency of decision.* When the picture is drawn John's way, no one in his right mind is going to put off accepting Christ on the grounds that it will be just as easy to do it later—after being eaten by vultures and spending time in the lake of fire, maybe? No, within Revelation itself, John is proved a very competent evangelist and one entirely capable of preaching for a decision *with urgency.*

Each of the points above concerns that which we can be sure John does teach; but does he teach universalism? Let us take great care and show true caution in our conclusions. I think it would be wrong to come out dogmatically, saying that John teaches that all men eventually will be saved. That would be to go further than the evidence allows. Granted, he says a number of things that could be taken to imply this; but he never comes out to state it as a fact—and he does say some other things that could be taken to imply a different conclusion.

But as it would be wrong to assert that he teaches that *all men will be saved*, just as wrong would it be to assert that he teaches that *some men never can be saved;* he doesn't say that, either! As much as we can say with confidence, then, is that John teaches that we dare never deny the *possibility* of *any* person's being saved—if "the kings of the earth" can find their way to redemption, then it's a possibility for anyone! Don't ever say that you know for a fact what is the ultimate destiny of any man—be he Adolf Hitler, Cain, or Judas Iscariot. We dare not be dogmatic as to what God *will* do—whether save all or only some. But even more, we dare not suggest that God is limited in what he *can* do. Who are we to say how many people or which people God in his love and grace will be able to get to and win? Who are we to say that, at some point, God quits loving people and working for their redemption, the redemption for which he gave his only Son? No, John does not make a universalistic claim about what God will do; but neither is he willing to make a dogmatic assertion about what God will not do. What we can and must say is that John attributes to and leaves with God "the universalistic possibility."

It should be said that the rest of the New Testament has the net effect of doing this, too—although not quite in the way John does. Revelation, as we have seen, comes out rather directly in support of "the universalistic possibility"; the remainder of the New Testament as much as forces the same conclusion by failing to give unanimous support to any other alternative.

Scattered throughout the New Testament are a number of passages that would seem rather clearly to point toward some sort of universalism. Paul's "Therefore God raised him to the heights and bestowed on him the name above all names, that at the name of Jesus every knee should bow—in heaven, on earth, and in the depths—and every tongue confess, 'Jesus Christ is Lord,' to the glory of God the Father" (Philippians 2:9-11) is just one example. Conversely, there is another group of passages that seem, just as clearly, to point toward a doctrine of eternal damnation. And there is no way of deciding for or against either group on the basis of the authenticity, dating, or authority of its texts.

The common way of handling this dilemma is perhaps the least permissible. The expositor simply latches onto the verses he personally prefers, uses them to "prove" his position, and conveniently ignores even the presence of an equally weighty body of scripture pointing toward a different conclusion. The much more honest solution would be simply to leave the issue open, refusing to become dogmatic either way. Indeed, Scripture may be wanting to tell us that this question regarding the ultimate destiny of individuals is not one we need to have answered, not one that affects our present opportunities and obligations, not one that needs to cause division between Christian and Christian. We know what our present Christian responsibility is and what we should be doing about it. The rest safely can be left to God, because our "doctrine" won't change things in any case. The "universalistic possibility" must be attributed to and left with God.

CLOSING EXHORTATIONS

6   Then he said to me, 'These words are trustworthy and true. The Lord   (22:6-21)
    God who inspires the prophets has sent his angel to show his servants
7   what must shortly happen. And, remember, I am coming soon!'
        Happy is the man who heeds the words of prophecy contained in this
8   book! It is I, John, who heard and saw these things. And when I had
    heard and seen them, I fell in worship at the feet of the angel who had
9   shown them to me. But he said to me, 'No, not that! I am but a
    fellow-servant with you and your brothers the prophets and those who
10 heed the words of this book. It is God you must worship.' Then he told
    me, 'Do not seal up the words of prophecy in this book, for the hour of
11 fulfilment is near. Meanwhile, let the evil-doer go on doing evil and the
    filthy-minded wallow in his filth, but let the good man persevere in his
    goodness and the dedicated man be true to his dedication.'
12   'Yes, I am coming soon, and bringing my recompense with me, to
13 requite everyone according to his deeds! I am the Alpha and the
    Omega, the first and the last, the beginning and the end.'
14   Happy are those who wash their robes clean! They will have the right
15 to the tree of life and will enter by the gates of the city. Outside are

dogs, sorcerers and fornicators, murderers and idolaters, and all who love and practise deceit.

'I, Jesus, have sent my angel to you with this testimony for the churches. I am the scion and offspring of David, the bright star of dawn.' 16

'Come!' say the Spirit and the bride. 17

'Come!' let each hearer reply.

Come forward, you who are thirsty; accept the water of life, a free gift to all who desire it.

For my part, I give this warning to everyone who is listening to the words of prophecy in this book: should anyone add to them, God will add to him the plagues described in this book; should anyone take away from the words in this book of prophecy, God will take away from him his share in the tree of life and the Holy City, described in this book. 18 19

He who gives this testimony speaks: 'Yes, I am coming soon!' 20

Amen. Come, Lord Jesus!

The grace of the Lord Jesus be with you all. 21

This passage is an enlargement upon the third section of the introductory overview (21:6-8). It is interesting to note how many of the ideas are ones we have encountered earlier, in much the same form even. A number of them come right out of the opening chapters of the book. The phenomenon certainly is not accidental. John is like the good preacher who "tells 'em what he is goin' to tell 'em; then he tells 'em; and now he tells 'em what he told 'em." With this section, we come to know for a certainty what John intended should be the central purposes and emphases of the book as a whole.

Verses 6-7 open with the familiar theme that is absolutely vital to John's concept of the book: these things "must *shortly* happen"; "I am coming *soon*." Recall once more that those words obviously were meant to be read by first-century Christians before they were meant for us. They cannot be taken as a disclosure confirming that Jesus will return in the last quarter of the twentieth century.

John is not claiming any sort of inside information regarding either the time or any other calendarizing details having to do with the end of history. He is saying, rather, "Although the eschatological whens and hows of God's plan for history are far beyond our ken—and properly so—you dare not treat this message as a science-fiction story, something interesting and even curious, fun to speculate about, but nevertheless remote, unreal, and irrelevant to the actual situations you face and decisions you must make. What I have written may be *future* history, but it is nonetheless *your* history." Whatever the hour may be on God's clock, Christian eschatology always has a "soonness" about it; it describes a history that is sure and not "iffy," a history, indeed, which even now is in process. It is the one "future" that incorporates our "now" and can tell us what that "now" means and where it is headed. Christian eschatology always must be read, not as a speculation about what may happen *then*, but as a "soon-coming" which must be lived out in expectation *now*.

Thus, the beatitude in verse 7 specifies blessedness for the one who "*heeds* the words," or "*keeps* the sayings." That injunction points one to a task quite different from doping out a calendar and scenario for the consummation of history. God can and will handle that one without our help and without regard to our shrewd guesses and clever readings. To "heed" and to "keep" points us, rather, to the quality of our own loyalties, our present ethical choices and actions. And there is not the slightest doubt but that this is where John wants his book to come out.

Verses 8-9 reiterate John's earlier warning against angel worship. "It is *God* you must worship." And just as he warns against worshipping the *messengers* of the revelation—whether the angel or the prophet-author—so, I am sure, he would warn against worshipping the revelation itself. John is speaking strictly: "It is *God* you must worship."

Verse 10 puts us back into the "soonness" emphasis; and verse 11 gives it a very difficult and troublesome twist. What does John have in mind with his "let the evil-doer go on doing evil"? First off, we can speak with some assurance about what John does *not* mean. He cannot be expressing a discouragement of evangelism; we already have seen to some extent and have yet to see to how great an extent Revelation is an evangelistic appeal. John hardly can be running down evangelism in the very same passage where he is intent on playing it up. Likewise, John cannot mean to be saying that ethical and moral distinctions are of no importance; his whole book—including verses 14-15, just two verses ahead—contradicts such a reading.

I take John to be saying, rather, that even though it is one of our highest obligations to invite our fellow men to give their loyalty to Jesus and live out its implications, it nevertheless is not our place to try to stop them if they insist on going another way. What they choose to do with the Christian invitation is a matter between them and God—which matter will be properly cared for without our interference or well-meaning help. You preach the everlasting gospel that gives the evil-doer the choice; but if he chooses not to take the opportunity, you "let the evil-doer go on doing evil"; God doesn't need your moralistic manipulations in dispensing either salvation or judgment.

If this is the counsel John intends, it is one much needed in our day. It is needed by those evangelizers who are determined to irritate people into accepting Christ, who will not respect the evil-doer's right to say "no" but continue to twist his arm until he will say "uncle" in the words *they* want to hear. It is needed just as much by those who seem to think that heaping imprecation and hell-fire upon evil-doing U.S. presidents and other such moral perverts will change the character of the world. Although it is a hard saying, John is correct in calling us to "let the evil-doer go on doing evil" and concentrate, rather, on being a good man who perseveres in his goodness and is true to his dedication.

Verses 12-15 continue the "soonness" theme but proceed to make specific the ethical decision to which the "soonness" lends urgency. "Soonness" plus "the certainty of recompense" equals "urgency." The coming of Jesus will mark an administration of justice in which consequences are in direct correlation to the character of one's deeds. One of the gross "wrongnesses" of the world is that such correlation currently does not obtain; in the justice of God's kingdom, it will. There is, then, a real urgency in getting "right" before that time comes.

Verse 14 makes it plain that getting "right" is not simply a matter of deciding that now I will be a good boy. There is only one way of getting clean, and that is by letting one's robe be *washed* clean in the blood of the Lamb. For John, the ultimate distinction between man and man is that of ethical behavior and moral uprightness (in the broadest possible sense of those terms); however, he also is certain that no person has a chance of achieving that sort of authenticity through his own moral striving but only as he experiences both the forgiveness and enablement that come from Jesus alone. John's demand for ethical rightness and his call for a personal allegiance to Jesus are not two foci but one and the same thing; *having* a clean robe and *washing* it in the blood of the Lamb are inseparable conditions.

The phrase that concludes verse 14, "will enter by the gates of the city," more closely should be translated "may be entering." The wording rather clearly points to a transaction that continues beyond the establishment of the city. But again John is quick to specify that in-coming traffic dare not be understood to imply the entrance of evil into the city. What is certain is that, as long as a person is one of the kinds John enumerates, he is outside; only those with washed robes may enter. (It would not be wise to try to read into this verse any Johannine prejudice against puppy-dogs; he is talking about a quality of dogdom that is the perquisite of human beings rather than canines.)

Quite clearly, the material from verse 16 to the end of the book constitutes a great invitation-dialog on the theme "come"—except that verses 18-19 form a rather obtrusive interruption. Not only do they interrupt, they may also betray something of the "gnostic" mentality we earlier attributed to the Interpolator. That is, they *could* be taken as implying that Revelation is a magical writing designed to communicate esoteric knowledge and power to initiated "lovers of wisdom" and that tampering with the occult formulations would bring supernatural curses upon the head of the guilty one. If this is how the passage is meant to be read, then it is quite unlike John. However, if the passage means to say simply that Revelation is a presentation of the Christian gospel and that anyone who presumes to teach a different gospel from what God has revealed in Christ is bringing serious consequences upon himself—then it is quite conceivable that John wrote these words. But the matter is not worth arguing one way or the other; the important thing is not to allow this warning to break up the great passage in which it appears.

In verse 16, Jesus appears; he comes to authorize and confirm the gospel which Revelation proclaims and to present himself as being the *Messiah*—God's chosen one earlier described as the *Lion* of Judah (whom we also know to be the Lamb)—and "the bright morning star," the celestial firstfruit whose rising introduces and guarantees the coming of total LIGHT. John undoubtedly wants this line to call to mind everything we have learned about Jesus from the foregoing.

Jesus has appeared; and the response of the Spirit and bride undoubtedly is addressed to him. "Come to us, Lord Jesus!" they say. This pairing of the Spirit and the bride is most significant. "The bride," we know, is the church, the community of those who bear the Lamb's mark and make their martyr-witness to him. The Spirit is the presence of God as it constitutes, motivates, and empowers the faith community. The New Testament specifically identifies the Spirit as the mode of God's working that sustains history from the time of Jesus' earthly leave-taking until his return. The Spirit and the bride are together and speak together. Outside the Spirit, the bride cannot be "bride" and has no true existence. And just so, the primary assignment and work station of the Spirit is with the bride; here is where the operation of the Spirit can be expected and encountered. And the prayer of the bride is also the prayer of the Holy Spirit himself, "Come to us, Lord Jesus!"

But John does well not to leave the matter at this somewhat mystical level. " 'Come to us, Lord Jesus!' let *each hearer* reply." The bride—and indeed, in one sense, even the Spirit himself—cannot pray until individual Christians are ready to take up the prayer for themselves. You, my friend, are not a spectator to the scene portrayed here but a participant. How well, how truly, are *you* praying for the coming of the Lord Jesus?

Christians today are full of prayers for the coming of peace, righteousness, and social justice; but until we are willing to couch those petitions as a prayer for *the coming of Jesus*, they are not what John calls for. He knows that it is only in the coming of the Lord Jesus that there is hope of these other achievements. How well, how truly, are *you* praying for the coming of the Lord Jesus?

The theme word is "come"; and John plays it in perhaps three different modes. Thus far it has been the church's *prayer* that the Lord Jesus will come to it and to the world. Now it shall be Jesus' *invitation* for the church—all who desire it—to come to him and to the end-state blessings he is prepared to give. Finally, the "come" reference is to *the actual event* of that final coming in which he comes to us even as we come to him.

So the final line of verse 17 is an invitation, an invitation into LIFE, the second-order life of men dwelling in the direct presence of God with no barrier or hindrance between them. The invitation offers "a *free* gift to *all* who desire it"; here is a footnote specimen for our collection of "universalistic" texts—and a beauty it is, too! And the first line of verse 20 caps that invitation with Jesus' own most strong and solemn affirmation of his promise: "Yes, I *am* coming soon!"

To which the faithful church responds with the word that is most truly and rightly hers: "Amen (may it be so)!" The church is the church only as she says "Amen!" In a very real sense, all the church has to do to be the church, all she is called to do, is to say "Amen!" If the church continually responds with a "may it be so" to the commands and promises of God and if she conducts herself in such way as to *allow* it to be so, as to *help* it be so, what more is there that she can or should do?

And when Jesus says, "Yes, I am coming soon," and the church responds with its "Amen!"– this *is* to pray, "Come, Lord Jesus." That little prayer in verse 20 is the least original line in Revelation. John is writing in Greek, and these words, along with the rest, are in Greek; but John's earliest readers, and anyone else who knows, immediately would recognize the phrase as a translation of the original, early Christian, Aramaic prayer, *Maranatha!*

All the evidence indicates that this was the earliest, dominant, and central prayer of the original Christian community. It was used at the high point of the worship experience, in the taking of the bread and cup during the regular love feasts—and undoubtedly upon many other occasions as well. It was so precious a possession that the original Aramaic wording often was retained even in entirely Greek-speaking congregations. "*Maranatha:* come, Lord Jesus!"

And suddenly something comes clear. Revelation is not—as it so often has been seen—a late and rather foreign appendage to the normative New Testament tradition. Not at all! Although done in a style and language different from what is customary with the other writers, John's work actually is an exposition of the prayer that was right at the center of the New Testament faith. Consequently, perhaps the most valuable thing Revelation can do for us is to awaken an appreciation for this orientation that was so essential to the original gospel—teaching *us*, with meaning and understanding, to join those first brothers and sisters of the faith in praying, "*Maranatha:* come, Lord Jesus! Amen!"

John closes, then, by pronouncing his own benediction upon the beloved brethren to whom his work is addressed.

Now when the last word of the book is found to be "Come!"—what does that tell us about the book itself? It tells us that Revelation is first and foremost an *evangelistic appeal*. This . . . this . . . this . . . always and everywhere *this*—and never ever a convoluted cryptogram with which to crystal-ball hidden events out of a secret future. John's interest is a revelation of Jesus Christ, the *gospel*. And the "good news" embodied in that gospel takes the form of an invitation: "Come! . . . come! . . . come!" (and not merely to "the church in the valley by the wildwood" but to the church which is the bride of Christ in the new Jerusalem). John's—from first to last—is the "Come!" book. And the respect in which he even adds to the evangelistic invitation of the remainder of the New Testament is in stressing that the one to whom we are invited to come is himself "the *Coming* One," the one who has promised himself in a soon-coming that will establish a presence and knowledge and enjoyment of God far to surpass anything man has yet known or dreamed.

So "Come to us, Lord Jesus!" the bride prays through the Spirit. "Come to us, Lord Jesus!" let *you*, along with every other hearer, reply. "Come forward," the Coming One invites, "and take from me the gift of life that is free to all who desire it; for it is true that I am coming *soon!*" "Oh, may it indeed be so!" the expectant—the perpetually expectant—community cries. "Amen! Come, Lord Jesus!"

An Epilogue

A goodly number of scholars have suggested that Revelation is a composite work patched together out of apocalyptic fragments from different hands, different traditions, and different times. Frankly, I find the proposal completely incredible; Revelation strikes me, rather, as being the most finely crafted book of the Bible. The author comes across as a consummate artisan *and artist.* (I intend that attribution as applying to the Holy Spirit just as much as to John; my conviction is that the Spirit normally appropriates and uses the gifts of his instrument rather than simply overriding them.)

The John-Spirit artistry is seen particularly in the ability to hold a great diversity of thought and imagery into true coherence. It shows up in three different ways.

(1) John introduces a symbol in one scene, develops some aspects of it, then drops it and goes on to something else. Yet, in a later scene, he will circle back to pick up the symbol again—bringing recollection of the meaning with which he had endowed it earlier—but in a way that, rather than being simply repetitious, adds new and growing insight. The changing use of the symbol makes it a vehicle of newness and diversity; the constancy of the symbol itself makes for a profound unity. As just one example, recall what John accomplishes with the Lamb symbol in the course of the book as a whole.

(2) In other cases, John introduces and reintroduces the same idea but states it through differing images and symbols. Again, there is a basic unity of thought; but the diversity of form keeps things from becoming redundant and boring. As an example in this

case, recall how many were the different ways John found to affirm the universality of God's love and outreach toward man.

(3) Finally, in and through the flux of image and idea, it is thrilling to discover the pattern and symmetry of the structure underlying the whole. The outline and chart inside our covers will recall what we have in mind; Revelation, obviously, is a book that was "built" (as a cathedral is built) rather than simply being "spun out." John was able to display great freedom and variety in detail even while forming the whole as a controlled and unified vision.

John can keep any number of themes going at once, giving the prominence first to one and then another, each being appropriately developed as it progresses, and each being kept in perfect phase with the others so as to bring them all out at the same place. And then, looking back, one realizes that all the individual-theme patterns were being woven together to form one, over-all pattern which included each but was greater than the sum of them all. I know of only one other artist who could match it—another man named "John."

Johann Sebastian Bach inscribed his *musical* polyphony *Soli Deo Gloria*. John the Revelator's work obviously bears the inscription on every page—whether or not the words "to God alone be the glory" appear. My desire is that this book be dedicated the same way:

SOLI DEO GLORIA!

THE REVELATION OF JESUS CHRIST—Made Known to John

I. **The Introduction to the Book (1:1-20)**
   A. The Commission (1:1-3)
   B. The Greeting (1:4-8)
   C. John and the Revealer (1:9-20)

II. **The Revealer's Letters to Seven Actual Churches of the End-Time (2:1—3:22)**
   A. To Ephesus (2:1-7)
   B. To Smyrna (2:8-11)
   C. To Pergamum (2:12-17)
   D. To Thyatira (2:18-29)
   E. To Sardis (3:1-6)
   F. To Philadelphia (3:7-13)
   G. To Laodicea (3:14-22)

III. **The Control of History in the End-Time (4:1—5:14)**
   A. The Throne of God (4:1-11)
   B. The Scroll of the Future (5:1-5)
   C. The Lamb (5:6-14)

IV. **The End-Time as Seven Seals (6:1—8:1)**
   A. Seal 1 (6:1-2) ⎫
   B. Seal 2 (6:3-4) ⎬ The Four Horsemen
   C. Seal 3 (6:5-6) ⎪
   D. Seal 4 (6:7-8) ⎭
   E. Seal 5 (6:9-11) ⎫ The Saints and the Kings
   F. Seal 6 (6:12-17) ⎭
   G. The Seal Interlude: The Church—Below and Above (7:1-17)
      Part A: The Church of the Living (7:1-8)
      Part B: The Church of Those Who Have Died (7:9-17)
   H. Seal 7: The Coming of the End (8:1)

V. **The End-Time as Seven Trumpets (8:2—11:19)**
   A. Introduction to the Trumpets (8:2-6)
   B. Trumpet 1 (8:7) ⎫
   C. Trumpet 2 (8:8-9) ⎬ The Four Plagues
   D. Trumpet 3 (8:10-11) ⎪
   E. Trumpet 4 (8:12) ⎭
   F. Trumpet 5: The Warrior Locusts (8:13—9:12)
   G. Trumpet 6: The Demonic Cavalry (9:13-21)
   H. The Trumpet Interlude: The Scroll and Its Contents (10:1—11:13)
      Part A. The Eating of the Scroll (10:1-11)
      Part B: The Fate of the Church (11:1-13)
   I. Trumpet 7: Victory to Our God! (11:14-19)